Russian Research Center Studies 65

Nikolai Strakhov

Nikolai Strakhov

Linda Gerstein

Harvard University Press   Cambridge, Massachusetts   1971

The Russian Research Center of Harvard University is supported by a grant
from the Ford Foundation. The Center carries out interdisciplinary study
of Russian institutions and behavior and related subjects.

Library of Congress Catalog Card Number 79-139720
SBN 674-62475-0
Printed in the United States of America

For George

Acknowledgments

I am very happy to express, with this book, my admiration for and my thanks to Richard Pipes, both for the model of scholarly seriousness and for the personal encouragement, confidence, and friendship that he has given to me over the past dozen years. To Harvard's Russian Research Center and to Haverford College, for various commodious arrangements financial and otherwise; to Mildred Hargreaves, for superb clerical assistance twice over; and especially to Sara Winter Lake, for research help of a consistency and a devotion far beyond the normal obligations of student and friend, I am deeply grateful. The photograph of Strakhov was taken in the 1880's and is reprinted here from *Literaturnoe nasledstvo,* XXXVII-XXXVIII (1939), 153.

George knows why this book is dedicated to him.

Haverford College   L. G.
December, 1970

Contents

Introduction

Nikolai Nikolaevich Strakhov was a conservative. It is important to make such a naked statement at the beginning of this study because it explains many of the historiographical problems. It is primarily because Strakhov was classified as a conservative that we know so little about him; few historians have tried to understand his work.

Historians act as barometers of the social conscience, and have a tendency to create historical myths about the past which react reciprocally with social behavior in the present. In Russian studies the historiographical problem is especially acute. Russian history developed as a discipline in a very self-conscious manner, mainly as a result of the tardiness and haste of Westernization. Historians occupied a conspicuous portion of that group known as "the Russian intelligentsia": that is, of that expanding collection of Westernized thinkers for whom there was no permissible political atmosphere in which to express their enlightenment, much less a political arena in which to act. In lieu of the political rubric, the "intelligent" used other rubrics in which to express dissatisfaction. Literature and history were the favored tools; the urgency of the Russian need for self-expression led to unique distortions.

Liberals, for instance, found it necessary to seek in Russia's past both for evidence of the illegitimacy of the autocratic regime and for evidence of the latent existence of Russian democratic instincts. This would be proof, for them, that Russia had a liberal future. Herzen exemplified both tendencies. He insisted that Peter the Great was illegitimate – the son of his mother's German lover – and on the basis of an abortive officers' plot in 1825, he created by fiat a revolutionary consciousness in Russian society. Other historians, professing a peasant-oriented nationalism, discovered in Russian history a free communal system of land ownership that promised an alternative to a Westernized industrialization.

Perhaps the greatest myth in Russian historiography is that of the revolutionary movement. Following Herzen, the liberal historians at the end of the nineteenth century were eager to eulogize the martyrs of the battle against autocracy; in dealing almost exclusively with the radicals, they distorted their subject. The Revolution of 1917 only repeated this pattern by making it necessary not only to justify the revolution but to demonstrate both its logic and its inevitability. The new generation of Soviet Russian historians began to see more liberal elements in the Russian past than the nineteenth century had ever imagined. Peter Struve, as a Marxist in the 1890's, had done his best to prove that Marxism was valid for Russia and that the nation was already about to embark on a preparatory capitalist industrial revolution. Soviet historians later discovered that Russia's industrial development had occurred two centuries before the revolution and that consequently the socialist revolution of 1917 was perfectly consistent with the Marxist pattern.

Strakhov's life takes on a special significance for the historian of ideas because the radical myths make him such a perfect example of purposeful historical forgetfulness. In this respect, he shares the fate of most Russian conservatives. Strakhov was born in 1828, the same year as his great friend Leo Tolstoy and his great opponent Nikolai Chernyshevsky. His adult lifetime spans the entire second half of the century, and he was involved in most of the major intellectual controversies of his time. He was personally close to the giants of his period: Tolstoy, Dostoevsky, Vladimir Solovev. He engaged in serious polemics with the leading intellectuals of the radical movement: Chernyshevsky, Pisarev, Mikhailovsky. His concerns were the major ones of his era: Positivism, Nihilism, Materialism, Darwinism.

It is often said that Strakhov was "on the losing side" of these issues because his attitude toward them was negative, but this assertion only perpetuates the radical historical myth. It is true that his view was usually a minority view at its voicing. On the other hand, his career does not present an unmitigated picture of out-of-jointedness; in the last decade of his life there was a gradual acceptance of his attitudes. When the generation of the 1890's rejected the positivist creed of its fathers, it found Strakhov a welcome ally.

Strakhov has always been represented as a Slavophile, but the term is inadequate. Strakhov's was a Slavophilism grown up. He indulged in no idealization of the past—his concerns were solely for the present and the future. He was completely conversant with the European intellectual scene and, hence, was better equipped than his early predecessors—or even his contemporary, Dostoevsky—for that journalism in which Slavophilism finally found its métier.

The usual description of Strakhov as an "antipositivist" is similarly misleading. He was indeed the most vociferous defender of philosophical idealism in the 1860's when it was under attack from the "nihilists." Strakhov continually criticized the very essence of materialism, utilitarianism, and empiricism as theoretical positions, and in connection with these attacks he rejected the assertion that man could find in science the answers to life's essential questions. But he himself professed a positivism—one severely limited in its definition, but perhaps better fitted to the true meaning of the term. A biologist by training and well aware of the importance of the scientific method, he asked only that it be restricted to its legitimate field of operation and not be forced to deal with philosophical issues for which it was unsuited. His most consistent concern was the defense of science from the antirationalists (of which his friend, Tolstoy, was occasionally one) and the spiritualists, who wished to "scientize" the pursuit of spiritual truth.

Thus, we have a curious picture: a Slavophile who knew the European milieu as well as any European and who devoted his creative energy to its examination; an anti-positivist who worked his whole life as a scientist and a defender of the purity of science as an intellectual discipline. An examination of the tensions of Strakhov's thought will illustrate, I hope, some of the richness and complexity of Russian intellectual life in the nineteenth century.

Nikolai Strakhov

[I]

The Education of a Seminarist

Konstantin Leontev often visited Strakhov's rooms in the 1870's, and the two men customarily sat late into the night in conversation. Once, when Strakhov gently disagreed with an extravagent claim about the hypothetical virtues of the Russian aristocracy, Leontev jumped up and began to pace angrily about the room. "You!" he shouted, "*you* cannot understand what I am talking about, Nikolai Nikolaevich, you will *never* understand! Because — you — pardon me, Nikolai Nikolaevich — you are still just a *seminarist!*"[1]

Indeed, as any Russian would immediately perceive from the family name, Strakhov had a clerical background. He had received that same seminary education that nourished so many nineteenth-century Russian intellectuals, from the bureaucrat Mikhail Speransky to the radical Nikolai Chernyshevsky. When Leontev thus disdainfully drew attention to Strakhov's background, he was reflecting on a social fact that was to have a profound influence on Strakhov's career. During his whole life he was associated with the Slavophile movement, a movement epitomized by a man born into the archetypal Russian noble family, Ivan Aksakov. Strakhov's origins always put him out of harmony with the aristocratic elements of Slavophilism; he did not have that nostalgia for the country manor which permeated their writings.

The system of social caste laid down by Peter the Great had been rigidly enforced. Sons of priests were expected to become priests also, and they left home for the seminary at an early age. But social stratification loosened as early as the end of the eighteenth century; young men trained in the seminaries deserted their clerical heritage, and on government stipend they attended the secular universities in the large cities. Under the influence of an urban environment and a secular curriculum, they soon merged with other young men of indeterminate background who were similarly

1. D. I. Stakheev, "Gruppy i portrety" (Groups and portraits), *Istoricheskii vestnik* (January 1907), p. 90.

outside the caste system, such as the sons of petty government officials and doctors. Many of these *raznochintsy* (men-of-various-classes and hence "classless men") became writers, and some of them were the most famous men of their time. The careers of Vissarion Belinsky and Fedor Dostoevsky (both doctors' sons) and of Chernyshevsky and Nikolai Dobroliubov (sons of priests) testify to the strength of the intellectual achievements of the raznochintsy. Their appearance was one of the earliest symptoms of the disintegration of the old order in Russia.

Modernization — which seemed to mean, almost by definition, Westernization — was the original negative impulse for the Slavophile movement. Ivan Aksakov's father, Sergei, wrote the famous novel, *A Family Chronicle,* which is unequivocal in its nostalgia for the eighteenth century. It was this aspect of the movement which rapidly gave it a reputation for archaism. Even in the 1840's, when the Slavophile ideology was just being developed in Moscow circles, it was almost out of date; nothing illustrates this historical fact better than the growth of the raznochintsy. In this sense, and in defiance of Leontev's snobbery, Strakhov's social background gave him a psychological and emotional advantage over the early Slavophiles. He was more modern: he was infinitely more at home with the latest philosophies and, consequently, with the latest trends of European thought.

Like other raznochintsy, Strakhov came from the provinces rather than from the world of official St. Petersburg or aristocratic Moscow. He was born in 1828 in the small town of Belgorod, near Kharkov. His mother was a Savchenko, a family of petty gentry origin which had long intermarried with the local clergy. Her brother, in fact, was the rector of the seminary in Kamenets-Podolsk, and it was not surprising that she married a priest. Nikolai Petrovich Strakhov had some intellectual pretensions: he was a lecturer at the Belgorod seminary and an amateur collector of books. His son inherited the latter passion.

There were at least three other children. Strakhov was always reticent about his family, and biographical details can only be inferred.[2] The father died when Nikolai was six years old, and the family went to live with the mother's brother, a man with whom Strakhov was never on very good terms. When the uncle was transferred to the seminary in Kostroma in the northeast, the Strakhov family went with him. This was in 1838 when Strakhov was eleven years old; he immediately entered the local seminary, a very old and very impoverished institution.[3]

It is fascinating, in view of the scope of Strakhov's erudition as an adult, to consider the poverty of intellectual resources available to him in his early years. Dobroliubov, for instance, with a similar background, had a great advantage in the fact that his father managed the wealthiest parish in town and was constantly surrounded by well-educated men.[4] Strakhov remembered the seminary in later years with some nostalgic affection, but there is little doubt that his earliest reaction was sharply critical. In 1862, he wrote an essay on Dobroliubov, whose early life had so resembled his own. Although he spoke of the "spiritual strength hidden within the seminary," he noted:

Nevertheless, one must not blind oneself to its peculiarities. The seminarists had a choked and stifled development which prevented them from maturing completely. If there is any being who can be said to be truly cut off from his native soil, it is the seminarist. Torn from his parental home, already mutilated by the heavy hand of life, the eight-year-old boy comes to a provincial town . . . The seminary absorbs his entire life, for only there can he find the attractions of comradeship, knowledge,

2. There are two primary sources: a short biography which he wrote himself for the newspaper *Niva* in 1888 and an autobiographical memoir, unavailable to the scholar, which he wrote for his friend B. V. Nikolsky. This memoir was utilized by Nikolsky in a long essay which he published in *Istoricheskii vestnik* (April 1896), pp. 215–268, and which unexpectedly turned into an obituary. We have only Nikolsky's extensive quotations from the memoir. Aside from these two sources, some details can be gleaned from his correspondence.

3. B. V. Titlinov, *Dukhovnaia shkola v Rossii v XIX stoletii* (Vilna, 1909), p. 6.

4. A. L. Volynsky, *Russkie kritiki* (St. Petersburg, 1896), p. 136.

excitement. For the seminarist there is nothing to love
except what he gets at school. And there is something
remote and alien about this world . . . The only goal is to be
cleverer than the others; the only measure of human worth
is the intellect; the only passion is egotism.

It is impossible to conceive how much the seminarist is
dominated by the pursuit of knowledge. One knows,
however, what happens to such an interest: it is usually
quenched by a lazy, backward, and ignorant atmosphere;
the most brilliant and talented of the students become
the most idle. The more fortunate ones are those who
develop a reaction against all the principles which they had
once accepted without question. And then the entire edifice
which was built up from birth on these principles
crumbles; the greater its former influence, the more
total its destruction. Everything is scattered to ashes. And
what remains? Strong passions and an emptiness and
alienation from life that one finds in almost no other
situation.[5]

Most radicals with clerical backgrounds were violent in their
repudiation of the experience. Their attitude was typified in a book
written in the same year as Strakhov's essay, Nikolai Pomialov-
sky's *Seminary Sketches,* containing a biting denunciation of the
cramping atmosphere. Strakhov, as a raznochinets, did indeed
reject in part the seminary of his youth; the fact that he took up
both science and journalism testify to this. But the bitterness here
is more suggestive of Dobroliubov's reaction to the seminary than
of Strakhov's. Strakhov did not derive from it that urge for destruction which he described as so common; for him, "the edifice"
did not entirely "crumble." Despite the mean aspects of those
years, he retained a sympathy for religious questions and Russian
culture which was alien to men such as Dobroliubov. This side of
his seminary memories, the positive side, found a symbol for
Strakhov in the figure of Nikolai Karamzin, and in later years,
when Karamzin was under attack from the liberals for his con-

5. N. N. Strakhov, *Kriticheskie stati* (Kiev, 1902), "Dobroliubov," pp. 299–300.

servatism, Strakhov defended both him and, suitably, his seminary.

I was raised in a wild and isolated place, in a dark and ignorant institution . . . It was in the beginning of the 1840's, with Lermontov just dead and *Dead Souls* and Belinsky and *Otechestvennye Zapiski* in its heyday . . . And what did our seminary know of such things? Nothing. It had not the slightest understanding of them; it was as if we were situated, not on the confluence of the Volga and the Kostroma, but in some wild, pre-Columbus America. This enchanted kingdom was truly bewitched by a terrible poverty, an insurmountable laziness, and an impenetrable ignorance. No one, from the first to the last of six or seven hundred pupils, did anything at all . . . One lived as if the only way to live was in indifference and tranquility . . . as if under the pretence of lofty concerns one could even forget Latin and Greek — the only form of knowledge with which, at first, each seminarist was adorned.

Our seminary was in a large, run-down and dilapidated monastery, which by this time housed not more than ten monks. It was old, dating from the fifteenth century; it had fortification walls built against the Tatars and other wild tribes, and one could still climb them. There were embrasures for cannon and guns, turrets, underground passages — we lived, so to speak, continually surrounded by history.

Into this broad and empty ruin, every morning, crowded many young boys from the towns; they collected along the walls in buildings more like stables for horses than human habitation. They were by and large children of clergy and hence very rustic, with rude manners and primitive dress: in bast shoes and raw sheepskin coats in the winter, more civilized only in the summer in colored tunics, under which trousers need not be worn. They were such good boys! Their goodness, honesty, and sweetness fill me to tenderness now when I remember those distant years.

Only one thing was bad: the instruction was wretched.

No one read at all, since books were a rarity for students.
The instructors, who had better opportunities for
knowledge, preferred card playing, and drinking and eating
bouts. The idleness was beyond belief. The students, even
after they had congregated in the morning, were often
left alone, since the instructors either came very late or
did not show up at all. What a time we had! We spent long
hours singing peasant songs, running about, making
noise, quarreling—especially quarreling . . .
Even then I had a passion for knowledge which clearly
showed me that Fate would lead me to the unhappy realm
of Russian literature. I frequented the rarely used
seminary library. The librarian, one of the oldest instructors,
was very kind to me and called me his "special student."
He gave me open access to the dust-covered pile of books
. . . There were many eighteenth-century books and a few
from the beginning of the nineteenth century, but none
more recent . . . Hence I did not hear at all of Gogol,
Belinsky—or even Pushkin and Griboedov . . . Our books
stopped in the first decade of the nineteenth century:
Lomonosov, Derzhavin, Karamzin . . . my true love was
Karamzin. I read and reread his *Vestnik Evropy* and his
Letters of a Russian Traveler . . . I knew the first volume
of his *History* almost by heart. Karamzin was to me my
contemporary.[6]

The benevolent nostalgia in the description is unmistakable,
and there are other similar passages from Strakhov's pen. We are
faced, in looking at the very beginning of Strakhov's intellectual
life, with something in the nature of a paradox. The seminary
legacy was an ambivalent one for him; it pushed him simultane-
ously into both science and metaphysics. Boris Nikolsky and
others after him have taken passages like the one above as proof
that the seminary implanted a "profound religious impulse" in
Strakhov.[7] The implication is that Strakhov learned to seek God

6. N. N. Strakhov, *Kriticheskie stati*, "Vzdokh na grobe Karamzina" (A sigh on
the tomb of Karamzin), pp. 203–205.
7. B. V. Nikolsky, "Nikolai Nikolaevich Strakhov," *Istoricheskii vestnik* (April
1896), p. 222.

at the Bogoiavlensky monastery and continued to seek God his entire life in the same terms. This is an easy, but rather inadequate, conclusion. Why did Strakhov derive a "religious" impulse from the seminary and Dobroliubov derive the opposite impulse? Or, more simply, why did Strakhov not become a priest? The religion of his youth, traditional enough within the confines of the seminary, did not last a lifetime. Strakhov's "religious impulse," as we shall see, was of a very special kind. It was not synonymous with orthodox theism; in fact, Strakhov transmuted the religious impulse into a philosophical quest that sought The Beautiful and The True more fervently than God. The final legacy of the Bogoiavlensky monastery was philosophical idealism. Its beginnings are found in the university experience which followed the seminary.

The physical and intellectual poverty of the dismal northeastern town ended for Strakhov at the end of 1844. Having completed his seminary course creditably, he was sent to St. Petersburg to complete his education. He immediately enrolled in the Juridical Faculty of the university as an auditor. At the same time he began to prepare himself for the entrance examinations for the Mathematical Faculty, which he passed in August of 1845, and hence began an education in an area which, on the surface, would appear to contradict the religious heritage of Kostroma.

Some commentators have tried to explain away the move to science as an accidental event, or one which occurred because of an ulterior, and ultimately religious, motive on Strakhov's part. The fact that Strakhov *began* his studies in the Juridical Faculty has been explained by his friend Nikolsky as a reflection of the patriotism gleaned from the seminary.[8] Edward Thaden has discovered a manuscript in the archives of Pushkinsky Dom which, he feels, corroborates this statement;[9] "The Governmental Institutions of the Russian Empire" was a copybook exercise which Strakhov diligently composed as study notes for his first year as an auditor and which he filled with autocratic comments and

8. Nikolsky, "Strakhov," p. 222.
9. E. C. Thaden, *Conservative Nationalism in Nineteenth-Century Russia* (Seattle, 1964), p. 87.

patriotic remarks. But it seems to me more likely that Strakhov entered the Juridical Faculty at first simply from motives of insecurity. One can imagine the bewildering impact of St. Petersburg on the sixteen-year-old from the provinces, alone for the first time. Familiar with rhetoric and "philosophy" from the seminary, he would quite naturally turn first to the Juridical Faculty. At the same time, he immediately began to study mathematics, a field in which he had been very poorly prepared in Kostroma.[10] "I personally wanted to study natural sciences, but mathematics was the subject closest to it which also provided a stipend of six rubles a month."[11]

Strakhov's sojourn at the university in the late 1840's coincided with an upsurge of radical student activity. Belinsky was the center of attention; Mikhail Butashevich-Petrashevsky's reading circle devoted itself to Charles Fourier; other groups read Ludwig Feuerbach and the Left Hegelians. But Strakhov, according to his own testimony, was affected only negatively by the radicalism. "All around me lay the formula of negation and doubt: 'God doesn't exist and the Tsar isn't necessary!' It did not impress me much, but I realized that behind all of it was the authority of Science . . . And so, if I wanted to stand on a level with my own time and have an independent attitude toward it, I had to become familiar with the natural sciences."[12]

This is Strakhov speaking at the very end of his life to his very religious friend Nikolsky. Indeed, it would have been very strange had a young man of seventeen been so deviously provident at that stage of his life. Nikolsky commented: "Here we see the early stages of his *Struggle with the West* in defense of *The World as a Whole*."[13] This is the advantage of hindsight. Obviously, however, Strakhov at the time was more of a seminarist than he admitted later. Most important in the testimony is the phrase, "If I

10. Titlinov, *Dukhovnaia shkola*, p. 174.
11. Nikolsky, "Strakhov," p. 222.
12. Nikolsky, "Strakhov," p. 223.
13. Nikolsky, "Strakhov," p. 223. Nikolsky refers to two of Strakhov's later books.

wanted to stand on a level with my own time . . . " It is likely that Strakhov's choice of science was sparked by that same fascination with knowledge which he himself, in the essay on Dobroliubov, admitted to be integral to the seminary experience of that time. He never lost his fascination with ideas.

At this point I would like to note again that Strakhov's interests were very different from those of the typical Slavophile. The patriotic and religious heritage of the seminary did not preclude, for him, an absorption in the most "modern" and up-to-date of European influences on Russian life—that associated with the natural sciences. Science was the keystone of the "destructive" program of the radical Westernizers of the 1860's, and Strakhov's interest in science drew him closer, in some respects, to his fellow seminarists than to his Slavophile friends.

The happy financial situation in the Mathematical Faculty did not last, however. About a year after he entered, Strakhov and his uncle quarreled. The story is obscure; the uncle lodged a complaint against Strakhov with the warden of the university, and as a consequence Strakhov lost his stipend. Strakhov lasted for another six months without help; finally, in desperation, he transferred to the Chief Pedagogical Institute at the state's expense.

This was a normal school, and Strakhov obligated himself to a ten-year period of service as a teacher upon graduation. Just before he entered in 1847, the institute had revised its course to become less pedagogical and more theoretical.[14] Moreover, it had a rather distinguished faculty in the sciences.[15] Most seminary students joined the Philological Faculty when they entered the institute; the gymnasium students were the ones to study mathematics, and a certain social segregation was usually maintained.[16] Strakhov was again an exception. In 1851 Strakhov completed the course, for which he wrote his only purely mathematical work,

14. W. H. E. Jackson, *Russia's Educational Heritage* (Pittsburgh, 1950), p. 131.
15. Nikolsky, "Strakhov," p. 234.
16. I. M. I. Shemanovsky, "Vospominaniia o zhizni v glavnom pedagogicheskoi institute 1853–1857 gg." (Memoirs of life in the Chief Pedagogical Institute, 1853–1857), *Literaturnoe nasledstvo*, XXV–XXVI (1936), 271.

"Reshenie neravenstve pervoi stepeni" (A solution of mathematical inequality of the first degree). It was published in 1864.

Strakhov's memories of the institute were not pleasant. No doubt the circumstances of his entrance, his forced departure from the university, had something to do with his distaste. He noted the fact that Dobroliubov had attended the same institute, "which probably could only have produced a negative attitude toward life . . . that Pedagogical Institute which is worse than all others."[17] The most disagreeable aspect was undoubtedly the service in the provinces, which he had thought to have left behind him in 1844. But, in fact, Strakhov was fortunate; after a year in Odessa, he was transferred to a gymnasium in St. Petersburg, where for nine years he taught natural history at a small, but adequate salary.

While working as a gymnasium teacher, Strakhov pursued his academic studies. His salary enabled him to enroll in the university for graduate work in biology. This determination to pursue his studies distinguished him from those of his contemporaries who had a more dilettante attitude toward the sciences; it also tends to disprove Nikolsky's contention that Strakhov studied science only to prove the nihilists wrong. We have, then, what appears to be a rather typical picture of a young man from the provinces, of obscure clerical origins, beginning to make his way into the intellectual world of St. Petersburg in the 1850's through pursuit of the century's "new knowledge," natural science – in fact, a picture, like that of Chernyshevsky and Dobroliubov, of the Russian seminarist who would form the backbone of the new radical intelligentsia.

Although Strakhov's life during this period appears outwardly rather dull, the excitement of St. Petersburg did not pass him by. Like that of so many other young men in similar situations throughout Russia, his ambition was to be a writer, and he led a feverish "inner life." It is this interest which makes his life so

17. Strakhov, *Kriticheskie stati,* p. 299.

different in tone from those of his more politically radical fellow seminarists. He submerged himself in German literature. He followed all the journals. From his earliest years in St. Petersburg he wrote poetry and short stories. The poems, preserved in little notebooks and partly published at the end of his life, present the picture of a typical young romantic.[18] Here is an early one:

> *Again I grieve, my light-filled day*
> *Has passed by sickly grieving,*
> *As the shadow of a cloud hurries*
> *Across a sun-brightened cornfield.*
>
> *Here I sit and think of her.*
> *Smoke whirls around played by the wind*
> *And, like the dreams I've dreamt of love,*
> *Floats, forms a ring, and disappears.*

Another poem, dedicated to his young friend Platon Kuskov (a future poet), describes in a long series of iambic monometers the anguish of a morose and distant future. It had not taken the seminarist from Kostroma long to move from an acquaintance exclusively with Karamzin's *History* to the realm of European literature. Schiller's *Die Ideale* especially fascinated him (as it did so many other young Russians); he translated it and was inspired by it to write his own verses.

The poems of the 1850's are full of life's sadness and the artist's loneliness. A typical example, from 1853:

> *In a moment of spiritual weakness,*
> *Don't trust yourself, poet!*
> *All is false in the everyday world;*
> *In ecstasy alone there is no lie.*

18. They were published in Strakhov's *Vospominaniia i otryvki* (St. Petersburg, 1892) and previously in the journals *Russkoe obozrenie* and *Niva*. Strakhov handed the notebooks over to his oldest friend, Platon Kuskov, on his deathbed. When Kuskov died in 1909, he gave them to Strakhov's last and youngest friend, V. V. Rozanov.

Look—people themselves have no idea
Of what it is that moves them,
Or that there is a fiery torrent
Coursing through their fluttering hearts.

And so, like joyful, ignorant children
Without reflection in their passions,
They are pitiless and malicious
As children often can be.

Don't envy them their happiness;
Don't seek from them their praise;
Don't follow after everyday happiness,
Or bend yourself before it.

Only the pure spirit of the poet
Must be cherished as the highest gift;
Your rapture, as a torch of light,
Must be cherished in the muck of the world.

In a moment of spiritual weakness,
Don't trust yourself, poet!
All is false in the everyday world,
In ecstasy alone there is no lie.

This is a poem that Eugene Onegin, or any one of Ivan Turgenev's superfluous heroes, might have written. It was the fashionable literary pose of the time.

There was also a more jocular side to his personality. In 1935 a member of the Ukrainian Academy of Sciences discovered the manuscript of a story by Strakhov written in 1850 and called "In the Mornings." The story was in the form of a diary, short on plot and long on philosophical reflections. Strakhov wrote it during a vacation from the Pedagogical Institute, and he immediately sent it off to Nikolai Nekrasov, the editor of *Sovremennik* (The contemporary). This was a rather daring move for the young mathematics student; the seminarist was quick to cast off his shyness. When Nekrasov sent no reply, Strakhov wrote again to him:

I would be very much obliged to the editor of
Sovremennik if he would give me, through his office,
some news of my manuscript "In the Mornings." I have
complete faith in the high quality of this work (otherwise
I would not have sent it), and also in the acute
penetration of the Editor. Therefore, I have no doubts
about the story's fate. Especially if the Editor, as would
be quite desirable to me, would look upon the manuscript
from the highest psychological point of view, as upon
evidence of the intellectual and moral activity of a
man in a given set of circumstances and at a given moment
of his life. Developing this conception, the Editor will
easily sense that the readers will be as touched and
attracted on reading "In the Mornings" in the press as the
Editor, I am sure, was himself on reading it in the
hard-to-read manuscript form. All the same, I'd like to
know if you are going to print the thing or not?

> The One who Took the Trouble
> to Write "In the Mornings"

Nekrasov's answer was short and to the point:

I have the honor to inform you that you will receive
an answer about your manuscript not earlier than in six
month's time, because we read it "only in the mornings."

> The Director of the Office of
> *Sovremennik,* Morgenrot

Undaunted, Strakhov wrote again:

For the Editor, if I have succeeded in guessing
correctly, it would not be unsuitable to say that
"Morning" is not exactly as attractive as I had thought;
and one could even say that it is so boring that even for
two of them to conquer it it would take precisely one
month, and that only if read in the mornings after enough
sleep.

But instead, probably completely accidentally, a thought
was expressed which completely contradicts the
foregoing assumption: to wit, that the Editor intends
to hold on to the manuscript for reading purposes for
one-half year, or six months. If the manuscript is so
unsuitable, then would it not be proper to return it to me
immediately?

I am willing to wait for *an answer about my
manuscript,* if the Editor wishes to write one, for as
many months or years as is convenient; but I respectfully
request that the manuscript itself be returned to me
immediately!

Idem qui pridem[19]

The manuscript was finally returned, with Nekrasov's comments on the cover in red crayon. "The author has talent, his tone
is good, his manner is rather original. But we can't print this story
— the censor would find it scandalous, immoral — and would refuse
to print it." This comment fascinates a biographer; unfortunately,
the manuscript is virtually unreadable. The Russian editor, A.
Nazarevsky, says that from what little he could read of the tat-
tered pages, there were very few "scandalous" passages in the
story.[20] Nazarevsky concludes that Nekrasov refused the story
because he recognized the future reactionary Strakhov in this
early piece. The story does indeed sound as if it had suggestions of
Dostoevsky's underground man; but this was also part of the
standard "superfluous man" pose, and hardly reactionary in 1850.
Perhaps Nekrasov was really afraid of the censor, or perhaps he
simply did not like the story. In any case, we no longer have the
evidence to assess it. But the letters to Nekrasov that accompany
the manuscript are in a way as interesting. They demonstrate the

19. The letters are reproduced in A. Nazarevsky, "Pomety Nekrasova na rukopisi N. N. Strakhova" (Nekrasov's notes on a manuscript by N. N. Strakhov),
Literaturnoe nasledstvo, LIII–LIV (1949), 85–86.

20. Nazarevsky, "Nekrasov's Notes," p. 86.

satirical humor and spirit which would be characteristic of Strakhov as a journalist in the following decade.

It was not at all unusual, of course, for a young man in St. Petersburg in the 1850's to read German poetry and write stories full of *angst*. Chernyshevsky, for instance, read widely in German literature in his youth. However, romanticism did not affect Chernyshevsky deeply, and he soon abandoned it in favor of more politically oriented literature. The Slavophiles were also greatly influenced by German thought. What distinguishes Strakhov from both is the hold which European literature had over him. He never forgot Schiller, even when he was later so impressed by Pushkin and Tolstoy. He was not only influenced by Hegel (everyone was at the time, Slavophile and Westernizer), but he did not hesitate to call himself openly a Hegelian. He was not at all adverse to being identified with Western philosophy, and this philosophical romanticism penetrated his science also.

In 1855 Strakhov published a review of a biology textbook at the author's request.[21] This indicates his success in the other facet of his life in the 1850's: the completion of his education as a biologist. In 1857 he finished his thesis for a master's degree. The thesis was published in the *Zhurnal Ministcrstva Narodnogo Prosveshcheniia* (Journal of the Ministry of Public Education), and separately as a book in that year. But apparently the oral defense went so badly that he was unable to obtain a chair in St. Petersburg or Moscow. He was offered a position in Kazan, but by this time he was loath to leave the capital. In later years his friend Dmitry Stakheev suggested that Strakhov was robbed of his rightful chair because he did not know how to "pull the proper strings."[22] But in any case, Strakhov settled for an entirely different sort of audience.

He was still at this time teaching in the gymnasium. After the thesis was published, Strakhov decided to supplement his income

21. Nikolsky, "Strakhov," p. 235.
22. D. I. Stakheev, "Pustynnozhitel" (The hermit), in his *Sobranie sochinenii*, II (St. Petersburg, 1902), 176.

by writing the monthly scientific column in the *Zhurnal Ministerstva Narodnogo Prosveshcheniia.*[23] This was the first step; with the end of any prospects for an academic career in St. Petersburg, Strakhov decided to devote himself entirely to journalism. He had acquired in the apprentice years of the 1850's a solid knowledge of German philosophy and European literature. His education in the natural sciences added to his resources, and he was well equipped for the Russian literary world. Within a year he had published a series of short articles called "Physiological letters" in *Russkii mir* (Russian world),[24] an excursion into the field of the philosophy of nature, which was a combination of his two talents. Strakhov's articles were soon noticed by influential literary men, and in the following year he was invited to collaborate on a new journal, *Svetoch* (Torch). The invitation to write for *Svetoch* turned out to be the turning point in Strakhov's career.

23. It was called "Novosti po chasti nauk estestvennykh" (Scientific news).
24. N. N. Strakhov, "Fiziologicheskie pisma" (Physiological letters), *Russkii mir*, nos. 2, 22, 59 (1859). I shall discuss the articles in the next chapter.

II

The World of St. Petersburg Journalism

The busy literary circles surrounding the journals of Moscow and St. Petersburg in Russia of the mid-nineteenth century present a confusing picture to today's reader. The intensity of the atmosphere, the significance attached to each new issue of a journal, the sharpness of the polemics – all seem out of proportion to a society which takes intellectual pluralism for granted. But if we wish to appreciate the quality of intellectual life in Russia a century ago, we must redefine our conception of "journalism" and its significance.

The flowering of Russian journalism is closely connected with the growth of the raznochintsy intelligentsia. The invasion of the universities by new classes of young men, which so quickly began to erode the old social-class differentiations, at the same time presented contemporary society with an enormous pool of intellectual energy – a resource which at first seemed destined to remain untapped because of Russia's backwardness.

One of the outstanding characteristics of old societies is the exceedingly limited nature of available social options. In the Russia of 1830, for instance, an educated person could run a landed estate, become an army officer, or enter the state civil service; none of these options delivered any great intellectual satisfaction, and in almost all cases "good birth" was a qualification for real success. (The career of Speransky is, of course, an exception to this general rule.) Thus, the seminarist who had managed to acquire a university degree by dint of brains and luck found himself in a dilemma. The liberal professions, with the very slight exception of academic life, were almost nonexistent before 1870. Russian literature speaks frequently and poignantly of the superfluousness of the alienated Russian nobleman who found country life boring and civil service impossible, but the dilemma of uselessness was much more distressing to the raznochinets, who had been educated out of his former class and left without a niche into which to move. It was in such a situation that Russian journalism was born, and it developed in the second quarter of the nineteenth century to form a context of social action for the new intelligentsia. Thus, Nikolai Strakhov was behaving in a manner characteristic of his social peers when, failing to find a place in the academic hierarchy, he turned to the world of the journals.

But one cannot explain the significance of Russian journalism by referring only to the sociological vacuum which it filled. The journal *Svetoch* provided more than just a job for Strakhov; it was his entrance ticket into the only intellectual forum of his age. The uniqueness of the journals in this respect is a function of the relative political and intellectual immaturity of contemporary Russian society.

Public political life was nonexistent under Nicholas I and the bureaucratic autocracy which was his political style. Those forms of discourse which absorbed so much intellectual energy for Western Europe—parliamentary debates, political speeches, political clubs, electoral campaigns, public meetings—were entirely absent. This is an obvious point, but one must consider what it meant in real terms for Russians who had been educated to an interest in political matters. In the same way, university life was a very restricted affair during most of the nineteenth century. The combined effect of bureaucratic restrictions and the direct police control of the Ministry of Education was crippling. Universities had a hard enough time acting simply as transmitters of information, much less serving as centers of intellectual discourse. The journals, rather than politics or academic life, served as the sole forum of debate and organ of communication; the fact that so much depended on them gave a unique stamp to their character.

Thus, the Russian "fat journal," as it was called, was an institution in itself, although its nature changed in the course of the century. When it first appeared in the form of Karamzin's *Vestnik Evropy* (The messenger of Europe) it was a miniature "university"; mainly through translation of various European essays and literary works, it acted as an agent of Westernization, the arbiter of taste, and the creator of standards for several generations of Russian gentlemen. But by mid-century the journals were beginning to play a more independent, and at the same time more serious, role. Partly under the influence of Belinsky's essays and Nekrasov's editorial and publishing activities in the 1840's, but also as a result of the death of Nicholas I and the partial political thaw which followed, some of the Russian journals slowly began to assume the task of social criticism and political commentary. It was at this point, in the third quarter of the nineteenth century, that the Russian journals reached their peak and played their really vital role in Russian intellectual history, and it was at this point that Nikolai Strakhov began his career in Russian journalism on Miliukov's *Svetoch.*

Svetoch itself, as it turned out, was no great literary success; it lasted barely a year. But its editor, A. P. Miliukov, was a well-known figure whose weekly Tuesday evenings were attended by all the literary lights; it was here that Strakov was to meet both Dostoevsky and Grigorev and in the following year begin his long and fruitful collaboration with them. Moreover, in the course of one year, Miliukov published four of Strakhov's articles, which gave to the young writer a respectable, albeit limited, literary reputation.

The critic Nikolai Mikhailovsky, who had a knack for destroying his opponents by apt images (he once called Dostoevsky "the cruel talent"), compared Strakhov to Don Quixote fighting the giants.[1] It is curious, and at the same time very characteristic of Strakhov, that although he came out of a typical seminarist background and chose a typical seminarist career, he appeared nevertheless in a guise very uncharacteristic for his type. From his very first article he was a nonconformist, defying the dominant intellectual trend of the 1860's with his insistent philosophical idealism.

It is perhaps not so surprising that Russian journalism should burst forth in a radical form in the late 1850's, given the history of severe censorship suddenly lifted after Nicholas's death. This

1. N. K. Mikhailovsky, "Iz literaturnykh i zhurnalnykh zametok 1872 g." (Literary and journalistic remarks for 1872), in his *Polnoe sobranie sochinenii* (St. Petersburg, 1896), I, 706.

radicalism, however, was not expressed in directly political terms. Russia had not changed to the point where one could openly criticize the tsar's government. Rebellion was a much more subtle matter. Although it was dangerous to criticize the institution of serfdom or the Orthodox Church, often enough one could get away with professing an extreme philosophical materialism or even atheism. If the critique was *general* enough and couched in vague abstractions, it was permissible. One could criticize the social and political situation, paradoxically, only by taking intellectual stands which were in very fundamental philosophical opposition to the status quo.

Thus, the language of Russian journalism was necessarily rather oblique, but this was more than a surface obliqueness. To speak of the Aesopian quality of Russia journalism implies that one has merely to read between the lines to get the underlying political message. In fact, it is more complicated than that. Russian thinkers were often as much the victims of their language as the creators of it. The habits of intellectual evasion in expression of ideas had real consequences in the formulation of ideas; Russian writers themselves became obsessed with their abstractions. They were as emotionally involved in the intricacies of their symbolic language as they might have been in a political debate in another society; the fervor of intellectual debate seems at times to have been the result of a displaced political passion. Nothing illustrates this quality as well as the attack by the radicals on philosophical idealism in the 1860's, and it was in philosophy's defense that Strakhov made his literary reputation.

The Russian enlightenment was in many ways a philosophical vacuum. Part of the responsibility rests with Nicholas I himself; in 1848 he closed down the philosophy faculties in Russian universities in the interests of social utility. To the tsar, European philosophers were a dangerous source of revolutionary ideas, which had had all too obvious fruit in the Decembrist affair, the Polish rebellion, and finally, the revolutions of 1848. Like Joseph de Maistre (who had spend part of his exile from revolutionary France in Russia), he feared "the Pugachevs of the universities." Hence, professional philosophers by 1860 were rare and known usually by scandal only. It was not until the 1890's, in fact, that philosophy as an academic discipline became fully respectable.

It was not for such "official" reasons, however, that Strakhov occupied such a lonely perch in his defense of philosophy in the world of St. Petersburg journalism. The journals were already taking a very independent stand toward official Russia on many issues. The irony was that the radicals of the 1860's, Strakhov's fellow raznochintsy from the seminaries, shared Nicholas's attitude in the interest of *their* version of social utility. This was the era of the birth of Russian positivism, which can be distinguished from its French progenitor (among other ways) by the extremism with which the Russian followers adopted it. One of the greatest exaggerations was the extent of their intolerance for metaphysics.

Auguste Comte's positivism did not necessarily deny metaphysical speculation as a region of human activity; Comte merely excluded metaphysics from the realm of certainty, and therefore considered it a more primitive form of knowledge. Comte's interests were social; he felt that certainty was only possible under scientific conditions, and hence that social science was the only fruitful area of contemporary human endeavor.

The Russian positivists, however—Chernyshevsky, Dmitry Pisarev and the men surrounding their journals *Sovremennik* and *Russkoe slovo* (The Russian word)—were more uncompromisingly antimetaphysical. For instance, Chernyshevsky's famous "The Anthropological Principle in Philosophy" (1860), was based on a denial of speculative philosophy's right to exist.

That part of Philosophy which deals with the problems of man, just like the other part which deals with the problems of external nature, is based on natural sciences. The principle underlying the philosophical view of human life and all its phenomena is the idea worked out by the natural sciences, of the unity of the human organism; the observations of physiologists, zoologists and medical men have driven away all thought of dualism in man.[2]

2. N. G. Chernyshevsky, "The Anthropological Principle in Philosophy," in *Selected Philosophical Essays* (Moscow, 1953), p. 70

To Pisarev, similarly, philosophy represented intellectual char-
latanism.

. . . Philosophy has no roots, lacks flesh and blood, and
boils down to mere playing on words. That is scholasticism,
an idle play of intellect that can be indulged in with equal
facility in England and Algiers, in the Celestial Empire
and present-day Italy. What is the significance of such
philosophy today? What are its rights to existence? . . .
Abstractions can provide interest and be understood
only by the abnormally developed and insignificant
minority.[3]

Chernyshevsky and Pisarev called themselves "materialists";
they meant by this term that they found sufficient explanation for
the major questions of life in the chemical and biological discoveries which were coming to light so rapidly at this time. They did
not, however, give their thoughts the philosophical scaffolding
which the eighteenth-century materialists, such as d'Holbach, had
used; they did not even employ the agnostic language of their supposed master, Feuerbach. They simply rejected metaphysical
speculation entirely.

Nevertheless, philosophy had its defenders in Russia, and Strakhov was one of the first to make a strong protest against the attack
of the radicals. It appeared in his first article in *Svetoch* in 1860,
"Znachenie gegelevskoi filosofii v nastoiashchee vremia" (The
significance of Hegelian philosophy in our time). The article
shows the results of over a decade of submergence in German
idealism, and it indicates how much he had made of the "religious
inspiration" of the clerical training of his early years.

Strakhov began with a quotation from Gogol: "How hard it is to
find the path towards truth!" Is there no way out? he asks. For
Strakhov the answer lies in philosophy; and Hegel is the archetypal philosopher. Hegel incorporates all philosophical systems;

3. D. I. Pisarev, "Nineteenth Century Scholasticism," in *Selected Philosophical, Social and Political Essays* (Moscow, 1958), pp. 108–110.

he asks all the basic philosophical questions; and in answering them, he comes to terms with life as no other thinker has done before him.

When one reads over this first, and for Strakhov so important, article in the light of later claims made by scholars that he was a Hegelian,[4] it is most striking to observe how little of Hegel's technicalities are in it; Strakhov felt more kinship with Hegel's quest than with his solutions. Hegelianism is considered a synonym for German idealism, the key to all other idealist systems. He distinguishes Hegel from his predecessors only in that he feels Hegel to be in closer contact with the actual world. Strakhov's language is truly lyrical, as excited as the language of Nikolai Stankevich's circle in the 1830's. But it is Hegel's tone, not his intricacies, that Strakhov most appreciates. By far the liveliest part of Strakhov's article is his mockery of the materialists who had replaced Hegel in the public eye.

Who does not know the illustrious triumvirate: Karl Vogt, Moleschott, and Büchner? Karl Vogt, whom the advertisements of the German booksellers and the learned articles of Russian journals call "the ingenious," is just an ordinary naturalist. His colleagues do not even particularly respect him. He put together a zoological system which was immediately published, despite his own instincts to the contrary. Otherwise he has done some good work, but zoological, not philosophical. In regard to philosophy, however, he is not to blame; he let slip a few jokes, a few German witticisms — is it his fault that the public took them for deep philosophical concepts? . . .

Jacob Moleschott is much more serious than Vogt; with a thoroughly German temperament, he continually expostulates and quotes from Feuerbach . . . Moleschott is more serious than Vogt, but hardly more sound. He puts down,

4. D. I. Chizhevsky, *Gegel v Rossii* (Paris, 1939), pt. 4, ch. 3, passim; A. I. Vvedensky, *Obshchii smysl filosofii N. N. Strakhova* (Moscow, 1897), p. 2; N. Ia. Grot, "Pamiati N. N. Strakhova" (In memory of N. N. Strakhov), *Voprosy filosofii i psikhologii*, XXXII (1896), p. 308.

for instance, the subject-heading "Thought." You might think he was actually going to discuss the nature of Thought, but instead he tells us that if a man drinks champagne he then has cheerful thoughts, that a man with an empty stomach tends to be morose, etc.—in other words, that thought is dependent on the body . . . Moleschott has actually earned a well-deserved reputation as a physiologist for his research in this field. If the public takes physiology for philosophy it really is not his fault either.

Büchner without a doubt is the worst of the three—God only knows if he is any kind of a scholar at all. He is, indeed, a *Doktor*, but who in Germany is not? He has no scientific reputation, but of course he writes with great facility—a great merit! He has collected into a little book some rambling opinions on materialism, made up of the simplest and most naive propositions; they are put together without coherence, method, or originality—and here we have the latest "philosopher."⁵

"The significance of Hegelian philosophy in our time," then, is that it *is* significant. According to Strakhov, it is nonsense to say that philosophy has no role to play simply because a few scientists say so, or because there is currently a decline in philosophical voices; "Philosophy is not elected by majority vote like French emperors."⁶

Strakhov was to repeat his attack on Ludwig Büchner many times by exposing the philosophical confusions behind materialism as he saw it, and especially by questioning the pseudo-certitude of the "scientists." In an article commissioned by Mikhail Katkov in 1860 for *Russkii vestnik*, Strakhov tried to show that materialism actually has a metaphysical scaffolding, although the materialists themselves are not aware of it.⁷ Büchner, for instance,

5. N. N. Strakhov, *Filosofskie ocherki* (St. Petersburg, 1895), "Znachenie gegelevskoi filosofii v nastoiashchee vremia" (The significance of Hegelian philosophy in our time), pp. 5–7.

6. Strakhov, *Filosofskie ocherki*, p 9.

7. N. N. Strakhov, "Veshchestvo po ucheniiu materialistov" (Matter according to the materialists), *Russkii vestnik* (September 1860).

claims not to be an atomist, because his scientific idol, Emil Dubois-Reymond, has made atomism unfashionable. But Büchner not only invents the concepts "Force" and "Matter," he personifies them; in his writings they are merely products of his imagination.

Strakhov elaborated this theme later in an analysis of Feuerbach himself, "a great writer who in his time professed to have destroyed Hegel."[8] Strakhov's respect for Feuerbach (who, he made clear, was not responsible for the absurdities of some of his followers) did not prevent him from heavily attacking his philosophical assumptions and particularly his self-contradictory atomism. He tried to salvage Feuerbach by showing that he was not at all a materialist and thus in no way a progenitor of the Vogts and the Büchners. Feuerbach believed that essence is immanent in existence; the materialists do not understand Feuerbach's immanence. For Feuerbach, matter as an abstract principle has no existence whatsoever; individual bodies may indeed exist, but not matter.[9]

Strakhov's attacks on the materialists and his defense of metaphysics were not in any way a repudiation of his own identity as a scientist, however. In fact he depended on his scientific background for his metaphysical argumentation. One of the most interesting aspects of Strakhov's position is that his attack on materialism is an insider's attack. Even while assuming his new journalistic role as a Hegelian champion, he continued to write his scientific column for the *Zhurnal Ministerstva Narodnogo Prosveshcheniia*. Moreover, his first literary venture, the "Fiziologicheskie pisma" (Physiological letters) in *Russkii mir* in 1859, were followed by several more in *Svetoch* in 1860 of a similar nature. Strakhov appears in these articles not only as a popularizer of scientific advances but also as a philosopher of science who utilizes his knowledge of science for his metaphysics.

The "Physiological Letters" ask the basic question of the relationship of man to the world of nature and pose the answer in

8. N. N. Strakhov, "Feierbakh" (Feuerbach), *Epokha* (June 1864), and reprinted in *Filosofskie ocherki.*
9. Strakhov, "Feuerbach," in *Filosofskie ocherki,* p. 84.

traditional terms from German idealist *Naturphilosophie.* The physiologists tell us that man is an animal, composed of bits of matter which are no different in kind from the components of a simple stone. But man *feels* himself to be different; although he knows he is an animal, he does not feel limited to this simple physical dimension. Thus, man is both an animate organism and a spiritual being. Despite the claims of the materialists, who recognize only the existence of matter, man as an organism represents something more.[10]

The "Pisma ob organicheskoi zhizni" (Letters on life), published in *Svetoch* in 1860 and 1861, were devoted to a further elucidation of the unique qualities of organic nature. If growth were merely an instance of the movement of atoms, as the materialists suppose, then it would be a rather simple thing to create life. But the futile efforts of science have shown that this is an impossibility; growth involves not only movement *per se,* but movement in a forward direction: in other words, growth involves *development.* Organic growth seems to be a process toward perfection, and this perfection is the fundamental sign of life.

In thus stressing the internal element of organic development, Strakhov evokes a theme which was basic in the philosophical debates of his time. What he says about organic growth is in direct contradiction to the mechanistic theory of development held as a basic postulate by most contemporary materialists. One of the most tenacious intellectual heritages of the Enlightenment was a belief in the exclusiveness of the influence of environment over human development. In Montesquieu, in Beccaria, even in Jean-Jacques Rousseau one sees the indomitable conviction that the environment molds the organism, that man is no more than a product of the physical and social forces surrounding him. Strakhov, instead, stresses another element of development: the internal preconditions which make life more than just a mere response to external stimuli and give it a potential for transcend-

10. N. N. Strakhov, "Physiological Letters," published as part of "Pisma ob organicheskoi zhizni" (Letters on organic life) in *Mir kak tseloe* (St. Petersburg, 1872).

ing that environment. The essence of living, he suggests, lies in that potential.

In this emphasis on development and potential, Strakhov exhibits one of the most characteristic aspects of nineteenth-century biology, which one scholar has called its "post-Goethean romanticism."[11] Strakhov's insistence on the continuity of the biological process, his stress on metamorphosis rather than atomism, his view of the organism as a collective whole rather than an atomistic assembly of particulars—all would put him comfortably in the company of those rebels against the physics of being in the name of the metaphysics of becoming which we associate with pre-Darwinian biology.[12] Once life has been defined as the aspiration to perfection, one can see how closely Strakhov the scientist and Strakhov the philosopher are joined in the same quest. Those scholars who compartmentalize Strakhov into "scientist," "philosopher," and even "literary critic," present a misleading case; these roles were in fact identical, they illustrate the same battle against materialism waged on different fronts. Hegelian dialectic gives the only possible approach to a meaningful life in search of perfection. The articles on organic life are really supplements to the article on Hegel. Strakhov's quest was for a reality of the mind, higher than and of a different nature from the reality of the senses, perceived by the materialists. It involved a search for fundamentals rather than the narrow preoccupation with the concrete which characterized the positivist approach. In short, Stra-

---

11. Charles Gillispie, *The Edge of Objectivity* (Princeton, 1960), p. 199.
12. It is important at this point not to confuse what Strakhov is saying with vitalism. The vitalists represented a nineteenth-century biological school which postulated that animate organisms are imbued with a special "life force" which makes them *behave* differently from inanimate organisms, and thus makes them subject to different laws. Strakhov had specifically rejected vitalism as a materialist heresy in his master's dissertation and later in his essay on Claude Bernard. (See chapter V.) If one rejects materialism, then one need not invent forms of matter like "forces" to explain a form of life which does not seem to behave like matter. Strakhov is suggesting in this article that one can reject matter as a category entirely; one can simply divide life into the organic and the inorganic. Organic bodies obey the laws of physical phenomena ("man is an animal"), but not exclusively ("man is not only an animal, he is also a spiritual being").

khov through his scientific articles was preparing the case for philosophical idealism.

Given the predominance of the radical journalists, then, we can appreciate why Strakhov's first articles attracted attention. His frequent presence at Miliukov's literary evenings and those of other St. Petersburg publishers, such as Tiblen, brought him into contact with many of the leading radicals, including Chernyshevsky and L. F. Panteleev, who later recalled that "people said with regret that [Strakhov] had in vain rejected his real métier, which was natural science . . . because his dissertation was quite good. In the beginning of the 1860's, Nikolai Nikolaevich considered himself a great connoisseur of philosophy, especially German philosophy, and one of the most confirmed Hegelians."[13]

The Dostoevsky brothers, Fedor and Mikhail, were also friends of Miliukov. Fedor Dostoevsky already had a reputation as a writer and one who had suffered the rigors of exile. He was just now beginning to embark on a new career in journalism and with a new literary personality. Because he was in the process of elaborating an intellectual position, he was fascinated by Strakhov's articles. At the end of 1860, the brothers asked Strakhov if he would like to collaborate with them on a new journal.

This turned out to be a far more important venture for Strakhov than *Svetoch*. Dostoevsky was a daring editor, he was willing to allow space to a relative newcomer, and he was eventually successful in making his journal an exciting production. Strakhov, just past thirty and taking up a promising literary career after his academic failure, was terribly optimistic, in spite of — or perhaps, because of — the unpopularity of his views. Strakhov's enthusiasm was matched only by the reception of the new journal, *Vremia* (Time).

Vremia was one of the most interesting literary productions of the 1860's. Strakhov's service on it set the tone of all his future work, and his contribution to its literary personality was crucial.

13. L. F. Panteleev, *Iz vospominanii proshlogo* (Moscow, 1934), p. 193.

Although there were other journals which dissented from the radical dogma of Chernyshevsky and Pisarev (for instance, Katkov's *Russkii vestnik* [The Russian messenger] and the Slavophile *Den* [The day]), none was as consistently lively or as respected as *Vremia*. And, of course, posterity is grateful for the fact that *Vremia's* editorial policy had a literary incarnation in Dostoevsky's novels.

The intelligence and the liveliness of *Vremia* were precisely what made it so difficult to categorize the journal's position. Both contemporaries and later scholars have been puzzled (although rarely admitting it) in the effort to apply a label. Was the journal "conservative" or "liberal"? What did Dostoevsky mean by the slogan *pochvennichestvo*? Was there a change in editorial policy over time? How much was Strakhov responsible for the elaboration of editorial policy?

The answer to these questions can only be found within the context of the literary polemics of the day. It would be a useless exercise to try to define the journal in the framework of what Dostoevsky or Strakhov said a decade later, or in terms of any ex post facto category such as Slavophile. Those who were themselves involved in the subtleties of the issues were much less hasty in their definitions than later critics. To take an obvious case, which will be treated in more detail later, pochvennichestvo has been classified by most later (and hostile) critics as "conservative Slavophilism." But this is a most inadequate description, as I hope to show. Pochvennichestvo was indeed a *kind* of Slavophilism, but both "conservative" and "radical" are irrelevant adjectives for it; and Slavophilism itself was a very complex phenomenon.

At this point there is no need to add another voice to the chorus of argument about pochvennichestvo. Rather, I wish now to use the history of *Vremia* and its successor *Epokha* (Epoch) to respond to another concern: to illustrate the character of Russian journalism in the 1860's, its methods and its subject matter, and to show the way in which relatively minor incidents were seized upon to make more fundamental philosophical points. Strakhov in particular became a master at this game, and it is in this form that his literary personality emerged. We are now entering into the heart of the realm of obliqueness, of Aesopian language understandable only to initiates. Perhaps a warning is in order: it is a world which has to be approached with a certain amount of humor and sympathy, or else the superficial triviality of the issues is distressing.

The first issue of *Vremia,* for instance, was a brilliant literary success, but Strakhov's two contributions certainly were not. The issue opened with the first novel by Dostoevsky written since his exile, *The Insulted and Injured;* there were verses by Apollon Maikov and Apollon Grigorev; and there were even translations of three short stories by Edgar Allan Poe. However, Strakhov's "Zhiteli planet" (Life on other planets) was merely a long appendix to the "Letters on Life" in *Svetoch,* and made a rather murky impression. (The article makes sense chiefly in retrospect; it made a very appropriate opening chapter in Strakhov's first book, *The World as a Whole,* published a decade later.) Similarly, his "Zamechanie na 'otvete' P. Lavrova" (Remarks on Lavrov's answer) was merely a continuation of a discussion he had begun in *Svetoch* over the merits of P. L. Lavrov's *Ocherki voprosov prakticheskoi filosofii* (Essays on the problems of practical philosophy), not in itself a very spectacular subject for a new journal. Why begin in this way? The mystery disappears when we realize that the first issue of *Vremia* had found Strakhov already in the midst of a polemic, whose antecedents and consequences were much more striking than the articles themselves.

Lavrov was later to be known principally as a radical populist theorist; he fits quite clearly into what was called in those days "the progressive camp." Even in these earlier years, however, he combined in his philosophical writings that curious blend of positivism and ethical idealism which was to haunt the later populists. His serious approach to philosophical speculation aroused the ire of the leader of the Russian enlightenment, Chernyshevsky. Lavrov's book served as the pretext for Chernyshevsky's sensational attack on metaphysics in "The Anthropological Principle in Philosophy."[14] He rejected with vehemence both the philosophical trappings of Lavrov's method and the elements of Kantian subjectivism which he found buried beneath the "anthropological" positivism. But more striking in his "review" of the book, and in keeping with what later became known as his nihilism, was the fact that, even in such a review, Chernyshevsky was not particularly interested in Lavrov's book at all.

If Mr. Lavrov's pamphlet could serve only as a subject for
a critical review, and had we begun to read it with the idea
of analyzing the conceptions he expounds in it, we would
have stopped reading it after the very first page, because—
we shall be quite candid—we have not read most of the
numerous books the author has taken into consideration,
and we even think we shall never read them.[15]

Thus, when Strakhov attempted just that serious review of Lavrov's book which Chernyshevsky had rejected in the first sentences of his already famous article, he was taking a battle position.

Strakhov's first review of Lavrov's book, which had appeared in *Svetoch* shortly after Chernyshevsky's article, was also critical, but from a very different position.[16] Strakhov admired Lavrov's ethics while rejecting his attack on Hegel. The respectfulness of Lavrov's reply to Strakhov showed that he realized the implications of Strakhov's defense of his book, in view of Chernyshevsky's attack.[17] Strakhov's "Remarks on Lavrov's Answer," then, in the first issue of *Vremia*, appeared to further substantiate the point that the carefulness of the review is almost as important as the substance of the criticism.

The interchange between Lavrov, Chernyshevsky, and Strakhov began as a relatively private matter, but it soon became a very public affair. In the same month in which Lavrov had re-

14. In *Selected Philosophical Essays* (Moscow, 1953), pp. 49–135.
15. Chernyshevsky, "The Anthropological Principle in Philosophy," p. 49.
16. N. N Strakhov, in *Svetoch* (July 1860), pp. 1–13.
17. P. L. Lavrov, in *Otechestvennye zapiski* (December 1860).

plied to Strakhov, a very long and thorough attack on Chernyshevsky's "The Anthropological Principle in Philosophy" appeared
in the journal of the Kiev Theological Academy.[18] Pamphilus
Danilovich Iurkevich, a professor at the academy, had already
published several attacks on the materialists which had attracted
little attention outside theological circles, and it was unlikely that
this article would have met any different fate had it not been so
specifically directed against Chernyshevsky. Mikhail Katkov,
editor of the popular *Russkii vestnik*, had decided to make an
incident out of Chernyshevsky's article: he first echoed Strakhov's
defense of Lavrov,[19] then reprinted part of Iurkevich's article in
Russkii vestnik.[20]

Iurkevich's cause was taken up by people who, although un-
equipped to deal with the technical issues he had raised, were well
able to appreciate the implications of a rout of Chernyshevsky.
Katkov's championship of Iurkevich soon produced an uproar in
the journals. Chernyshevsky replied to both Iurkevich and Katkov.[21] *Otechestvennye zapiski* (Notes of the fatherland), which
had printed Lavrov's reply to Strakhov, also endorsed Iurkevich
by reprinting his article. At this point, Chernyshevsky wrote another attack on both journals.[22] Eventually most of the St. Petersburg press was involved in the polemic.

Why was there such an uproar about an article by an obscure
professor? It had, in fact, very little to do with Iurkevich or, for
that matter, Lavrov and Strakhov (who soon dropped out of the
debate). The issue evolved—or deteriorated—into a general polemic between Katkov and Chernyshevsky. The incident reveals
a significant aspect of St. Petersburg journalism; a minor book
review—in fact, a review of a review—could start a major polemic

18. P. D. Iurkevich, "Iz nauki o chelovecheskom dukhe" (On the science of the
human soul), *Trudy Kievskoi Dukhovnoi Akademii* (December 1860).
19. See especially Mikhail Katkov, "Starye bogi i novye bogi" (The old gods and
the new gods), *Russkii vestnik* (February 1861).
20. *Russkii vestnik* (April and May 1861).
21. Chernyshevsky, "Polemicheskie krasoty" (Polemical gems), *Sovremennik*
(June 1861).
22. Chernyshevsky, "Polemical Gems, II," *Sovremennik* (July, 1861).

if the parties involved (or even not yet involved) saw an opportunity for excitement. The polemic was passionately pursued. The real victim, unfortunately, was Iurkevich. He had exceeded his depth as a professor at a theological academy. With Katkov as vociferous sponsor he was offered the newly created chair of philosophy at Moscow University, and his course began in an atmosphere of intense student hostility. When he announced a series of public lectures on Büchner in 1863, there was a huge public demonstration and numerous protest letters in *Sovremennik*.[23] He did not really recover from the scandal for a decade.[24]

The second issue of *Vremia* was something of a repeat performance for Strakhov. In contrast to Dostoevsky's major contributions Strakhov merely contributed an off-hand remark.[25] The journal *Vek* (The century) had made a sneering reference to the great poet Schiller; Strakhov rebuked *Vek* in the name of the sanctity of art and the artist. It was not until the following month, when *Vek* had the audacity to sneer at Pushkin and was defended by Katkov, that a major confrontation began.

Vek was also a very new journal, which had appeared in the beginning of 1861 under the direction of a young poet, Petr Veinberg. The historian Konstantin Kavelin had been engaged to write a political column, but Veinberg, fearing that it was excessively dull, decided to lighten the journal with satirical *feuilletons* written by himself.[26] In so doing he unwittingly stirred up a hornet's nest.

At the end of February, *Vek* printed a piece by "Kamen Vinogorov." It took off from an account in the *Sankt-Peterburgskie vedomosti* (St. Petersburg gazette) of a recent literary evening in

23. A. Galaktionov and P. Nikandrov, *Istoriia russkoi filosofii* (Moscow, 1961), p. 306. On Iurkevich, see Volynsky, *Russkie kritiki*, pp. 320–365.

24. He was greatly admired in the early 1870's by the young Vladimir Solovev, then beginning his own, more famous, philosophical critique of positivism.

25. Especially important was Fedor Dostoevsky's "G.—bov i vopros ob iskusstve" (Mr.—bov and the art question), *Vremia* (February 1861). This was a refutation of Dobroliubov's utilitarian views on art.

26. P. [I.] Veinberg, "Bezobraznyi postupok *Veka*" (The 'ugly behavior' of *Vek*), *Istoricheskii vestnik* (May 1900), pp. 478–479.

the provincial town of Perm at which a Mme. Tolmacheva gave a public reading of Pushkin's unfinished short story "Egyptian Nights." The newspaper had related the following story: after the public reading, an officer wearing a St. George's medal had complained in an outrage that such an immoral story should not be read in the presence of ladies. The officer particularly objected to the passage in the story where Cleopatra asks, "Who among you young men would be willing to buy a night with me at the price of his life?" Mme. Tolmacheva, confronted by the officer with the St. George's medal, in great indignation defended both Pushkin's poetry and women's rights. *Vek,* commenting on the newspaper account, for some reason found Mme. Tolmacheva hysterically funny and was especially amused by the reported "expression of passion" which she allegedly wore as she recited the offending line by Pushkin. The poor lady was extoled in these terms: "O Orator, Reformer, and Emancipatoress! Now all the articles of John Stuart Mill, Mikhailov, and so forth seem superfluous; the universal campaign for female emancipation has begun with your bold new words!"[27]

The public reaction to *Vek's* comments was instantaneous. Once again, in no time at all both Mme. Tolmacheva and "Egyptian Nights" were side issues. Female emancipation was the current sacred radical cause, not only as an issue in itself but as a symbol for a general emancipation of the individual from the restraints of the old social order. M. L. Mikhailov, soon to be exiled for political activities, wrote an indignant letter to *Sankt-Peterburgskie vedomosti* about "Kamen Vinogorov's" insult to womanhood in *Vek* and also about his lack of social conscience and absence of moral sensitivity. "No man with a heart, aware of the present social position of women, could publicly so abuse a woman . . . simply because she dared to show her disdain for ignorant prejudice."[28]

Katkov took the opportunity to attack the radical Mikhailov by supporting *Vek,* just as he had supported Iurkevich and for the

27. Veinberg, "*Vek,*" p. 480.
28. Veinberg, "*Vek,*" p. 482.

same reason.[29] He was immediately rebutted by *Sovremennik* and *Russkoe slovo*, who defended Mikhailov and womanhood. Before long all the journals had hold of the scandal, including *Vremia*.

The irony of the scandal was that Veinberg had not meant it. Of all the targets for a radical counterattack, Veinberg was particularly unlikely. He was a liberal, a contributor to the radical *Iskra*, and above all a close friend of M. L. Mikhailov. In fact, his little satirical piece in *Vek* need not have been taken as illiberal. On the contrary, on the day in which it appeared he had met Nekrasov, editor of *Sovremennik*, on the street and was congratulated for its humor. "You've certainly given it to her; she had it coming," was Nekrasov's comment.[30] But after Mikhailov's indignant letter, Nekrasov changed his mind. The scandal, according to Veinberg's account, ruined *Vek*.

Vremia could not resist the polemic. Dostoevsky's inclination was to join the journalistic fray in a defense of humanitarianism.[31] An article in the May issue of *Vremia* placed the journal squarely on Mikhailov's side.

We are concerned with matters of lofty moral development. The sense of duty can take root in the soul of woman as easily as in the soul of man. We are convinced that only when this happens will the relations between men and women be defined clearly, justly, and humanely, and we wish to promote this as strongly as possible.[32]

But the most interesting part of the article had nothing at all to

29. Mikhail Katkov, "Nash iazyk, i kto svistuny?" (Our language, and who are the whistlers?), *Russkii vestnik* (March 1861).

30. Veinberg, *"Vek,"* pp. 481–483.

31. The incident is discussed partially in V. L. Komarovich, "Dostoevskii i 'Egipetskie nochi' Pushkina" (Dostoevsky and Pushkin's "Egyptian Nights"), *Pushkin i ego sovremenniki*, XXIX–XXX (Petrograd, 1918) 36–48; V. S. Dorovatovskaia-Liubimova, "Dostoevskii i shestidesiatniki" (Dostoevsky and the men of the sixties), in *Dostoevskii* (Moscow, 1928) pp. 5–60; V. Ia. Kirpotin, *Dostoevskii v shestidesiatye gody* (Moscow, 1966), pp. 97–105.

32. Fedor Dostoevsky, "Otvet 'Russkomu Vestniku' " (An answer to *Russkii vestnik*), *Vremia* (May 1861), p. 26.

do with the social issue; Dostoevsky also raised an aesthetic point, and in this case he was able to criticize both the slanders against Pushkin by Katkov and the ideological interpretation of the incident given by Mikhailov.

You [*Russkii vestnik*] speak of the tragedy, of the completing of this, as you call it, "fragment," but perhaps you do not understand that in an artistic sense it is impossible to develop and further fill out this fragment; then something *completely different* would result, something in a completely different form, perhaps of differing impact, perhaps of greater worth, but completely *other* than the present "Egyptian Nights," and consequently losing all the feeling and the meaning of the present "Egyptian Nights." Pushkin gave himself exactly the tasks (if it is possible that he assigned tasks to his inspiration beforehand) of presenting one and only one moment of Roman life, in such a way as to produce the fullest spiritual sensation, and so as to transmit in a few verses and images the whole spirit, the whole feeling of a moment of life in those times; and by this moment, by means of this little corner, a whole picture could be sketched in and become intelligible.[33]

This element of his article is very significant for Dostoevsky's views about aesthetics. He was later to make a similar defense of Pushkin in his famous memorial address in 1880. It is one of the strongest articles in which *Vremia* took up the cause of literature against the utilitarian critics who rated art less valuable than a pair of boots.[34] In view of the importance of this question for the novelist, it is very significant that most of Dostoevsky's thoughts about Pushkin's "Egyptian Nights" come directly from Strakhov's writings, although they appear in *Vremia* over Dostoevsky's signature. Strakhov had written several pieces about the incident at the time; one was published anonymously in the March issue of

33. Fedor Dostoevsky, "An Answer," p. 31.
34. On Dostoevsky's aesthetic views, see R. L. Jackson, *Dostoevsky's Quest for Form* (New Haven, 1966).

Vremia, but two shorter pieces were used only by incorporation into Dostoevsky's article in May.[35] Strakhov devoted his attention entirely to the aesthetic problems of the story and was completely indifferent to the social issue. He insisted that this story by Pushkin was most of all a personal statement of despair caused by the gulf which exists between a great poet and a sneering public. Pushkin identifies himself with the Italian improviser who is so mocked by the Russian audience in the story. "Indeed, one can still hear the Northern barbarians snickering at him now." In this respect, said Strakhov, *Vek* and *Sovremennik* are equally disrespectful. The conservatives complain that Pushkin's poem is *im*moral, the radicals complain that it is *a*moral; both are obviously insensitive to Pushkin's genius.

It is clear that Strakhov had a great influence over the expression of Dostoevsky's aesthetic views at this point in his life. Scholars who, like V. L. Komarovich and V. Ia. Kirpotin, emphasize the articles of these years as the formative ones for Dostoevsky, err in not recognizing this fact.[36] But there was, nevertheless, a great difference between the ways in which the two men approached the Pushkin episode; Dostoevsky saw it primarily as a social issue and a journalistic free-for-all, whereas Strakhov was concerned only with a defense of aesthetic principles from the utilitarians of right and left. As in the Iurkevich incident, Strakhov dropped out when the principles dropped out.

The two incidents which have been discussed are very good illustrations both of contemporary journalistic concerns and of *Vremia's* indirect technique of dealing with them in the first few months of its life. In both cases, *Vremia* played an ambiguous role, more provocative than decisive. Strakhov, having initiated a serious tone, was followed by a playful Dostoevsky, who in both cases seemed more interested in attacking Katkov than Chernyshevsky. There was some justification for considering *Vremia*

35. They were only published posthumously in a Strakhov volume in 1902, with the explanation. See Strakhov, *Kriticheskie stati*, p. 266.
36. Komarovich, "Dostoevsky and Pushkin's 'Egyptian Nights'"; Kirpotin, *Dostoevskii v shestidesiatye gody.*

friendly to the men on *Sovremennik*. This impression soon changed under the more energetic intervention of Strakhov.

In the late spring of 1861, Strakhov's importance for *Vremia* was fully realized; he finally appeared as *enfant terrible* with a series of anonymous letters which rapidly turned the journal into an uncompromising warrior against the radicals. "The battle against literary nihilism," as Strakhov was later to call it, started with a curious letter to the editor of *Vremia* in the April issue, signed with the initials N.K. It began with an epigram from Gogol: "I swear, the nineteenth century will be ashamed of these last five years!" It went on to criticize everything about St. Petersburg journalism, and especially its negativism; we on the Neva reject Pushkin, Schiller, Hegel, and hope to cater to the lowest common denominator of public taste by "whistling" instead of engaging in serious discourse.[37] The insults were generally venomous but undirected.

After two months, another letter appeared with the mask slightly lowered; it was signed "N. Ko." But the barb had found a very specific target.

Recently, in the beautiful month of May, two articles appeared which caught my involuntary attention . . . One of
them is by Mr. D. Pisarev in *Russkoe slovo*, under the title
of "The Scholasticism of the Nineteenth Century"; the other
is an article of Mr. N. Chernyshevsky in *Sovremennik*
under the heading "On the Causes of the Fall of Rome"
. . . To make a judgment about these articles, that is to
assess their worth, is exceedingly easy . . . If I, for example,
could write with the kind of authority with which *Russkii
vestnik* writes, then I would repeat the words of the learned
journal and would say, that the article of Mr. Chernyshevsky is *total nonsense,* and I would refer Mr. Pisarev to
what Mr. Antonovich said, that is, that *he does not possess*

37. The reference to "whistling" is a comment on *Svistok* (The whistle), Do-broliubov's satirical supplement to *Sovremennik*. Katkov was the first to call the radicals "whistlers" during the Iurkevich polemic.

even the understanding of what it is to think . . . But the
thing is not so easy to resolve . . . it is necessary to refute
these articles. But there is a terrible complication. It is easy
to see that it *is not worth it* to refute these articles. Judge
for yourself.[38]

To N. Ko., the articles by Chernyshevsky and Pisarev were
merely essays in childish negativeness: Chernyshevsky rejects
history and Pisarev rejects philosophy merely because they represent authorities which must be overthrown. Nevertheless, and
rather inconsistently, according to Strakhov, the two men have a
distressing faith both in their own logic and in that of respected
foreigners; they even take up issues simply because they are
European, even though they have no relevance to Russia. Pisarev
is the epitome of the trend, since he denies absolutely everything,
even truth and beauty. There is, it is true, something quite re-
freshing about Pisarev's total independence; perhaps it is that,
being barbarians, we cannot understand the normal preoccupa-
tions of civilized men. "But what if we take Pisarev up on it?
. . . When we all have enough to wear and enough to eat, what
then? Will we then be able to dabble in philosophy on a full
stomach?"[39]

N. Ko.'s target was the article in which Pisarev made his radical debut with a famous attack on the bastions of German romanticism: idealist aesthetics and idealist philosophy. I have already
quoted part of the article to illustrate the antimetaphysical tone
of radical thought;[40] using the evidence of Rudolf Haym's critique
of Hegel (*Hegel und seine Zeit*, first published in 1857, and in
Russian in 1861), he concluded that the study of philosophy was
on its way out. In a spirit very similar to Chernyshevsky's commentary on Lavrov, Pisarev ended his article with the following
paragraph:

38. N. N. Strakhov, *Is istorii literaturnogo nigilizma* (St. Petersburg, 1890),
pp. 15–16.
39. Strakhov, *Is istorii literaturnogo nigilizma*, p. 37.
40. Pisarev, "Nineteenth Century Scholasticism," pp. 108–110.

In speaking of our philosophical literature, I have mentioned only Mr. Lavrov. I consider it quite unnecessary to speak of Messrs. Strakhov and Edelson, who are so pallid and so stunted in stature as to be undeserving of mention, let alone of discussion. Reading their writings can only lead to yawns. They are so elementary and arid and boring that there is nothing in them to object to. Mr. Strakhov considers it necessary to prove that there is a difference between a man and a stone, while Mr. Edelson goes into raptures over the idea of the organism.[41]

Hence it is not surprising that N. Ko.'s attack appeared in *Vremia,* since N. Ko. was none other than Strakhov. Although his tone had now changed to heavy sarcasm and was to remain sarcastic, his message was that of his earlier essays. It was a declaration of war against materialism, utilitarianism, and positivist social science as illustrated by every issue of *Sovremennik* and *Russkoe slovo.*

The sarcasm of the tone, and the playfulness of the anonymity, at first disguised the thrust of the attack. N. K., then N. Ko. What would the next letter reveal? The surprise was that it revealed nothing, since it reverted to the signature N. K. and consisted of one long complaint. The radicals had counterattacked, but N. K. did not like the way in which they did it. Polemics were one thing, but personal insults were another. Thus, he suggested that instead of pretending to understand our critics and respond to them, perhaps we should simply forget intelligent discourse and set up a new institution in every journal, a monthly column entitled "Insults." In it one could simply list (1) horrible articles in *Russkii vestnik* this month, (2) horrible articles in *Otechestvennye zapiski* this month, (3) horrible articles in *Sovremennik* this month, and so on. One could simply throw names around and

41. Pisarev refers to Strakhov's "Letters on Organic Life." E. N. Edelson was one of Grigorev's closest friends, and later Strakhov's, also. He had been on *Moskvitianin* and later on *Russkoe slovo* in 1859, in the days when the poet A. A. Fet and Grigorev dominated the journal. The article in question was Edelson's "The idea of the Organism," which appeared in *Biblioteka dlia Chteniia* (March 1860).

completely avoid any issues. The one with the loudest voice would win the argument. Anyone, of course, can whistle and play the game; but the trouble lies in the fact that the significance of the whistle is counted in direct proportion to the significance of the whistler, and we are beginning to get an over-development of private authorities. They threaten you with: "Don't say that or I'll whistle at you!" They are even beginning to whistle at Pushkin now.[42]

This new letter added another dimension to the polemic with the radicals. N. K. had begun in apparent good spirits, swinging into his position with eager self-assurance. But he very shortly began to exhibit a certain peevishness, which reflected the fact that he had soon found it very difficult to challenge the dominance that the radicals had achieved in the St. Petersburg literary world. The triumph of radical journalism in the 1860's is an almost incredible story. Even under conditions of continual government suspicion and censorship (and eventual repression), the radicals managed to dominate simply by the assertiveness of their writings and the strength of their personalities. In fact, the self-assurance and conviction in their articles has even convinced most historians of the truth of their most cherished delusion: that they were the only important voice in Russia in the 1860's.

Strakhov was completely unprepared for this situation when he began his career on *Vremia,* but he had already been warned by a more sophisticated observer. One of the members of Miliukov's literary group, besides Dostoevsky, was the poet and critic Apollon Grigorev. Grigorev had admired Strakhov's work, and was invited to be a collaborator on the new *Vremia.*[43] In the early 1850's Grigorev had been one of the most active members of the "Young Editorial Board" of Mikhail Pogodin's *Moskvitianin* (The Muscovite). The success of this journal coincided with the last dark

42. Strakhov, *Iz istorii literaturnogo nigilizma,* p. 49.
43. N. N. Strakhov, "Vospominaniia ob A. A. Grigoreve" (Memoirs of Grigorev), published as a memorial to Grigorev in *Epokha* (September 1864). "Memoirs of Grigorev" was reprinted without censor's deletions in *A. A. Grigorev: Vospominaniia i stati,* ed. R. V. Ivanov-Razumnik (Moscow, 1930). The present reference is to the 1930 volume, p. 433.

years of the reign of Nicholas I, when liberal ideas could exist only in silent hearts. Pogodin and his journal have thus acquired the stigma of an association with the sterile patriotism of the Official Nationality of Nicholas I. But it is often forgotten that the "Young Editorial Board" (of which the playwright Aleksandr Ostrovsky was also a member) made of the journal a stunning literary endeavor; it was also the only outlet for philosophical thought in Russia at the time. Grigorev's thoughtful literary criticism was permeated with German idealism, and the young Strakhov of the 1850's, writing his own Schilleresque poetry, had admired him greatly. But *Moskvitianin* folded in 1856, along with the reign of Nicholas, and its demise signaled the new radical trend in Russian journalism. Nekrasov's *Sovremennik* soon captured young minds, with Chernyshevsky as star performer. Grigorev found himself alone, without any readers, and he thus began what he later called his "wanderings." He thought of himself, bitterly, as a "displaced person," without an opportunity to breathe or work. By the time Strakhov met him in 1860 he was at the nadir of his career, deprived by the radicals of what he considered his proper forum. In less than a decade since the heyday of *Moskvitianin*, the radicals had seized command. Grigorev was very skeptical about *Vremia*'s chances; but Strakhov, in his enthusiasm, refused to be alarmed.

The letters of N. Ko. from August of 1861 on indicate how short a time it took for Strakhov to be apprised of the danger. Grigorev's bitterness was in some degree justified. From now on the letters would alternate between an attempt to discuss the issues and a complaint about the radicals' effort to excommunicate their literary opponents. The arrogance of such "literary legislators," Strakhov once said, resembled that of the Caliph Omar who, upon being confronted with the Greek library at Alexandria after the Moslem conquest, said: "If these books repeat what is already in the Koran, they are superfluous; if they contradict it, they are harmful; hence, burn them!"[44]

44. Strakhov, *Iz istorii literaturnogo nigilizma*, p. 85.

The vehemence of the excommunication by the radicals is an important landmark in *Vremia*'s, and in Strakhov's, history. It was now quite clear that *Vremia* was an enemy. Despite Dostoevsky's exile, the humanitarianism of his novels, and his journalistic antipathy to Katkov, his journal was quite clearly devoting itself to an attempt to unseat the radicals. The counterattack launched by the radicals focused at first on Strakhov as N.K. and eventually on the question of the meaning of the slogan which *Vremia* took for itself: pochvennichestvo.

The most important item in the polemic appeared in print even before *Vremia*. It was customary to print an advance notice of policy, together with an appeal for subscriptions, several months before commencement of publication; such a notice, written by Dostoevsky, had appeared in various journals in September 1860.

The reforms of Peter the Great have been too expensive for us: they have separated us from the people . . . Peter's reforms, continuing right up to our own times, have reached their last limits. It is not possible to go further, indeed there is nowhere to go: there are no roads . . . We have become convinced, finally, that we also are a separate nationality . . . and that our task is to create for ourselves a new way, a native way, taken out of our own soil, from the soul of the people, and derived from national principles. We foresee that the nature of our future culture should be to the highest degree humanitarian, that the Russian idea, perhaps, will be a synthesis of all those ideas which Europe has developed with such firmness and vitality in each of her separate nationalities; and that perhaps all contradictions in these ideas will find their reconciliation and furthest development in Russian nationality . . . But first we must reconcile Peter's reforms with the popular spirit.[45]

45. O. F. Miller and N. N. Strakhov, eds., *Biografiia, pisma, i zametki iz zapisnoi knishki F. M. Dostoevskogo* (St. Petersburg, 1883), pp. 178–180. Strakhov's memoirs of Dostoevsky appeared in this volume; it was the first biography of Dostoevsky to be written and the source of much of our information about the details of his life.

The essence of the announcement was that *Vremia* would be the literary organ of this reconciliation between the Russian people and the educated classes. The real complaint was that the educated Russian, excessively Westernized, had been "cut off from the national soil *(pochva)*." It was from this phrase that the editorial board of *Vremia* acquired the nickname *pochvenniki* and their program pochvennichestvo.

Dostoevsky's use of the word pochva was a conceit common in the nineteenth century, a reflection of the popularity of biological imagery in this post-Newtonian era. As noted before, organicism was a characteristic trait of the romantic reaction to what was considered the mechanistic thought of the previous century. Strakhov's "Letters on Life" in *Svetoch* was only one of many examples of the utilization of this terminology. Grigorev, also, used the pages of *Svetoch, Vremia,* and other journals to develop what he called his "organic theory" of literature (which will be discussed later).

Although both Strakhov and Grigorev made important contributions to the theory of pochvennichestvo as *Vremia's* trademark, they had no exclusive monopoly on biological terminology even within the context of St. Petersburg journalism. Petr Veinberg, the poet who had published *Vek* with such disastrous results, recalls in his memoirs that he was part of a circle in 1858 that decided at one point to put out a new journal which would be called *Korni* (Roots). Veinberg sat in on the planning conferences; being thoroughly mystified by most of the conversation, he finally asked for a precise definition of their program. The answer was

"We wish to put down roots."
"Where, and what kind of roots?"
"Into the Russian soil, and the deeper
  they penetrate, the better."[46]

Miliukov's *Svetoch,* on which Strakhov, Grigorev, and Mikhail

46. Veinberg "*Vek*," p. 473.

Dostoevsky had all worked, had also taken "reconciliation" as a slogan.[47]

These associations with pochva tended to give the slogan a connotation that was distinctly Slavophile and, as it was thought in 1860, hence distinctly conservative. On the other hand, Dostoevsky's reputation was that of a political exile whose Siberian experiences were that very moment being chronicled in *Russkii mir* in his *Memoirs from the House of the Dead. The Insulted and Injured,* published in the first issues of *Vremia,* was clearly in the humanitarian tradition of *Poor Folk,* which had so pleased Belinsky in 1846. Hence both Chernyshevsky and Pisarev commented favorably on *Vremia's* first issue, and even M. A. Antonovich, later their most violent critic, admitted that he had been pleased at first with *Vremia.*[48]

However, from the very beginning Dostoevsky had given fair warning that his journal would not be easily categorized. *Vremia* opted for independence: "We are not here speaking of Slavophiles and Westernizers; their family quarrels leave us cold."[49] But it was more than anything the letters of N.K., with their very direct attack on the radical dogma, that finally provoked the onslaught.

As it turned out, *Vremia's* most vocal antagonist was not Chernyshevsky or Pisarev but M. A. Antonovich, a man of considerably less talent but much more venom. Antonovich has now been very much overshadowed by his illustrious colleagues, and with some intellectual justification, but in his own time he had considerable influence on *Sovremennik,* especially after Chernyshevsky's arrest in 1862. It is true that in the following decade he managed to make himself quite unpopular among the radicals for his criticisms of the populists, and he acquired a reputation for cantankerousness. But in the 1860's he was very orthodox indeed, especially

47. See "An Introductory Word," written by the editor in the first issue of *Svetoch* for 1860; also, the analysis of it by the radical journalist, Antonovich, in M. A. Antonovich, *Literaturno-kriticheskie stati* (Moscow, 1961), p. 466.

48. M. A. Antonovich, "O dukhe Vremeni" (On the spirit of *Vremia*), *Sovremennik* (April 1862).

49. Miller and Strakhov, *Biografiia,* p. 180.

about his antipathies; he often embarrassed Chernyshevsky and Pisarev by his single-minded dedication to the cause. He was one of the first to attack Iurkevich and the Kiev Theological Academy and was later to be one of the most violent in attacking Turgenev for *Fathers and Sons;* furthermore, he seemed to consider the very existence of *Vremia* a personal insult.

In the December 1861 issue of *Sovremennik* an article appeared by Antonovich entitled "O pochve (ne v agronomicheskom smysle, a v dukhe 'Vremeni')" (About the soil [not in an agricultural sense, but in *Vremia*'s sense]). The point, as if to nullify any future arguments, was that the definition of pochvennichestvo was really a very simple matter: pochvennichestvo is nothing more than old-fashioned Slavophilism as preached by the Official Nationalists of the 1840's. Antonovich simplified the problem of historians of Russian nationalism by merely combining in a single hypothetical whole the writings of the reactionary Faddei Bulgarin, the Slavophile Aleksei Khomiakov, and Nikolai Strakhov. They talk, he said, about their love for the people, and they talk about the need for educating them and helping them; but in fact the people need bread most of all, and this the pochvenniki refuse to give; their "reconciliation" is a reconciliation of the people to their poverty.

Strakhov's answer to Antonovich's charge was the most important of his contributions to pochvennichestvo; he saved *Vremia* from the charge of cruelty by lifting the issue onto another level. After all, there is something beautifully simple and just about Antonovich's charge, if it is taken on its own economic terms. Strakhov, however, as might be expected from his Hegelianism, was unable to accept the materialist assumption. His response is a classic statement of philosophical idealism. He does not deny the necessity for caring for physical needs; but

People always were, are, and will be idealists. Occasionally one hears it sarcastically said: bravo for humanity! Look how long people have been living on this earth and up to this time they have still not been able to arrange things so that no one starves to death. What an unjust reproach!

. . . Suppose people had set themselves the creation of
such a system as chief and only goal . . . Without doubt
they would achieve this goal. But that never happened;
people always wanted more . . . Idealism constitutes
the root of human misery [therefore] . . . if this is the root,
then the rectification of this evil should start from here
also. From this reasoning it is clear why many conclude
that one must *destroy idealism* . . . These people would
say . . . "Does your head hurt? Cut it off and the pain will
go away . . ." To take away man's idealism means just
that — to remove a man's head because it hurts. In the place
of the sick head we need a healthy head, not a headless
torso. A sick idealism should not be destroyed, but changed
into a healthy one.[50]

Moreover, people have always risked their lives in the name of
ideals. One cannot change human nature.

Do you want people to value bread and life more than they
do now? Hardly anyone will agree to that. For if man is
good for any reason, it is precisely because he never
will be content with satiety and merely earthly blessings;
always there are blessings that he puts above a full
stomach.[51]

Whether or not you consider Strakhov's response an apt one
depends on your own philosophical assumptions; Antonovich certainly did not. As a materialist, along with his colleagues, he did
not find idealism a cogent defense. He had once tried to refute
Strakhov's Hegelianism on more or less its own terms by the following stratagem: "One hundred theoretical rubles are useless
to a starving man."[52] Strakhov had replied to this display of philosophical ingenuity: "I sympathize with his sympathy for the

---

50. Strakhov, *Iz istorii literaturnogo nigilizma*, p. 122.
51. Strakhov, *Iz istorii literaturnogo nigilizma*, p. 124. Not only was Strakhov's
article a review of his previous articles, it was a statement of the basic points in
Dostoevsky's *Notes from Underground*, which was written two years later.
52. M. A. Antonovich, "O gegelevoi filosofii" (On Hegelian Philosophy), *Sovremennik* (August 1861).

starving man, but what has all this to do with philosophy?" One must, after all, distinguish between men and turkeys, and the same rules do not apply to both.

It is permissible to be ignorant of philosophy; in this there
is no harm; but it is not at all permissible to write about
philosophy when you know nothing . . . Knowledge is not
compulsory, indeed it is not accessible to everyone; it is
not possible to demand that everyone be a philosopher.
But everyone is obliged to be honest and an upright
person, and this is accessible to everyone.[53]

Antonovich took the advice in the long run and avoided such "philosophical" debates by moving onto surer, political grounds. "About the Spirit of *Vremia* and Mr. Kosits. as its Chief Expounder"[54] was a thoroughly political attack on N. Kosits., as the leading political reactionary of a reactionary journal, one which absolutely dismissed the need for social and economic progress and callously accepted the silent suffering of the Russian people. In other words, *Vremia* and *Sovremennik* were too far apart to engage in fruitful discussion.

Strakhov recognized the futility of it all. "Nothing but twaddle comes from twaddle," concluded N. Kositsa, using the full pseudonym, in May 1862.[55] When Antonovich goes to the point of dismissing such an eminent work as Nikolai Nikolaevich Strakhov's "Life on Other Planets" he has gone too far![56] The differences between the journals are simple, according to Strakhov. *Vremia* considers literature the most organic significant phenomenon in contemporary life and Pushkin the epitome of it; *Sovremennik*

53. N. N. Strakhov, "Ob indiushkakh i o Gegele" (About turkeys and Hegel), *Vremia* (September 1861); in Strakhov, *Iz istorii literaturnogo nigilizma*, pp. 73 and 79.

54. M. A. Antonovich, "O dukhe 'Vremeni' i o g. Kosits. kak nailushchem ego vyrazhenii" (About the spirit of *Vremia* and Mr. Kosits. as its chief expounder), *Sovremennik* (April 1862). Strakhov's pen name had unfolded considerably by this time.

55. Strakhov, *Iz istorii literaturnogo nigilizma*, p. 130.

56. This was Strakhov's first article in *Vremia*.

calls literature "mere chattering" and Pushkin a writer about military and erotic matters. *Vremia* considers it a duty to search everywhere for manifestations of the Russian spirit; *Sovremennik* considers *narodnost* an empty phrase. Of course, *Sovremennik* may not think that there is any *real* cause for argument here, but that is only because the people involved are complete cynics who do not realize that there are some people who value abstract truth above all material things.

The justness of the argument aside, the really significant point about Strakhov's debate with Antonovich is that he, for the first time and in unambiguous terms, defined pochvennichestvo within a philosophical context rather than a political one. If this rubric is accepted, then all arguments about Dostoevsky's humanitarianism or dislike of Katkov become irrelevant; as a defender of philosophical idealism and aesthetic idealism *Vremia* was clearly never in the radical camp. The most that one can say about the ambiguities are that it took some time for all this to become obvious. N. Kositsa's debate with *Sovremennik* clarified it.

The question of the *timing* of this effort at clarification is very important if we wish to understand the special role that Strakhov played on the journal. It is clear, both to contemporaries and to historians now, that *Vremia* underwent a certain change in the course of its first year; this could be crudely described as a shift in category from "democratic" to "conservative," although I have suggested already that these are not very helpful categories. Why the shift occurred, however, is a more interesting question.

Some observers have suggested that *Vremia*'s editorial policy was a direct reflection of Dostoevsky's political views, and that *Vremia*'s evolution was merely Dostoevsky's personal conversion. This is the view, for instance, of one of the most knowledgeable of Dostoevsky scholars, A. S. Dolinin.[57] Dolinin points to the change

57. A. S. Dolinin, *Poslednie romany Dostoevskogo* (Moscow, 1963), "Dostoevsky and Strakhov"; idem, "F. M. Dostoevskii i N. N. Strakhov," in *Shestidesiatye gody,* ed. N. K. Piksanov and O. V. Tsekhnovitser (Moscow, 1940), 238–254. Dolinin is the editor of Dostoevsky's correspondence and author of many books about the man and his work.

which seems to have occurred between the writing of *The Insulted and Injured* (1860) and *Notes from Underground* (1863). He feels that the crucial document is *Winter Notes on Summer Impressions* (1862), written on the important first trip to Europe with Strakhov as companion. Dolinin suggests that Strakhov's influence on Dostoevsky was decisive in the shift from radical to conservative; he points to the similarity between Strakhov's articles and the ideas of Dostoevsky's stories, and to the explicit acknowledgement of intellectual debt which Dostoevsky makes to Strakhov in his letters.

Other critics have elaborated Dolinin's interpretation of the "liberal" early Dostoevsky.[58] The work of V. Ia. Kirpotin is the most extreme example of this point of view. Kirpotin insists on the "democratic" label not only for Dostoevsky but for Grigorev also; he thus exceeds the efforts of his colleagues to "justify" Dostoevsky as at least an *early* liberal. According to Kirpotin, the only real conservative on the journal was Strakhov, and he was responsible for wooing Dostoevsky away from Belinsky's heritage and toward Slavophile conservatism "because he hated socialism with all the fibres of his niggardly soul."[59]

From an entirely opposite critical position, the neo-Kantian

58. V. L. Komarovich in "Dostoevskii i shestidesiatniki" (Dostoevsky and the men of the sixties), *Sovremennyi mir* (January 1917) analyzed the early *Vremia* articles as friendly to *Sovremennik*. The articles were bitter toward Katkov, they were reticent about Iurkevich, and they were only ambiguously critical of Dobroliubov. According to Komarovich, it was the extremism of *Sovremennik* which led to Dostoevsky's break with its editorial board. G. O. Berliner, *N. G. Chernyshevskii i ego literaturnye vragi* (Moscow, 1930), endorsed the image of the liberal Dostoevsky, emphasizing again his attack on Katkov.

59. V. Ia. Kirpotin, *Dostoevskii i Belinskii* (Moscow, 1960), p. 124. See also idem, *Publitsisty i kritiki* (Moscow, 1932). Kirpotin takes a closer, and more balanced, look at the activities of the pochvenniki in his *Dostoevskii v shestidesiatye gody* (Moscow, 1966); he admits that Grigorev's attitude toward Belinsky was very complicated. Nevertheless, he himself retains a most peculiarly hostile attitude toward Strakhov, which makes him completely unable to understand either Strakhov's ideas or the nature of the influence he had on Dostoevsky. His use of the relationship to Belinsky as a barometer of the social and political attitudes of the men of the sixties is unfortunate; he completely misrepresents Strakhov's view of Belinsky, which was far less hostile than Kirpotin seems to think.

critic A. L. Volynsky shares these opinions about Dostoevsky's early liberalism.[60] Although unsympathetic to Chernyshevsky, he is even more hostile to Katkov, and he emphasizes the significance of the polemic with Katkov's *Russkii vestnik* during the Iurkevich incident and the "Egyptian Nights" controversy. Volynsky claims that Strakhov was the only real enemy of the radicals, and that the polemic between *Vremia* and *Sovremennik* evolved only because Antonovich was too rigid to recognize that *Vremia* had very little in common with the Slavophiles.

All these interpretations assume that there was a real change in Dostoevsky and that Strakhov was the responsible party. A more recent commentator, S. S. Borshchevsky, makes a very different assessment.[61] Unlike Dolinin and Volynsky, he holds no particular brief for Dostoevsky. His hero is Mikhail Saltykov-Shchedrin, and he views the entire history of *Vremia* from the vantage point of Shchedrin's polemics with Dostoevsky after 1864. According to his analysis, which follows rather closely Shchedrin's contemporary accusations, Dostoevsky was a villain and a cynic. There was no change; he was always a reactionary. His attacks on Katkov were a diversionary tactic, because he feared an attack from the popular Chernyshevsky. Only after Chernyshevsky's arrest in 1862 did Dostoevsky's hypocrisy reveal itself.

Borshchesvsky's case is interesting, if a little overstated, because it depends so vitally on contradictory internal evidence. He relies heavily on Dostoevsky's articles in both their published and their earlier, unpublished form; they are still ambiguous, even with Borshchevsky's reading of them. He also uses as evidence Strakhov's reminiscences, which are unreliable because they were written fifteen years after the events in question.[62]

Strakhov saw Dostoevsky essentially as a journalist. By this he meant that Dostoevsky was not above simplifying or exaggerating

60. A. L. Volynsky, *Russkie kritiki.*
61. S. S. Borshchevsky, *Shchedrin i Dostoevskii* (Moscow, 1956).
62. Miller and Strakhov, *Biografiia.*

to make his points. He was able to prevaricate if he saw a journalistic advantage in it. Strakhov illustrates this with an anecdote which describes how Dostoevsky once tried to soften Strakhov's attacks on the radicals; he inserted a flattering comparison to Voltaire in the same sentence in which Strakhov was criticizing them most heavily.[63] Nevertheless, despite Dostoevsky's caution, Strakhov insists that Dostoevsky was as intellectually committed to the polemic with *Sovremennik* as Strakhov himself.

Strakhov uses the issue of the Slavophilism of pochvennichestvo to make his point. He suggests that, despite his early denials, Dostoevsky was naturally inclined toward Slavophilism from the beginning. He suggests also that the famous "Pushkin speech" of 1880, in which Dostoevsky's Slavophile views were most clearly expressed, can be traced back in detail to the *Vremia* subscription announcement of 1860.

Strakhov's reminiscences may perhaps have overemphasized the commitment to Slavophilism because he was so aware of the direction in which Dostoevsky traveled after the *Vremia* days; letters which were exchanged between Strakhov and Grigorev during the early months of *Vremia's* existence tend to corroborate Strakhov's analysis. The circumstances of the correspondence were slightly peculiar. Having been invited to participate in the publishing of *Vremia*, Grigorev suddenly disappeared in June 1861. The reasons for his departure were purely personal, involving a disagreeable wife and a young mistress; he moved to Orenburg as a teacher in a local school, and proceeded to bombard Strakhov with articles and letters. After Grigorev's death, Strakhov published the correspondence.

Grigorev was an intellectual despot; all of his letters have an accusatory tone, not toward Strakhov personally but toward *Vremia*. Grigorev wanted *Vremia* to come to terms with its own latent Slavophilism. He was indignant, for instance, at a suggestion from Dostoevsky that Grigorev's articles be anonymous. "I am not yet, thank God, a Bulgarin whose name would compromise

63. Miller and Strakhov, *Biografiia,* p. 235.

the journal!"[64] At one point, Mikhail Dostoevsky objected to praise of Khomiakov and Ivan Kireevsky in an article by Grigorev, who then became enraged. "I cannot and will not even renounce the right to put initials before the name of Pogodin, and even to address him as Mikhail Petrovich, and even to speak with respect of Shevyrev, freely bestowing praise and blame as I wish!"[65] He also protested that Mikhail Dostoevsky was cheapening his brother's talents by "driving him like a posthorse" and letting him write political drivel.[66] Grigorev always assumed that Strakhov shared his Slavophile views; indeed, as Strakhov put it in his reminiscences, "the matter came to its inevitable conclusion," and *Vremia* in time openly acknowledged this aspect of pochvennichestvo.

On the basis of this kind of evidence there seems to be little doubt that Borshchevsky is correct in questioning the "liberal" Dostoevsky of 1861. But it is not very helpful to suggest that *Vremia*'s slowness in defining itself was due to his depravity. I would like instead to suggest something of a modification; there were other factors involved besides Dostoevsky's personality.

I suspect, for instance, that Mikhail Dostoevsky's role in the formulation of editorial policy has been mistakenly minimized. It is true that Mikhail was editor-in-chief of the journal only because Fedor was under a police ban after his exile. Nevertheless, Mikhail Dostoevsky was a literary man himself, he had had the original idea for the journal, and I cannot imagine that he took his editorial duties casually.[67] He was a good business man (he ran a cigarette factory which put little "surprises" in each pack), and he was very much aware of the influence of public opinion. He exerted more control over editorial matters, perhaps for financial reasons, than Strakhov and others wished to admit.[68] Mikhail

64. Grigorev's letters were interleaved with Strakhov's comments and included at the end of Strakhov's "Memoirs of Grigorev." The specific letters are referred to by date. The above quotation is from Grigorev to Strakhov, August 12, 1861.
65. Grigorev to Strakhov, June 18, 1861, in "Memoirs of Grigorev."
66. Grigorev to Strakhov, June 18, 1861, in "Memoirs of Grigorev."
67. A. S. Dolinin, *F. M. Dostoevskii: Stati i materialy*, II (Moscow, 1925), 559.
68. Dolinin, *F. M. Dostoevskii*, I, 516.

Dostoevsky was especially cool toward the Slavophiles; this is evident both from Strakhov's reminiscences[69] and Grigorev's letters. Neither Strakhov nor Grigorev had a smooth relationship with Mikhail Dostoevsky. It would be reasonable to assume that he was partially responsible for the slowness with which *Vremia* aligned itself against the radicals.

Moreover, and much more important, when pochvennichestvo did finally emerge, it was as a philosophical and aesthetic doctrine rather than a political one, and in this Strakhov was a vital influence in Dostoevsky's evolution. There *was* no change from "democratic" to "conservative" politics in *Vremia,* but rather an ever increasing awareness of its own Hegelianism; Dostoevsky's articles became more idealist as N. Kositsa's letters became more important in the journal. When did Dostoevsky undergo his "conversion"? Scholars will always disagree on this point because Dostoevsky was so slow in his development. But the important point is that he did, finally, adhere to the views which Strakhov held so firmly, and he carried his views to the public at large in his novels. *Notes from Underground* alone has had more of an impact than all of N. Kositsa's letters.

Strakhov's pseudonymous creation, N. Kositsa, is a very nebulous character. The gradual unfolding of the pen name (not fully revealed until May of 1862 as "the pigtail") is amusing, but disturbing. What is the point of masking a pseudonym? It is a parody of his own device. When the full name was finally revealed, it revealed nothing. The name itself is borrowed from Pushkin, who had occasionally signed his journalistic sallies with the name "Feofilakt Kosichkin"; "kosichka" is the diminuitive form of "kositsa." Pushkin used it in 1831 in several articles directed against the conservative Official Nationalists Nikolai Grech and Bulgarin. Strakhov would seem to be disassociating himself from at least that form of right-wing nationalism.

The irony was that Kositsa was on the defensive because of the radicals in 1861, whereas Kosichkin had fought a rearguard ac-

---

69. Miller and Strakhov, *Biografiia,* p. 204.

tion against the conservatives in 1831; nevertheless, they used the same technique of sarcasm in replying to the "literary legislators." Pushkin always maintained the separateness of Kosichkin as a literary creation and at one point even had him discussing a play by Alexander Pushkin (*Boris Godunov*) in a silly tone, suggesting its similarity to a novel by Bulgarin because they both have the same set of characters![70] Strakhov did the same, and indeed his pen name was not widely identified. Moreover, in one of his letters Kositsa reveals that he had decided to make the acquaintance of Nikolai Nikolaevich Strakhov, whom he had always admired but who had ignored him in print. Kositsa sought out Strakhov in his office, and asked for an opinion of Kositsa's letters to *Vremia*.

"Useless," said Strakhov. "You try to be logical, but the readers don't want logic."

"But why do they attack me and insult me so?"

"Because logic is dangerous!"

Kositsa returned home greatly depressed.[71]

Despite the tone of elusive banter and the slightly off-center nature of Kositsa's attacks, there is little question that Kositsa's letters set the pace for *Vremia*. The subscription announcement for 1863 (which appeared in the September 1862 issue) was unequivocal in taking up Kositsa's position: "We stand for literature, we stand for art, we believe in their independence . . . We despise

70. Alexander Pushkin, "Torzhestvo druzhby, ili opravdannyi Aleksandr Anfimovich Orlov" (The triumph of a friendship; or Aleksandr Anfimovich Orlov justified), *Teleskop*, no. 13 (1831), pp 245–254; idem, "Neskolko slov o mizintse g. Bulgarina i o prochem" (Several words about Bulgarin's littlest finger and other matters), *Teleskop*, no. 15 (1831), pp. 255–261; both articles are reprinted in A. S. Pushkin, *Polnoe sobranie sochinenii v desiati tomakh* (Moscow, 1958), VII, 245–254 and 255–261.

71. Kositsa [N. N. Strakhov], "Hard Times," *Vremia* (October 1862), quoted from Strakhov, *Iz istorii literaturnogo nigilizma*, pp. 149–154.

the whistlers, who merely whistle for their supper."[72] Dostoevsky's opening article for 1863, (called "A Necessary Explanation of Various Bready and Nonbready Questions") was a violent attack on *Sovremennik*.

But it was Strakhov's last appearance in *Vremia* that was truly spectacular, both for himself and for the journal. His article, which appeared in the April 1863 issue, was signed simply "A Russian" and was called "A Fatal Question"; the actual fatality was *Vremia*, because the government closed the journal down entirely in reaction to Strakhov's article.

The "fatal question" concerned the meaning of the recent Polish revolt for Russian national consciousness. Strakhov's position was complex, and I shall discuss it later in connection with his Slavophilism. At this point I would like merely to note (1) the obliqueness of the language of the anonymous article—although signed "Russkii," the censors objected that it was unpatriotic, and (2) the extreme quality of the reaction—*Vremia* was suspended indefinitely. Elena Shtakenshneider, a prominent social figure, made the following entry in her diary:

Vremia has had a terrible misfortune, having been closed
because of Strakhov's article on Poland. I can't say exactly
what was in the article—this absurd "A fatal question"
which I never read to the end for lack of patience . . . Worst
of all, the article was not only hostile to the government
but offensive to public opinion as well. In Moscow they are
all up in arms for the cause of Russian honor, and yet the
article was signed "Russkii." Only with Strakhov, only
with *Vremia* . . . that mild, timid journal, so well-
intentioned and so dull—could this happen![73]

By the autumn of 1869, Mikhail Dostoevsky had succeeded in convincing the government censors that Strakhov's article had

72. Miller and Strakhov, *Biografiia*, p. 245. Dostoevsky's phrase was *"svistuny iz khleba"* (whistlers for bread).
73. E. A. Shtakenshneider, *Dnevnik i zapiski (1854–1886)* (Moscow, 1943), pp. 331–332.

only been published by mistake because he, Mikhail Dostoevsky, had been ill. He finally received permission to publish another journal under another name.[74] Thus, the journal recovered from the scandal, but Strakhov was haunted by the ban of the censors for fifteen years afterwards, never being allowed to have his name officially on the editorial board of any journal.

In the interval between the closing of *Vremia* and its reappearance as *Epokha*, Strakhov found himself in a difficult personal position. He was without an income and without his friends. Dostoevsky went abroad for the summer and was completely absorbed in plans for a new novel, *The Gambler;* Grigorev was diverted by a new journal; Strakhov and Mikhail Dostoevsky were barely speaking because of the circumstances of *Vremia's* demise. Strakhov occupied himself with translations of Heine and Kuno Fischer's *Geschichte der neuen Philosophie,* but in general it was a period of loneliness and debts, occasionally relieved by an article for *Biblioteka dlia chteniia* (The reader's library).

Strakhov, when he was on *Vremia,* had been in the habit of initiating polemics with his articles, and he continued the practice. *Epokha* was to find its major antagonist in Saltykov-Shchedrin, but Strakhov took him on even before *Epokha* appeared on the stands. In September 1863 a letter to the editor of *Biblioteka dlia chteniia,* signed "N. Nelishko," appeared in the guise of a review of a story by Shchedrin in the latest *Sovremennik.*[75]

Shchedrin had just now begun his career as a radical satirist, and his story was in character. But N. Nelishko pretended to misread it. With deliberate sarcasm, he concluded that Shchedrin was a sturdy defender of Family, Property, and philosophical idealism.

---

74. Dolinin, *F. M. Dostoevskii,* II, "K tsenzurnoi istorii zhurnalov Dostoevskogo" (The censorship of Dostoevsky's journals), 572.

75. It was planned as a letter from Kositsa, but the journal probably shied away from the incriminating pen name. "Nelishko" was perhaps an answer to Grigorev, who often signed his article *"lishnii chelovek"* (a superfluous man). Strakhov revealed the plans about the Kositsa letter to Dostoevsky on September 18, 1863. Strakhov's letters to Dostoevsky were edited and published by A. S. Dolinin in N. K. Piksanov, ed., *Shestidesiatye gody* (Moscow, 1940). I shall cite them by date.

Strakhov's little satire, which was so curiously biting, has been entirely ignored by commentators on the polemics of the era, but it had important literary consequences. Dostoevsky was delighted when he read it; he then decided that he would write his own satire of Shchedrin's story. Dostoevsky's satire was never finished; the skeleton of it exists only in his notebooks. But it was the germ of what several months later became *Notes from Underground*.[76]

By the end of 1863, it had already become clear that Mikhail Dostoevsky would get permission from the censors for the new journal *Epokha*. Strakhov, in celebration, planned a long, three-part essay for the opening issue. The target was well chosen: in the interval between *Vremia* and *Epokha*, Chernyshevsky had published *What Is to Be Done?*

If any one piece of writing can stand as a symbol for the mentality of the radicals of the 1860's, with all its weaknesses and virtues, it is this novel by Chernyshevsky. Written while the author was in prison and published just prior to his exile, the novel was a rallying point for revolutionary youth. Although it is quite common now to mock the novel for its sentimentality, it would be a great mistake to underestimate the impact of its message on generations of young Russians. Strakhov certainly was aware of its significance as a new enchiridion, the idealization of the philosophy of the full stomach with its sermon on social reform through rational and communal self-improvement.

Strakhov sarcastically entitled his essay "The Happy People." His criticism is not so much that the characters are unrealistic (as later critics have claimed) as that they are gruesome.

Everyone knows that human life is prey to various
misfortunes and kinds of suffering, that it is a difficult
thing to live in this world. And yet for these "new people"
life is easy; the whole novel is a tale of how skillfully they
are able to avoid any kind of inconvenience and
unhappiness . . . For them, temptation does not exist;
they never have unsettling desires; they never have to

76. Borshchevsky, *Shchedrin i Dostoevskii*, p. 88.

win a victory over their own impulses; they are so abstract,
so ascetic, that honesty, plain honesty, costs them
absolutely nothing.[77]

For Strakhov, the coldness and the self-confidence of the pre-
scriptions for life in the novel made corpses of the characters;
Chernyshevsky denied in one blow that Hegelian search for the
ideal that was the message of Strakhov's "Letters on Life." One
can imagine that it is both rational and easy to steal the wife of
one's best friend; but is it really possible to learn, like Rakhme-
tov, everything that is worth knowing in a period of six months?
This easy life, without travail, is like a Chinese painting without
shadows, representing a world without blood or nerves.

I cannot tell you how the message chilled me the first
time I read it! It seemed to me that anyone who is alive
while reading it should be seized with dread and should
answer without a moment's hesitation: I don't need your
kind of happiness! For this inhuman coldness, for this
terrible emptiness which you call happiness, for this
infallibility and indestructible tranquility I would not give
up at any price my present life which is hard and meager
but nevertheless full and warm and pulsing.[78]

Strakhov's article was never published in *Epokha*, and was in
fact never even finished. "Fedor Mikhailovich decided not to
print it."[79] The decision was probably reached because in November 1863 Dostoevsky had himself embarked on a similar, major
project. As was the case with Strakhov's little article on Shchedrin, Strakhov's ideas were incorporated into *Notes from Underground*.[80] Dolinin and other scholars have shown in great detail
how *Notes from Underground* was intended as an answer to

77. Strakhov, *Iz istorii literaturnogo nigilizma*, pp. 319–340.
78. Strakhov, *Iz istorii literaturnogo nigilizma*, p. 339.
79. Strakhov, *Iz istorii literaturnogo nigilizma*, p. 342.
80. F. M. Dostoevsky to M. M. Dostoevsky, November 19, 1863, in F. M. Dostoevsky, *Pisma*, ed. A. S. Dolinin, 4 vols. (Moscow, 1928–1930–1932–1959). Strakhov's

What Is to Be Done? Recently Borshchevsky has analyzed the novel as a refutation of Shchedrin's ideas also. The argument is self-evident in both cases, and the genesis of the argument appears to be Strakhov's articles. The mutuality of the intellectual relationship between Dostoevsky and Strakhov appears nowhere more clearly than in the former's novels. Unquestionably Strakhov was the philosophical teacher and the first to verbalize arguments that appear later in the novels, but it was of course Dostoevsky's genius that created the Underground Man and Raskolnikov and made them into literary forms which have universal significance.

Epokha had a much shorter lifetime than *Vremia* and on the whole had a less successful existence despite such achievements as *Notes from Underground*. Much more than its predecessor, *Epokha* became involved in sarcastic and petty polemics in which more energy was devoted to cruelty than to principle; the charge of triviality lies heavily on the journal. This is not to suggest that *Epokha* was unique among St. Petersburg journals in this respect; in fact, it is worth discussing largely because it was so typical.

Strakhov's new personality on the journal was emblematic; he appeared in the guise of "The Chronicler," and his "Zametki letopistsa" were fragmentary jottings on this and that, which were designed more often than not to be provocative. The pseudonym was not unusual for the times: Shchedrin had a column in *Sovremennik* for a time called "Khronika," and he wrote several books in the form of chronicles. Strakhov, however, used the Slavonic form of the word (*letopisets*), which betrays the fact that he considered the chronicle a Russian form; he would later show special interest in Pushkin's *Letopis sela Gorokhina* and in the "chronicle" aspect of Tolstoy's *War and Peace*.

---

article was updated and partially published only in 1865 after *Epokha* closed. *Epokha* did eventually publish a review of *What Is to be Done?* by Nikolai Ivanovich Solovev, whose ideas were paler versions of Strakhov's articles. Solovev concentrated on attacking Pisarev, Chernyshevsky, and Dobroliubov on literary matters; he was associated with Strakhov on all the journals of his career.

"The Notes of the Chronicler" appeared every month, with a dozen or so acid paragraphs and pointed barbs each time. The Chronicler was an unusual role for Strakhov. His usual biting humor and quick wit had always before been embedded in a more serious and sustained analysis. For this one year he attempted an impressionistic approach to journalism. Unfortunately, the "Notes" make very unsatisfactory reading at any distance in time. It is true that Kositsa was elusive, but the Chronicler is often trivial and obscure. Strakhov spoke, in his reminiscences of Dostoevsky, of his dislike of journalism precisely because it depended on an impression rather than an analysis, and he criticized Dostoevsky for this inclination. "Fedor Mikhailovich once said to me: 'You're always writing as if for your own *Complete Collected Works!*'"[81] The Chronicler was the one exception to this self-imposed rule, and it was not very successful.

Dostoevsky, however, had a field day on *Epokha;* the full force of his sarcasm and gift for parody was let loose on the radicals, and he found a worthy opponent in Saltykov-Shchedrin. The story of *Epokha* is more than anything else the story of their skillful mutual cruelties.

The polemic actually began in *Vremia,* although it was not apparent at the time. *Vremia* had printed a romantic poem by F. N. Berg called "The Birds." In March of 1863 someone on *Sovremennik* who called himself "A Young Pen" wrote a satire of Berg's poem called "The Fears of *Vremia.*" The not too subtle point was that *Vremia* was a secret member of the reactionary group around Katkov's journals but was afraid to admit it. Dostoevsky responded with a piece of (untranslatable) drivel:

> *Vek i Vek i Lev Kambek*
> *Lev Kambek i Vek i Vek*
> *Na pistonchike kornet*
> *Strakhov zhiteli planet*
> *Ro-ro-ro, ro-ro, ro-ro*
> *Molodoe pero,*

81. Miller and Strakhov, *Biografiia,* p. 220.

> *Us-us, us-us-us*
> *Akh, kakoi-zhe eto gus.*[82]

This devastating response failed to silence *Sovremennik*, and the association of *Vremia* with "birds" somehow stuck.

The publication of *Notes from Underground* in *Epokha* provoked a nasty response from Saltykov-Shchedrin in the form of a satire called "The Martins" (*strizhi*). The scene opened on the editorial offices of *Epokha*, where all the birds were gathered to discuss the first issue. They were all wearing mourning for the recently deceased *Vremia*. At one point the First Martin (Mikhail Dostoevsky) asks the Second Martin (Strakhov): "Have you been absolved yet?" "Oh yes, I've confessed and been forgiven." The First Martin suggests that they decide on an editorial policy. The Fourth Martin (Fedor Dostoevsky) at this point jumps up and announces that he has written a story entitled "Notes on the Immortality of the Soul" to illustrate the journal's program; he then proceeds to read it. "The Martins" was actually not a bad summary of the major philosophical points of Kositsa's letters and *Notes from Underground*.[83]

Shchedrin's parody provoked Dostoevsky into a retaliatory one, in which he took advantage of the fact that the two leading radical journals were at the moment arguing about the revolutionary

82. Fedor Dostoevsky, "Again 'A Young Pen,'" *Vremia* (March 1863). *Vek* was Veinberg's journal, which had begun the scandal over Pushkin's "Egyptian Nights." Lev Kambek was a reference to Dmitry Minaev, who wrote verses in *Iskra*, the satirical supplement of *Sovremennik*. Dostoevsky's poem reappeared in *The Possessed*, as a nightmare of Stephen Verkhovensky. The "Egyptian Nights" episode and Mikhailov's accusation that *Vek* had indulged in "ugly behavior" appeared as Varvara Petrovna's nightmare in the same novel. Both dreams illustrated the poison of St. Petersburg journalism in the 1860's. *"Molodoe pero"* (the young pen) turned out to have been Saltykov-Shchedrin.

83. In March 1863, "A Young Pen" had called the men on *Vremia* "birds, floating freely on the still air," in the satire of Berg's poem, "The Birds." Dostoevsky in his rebuttal acknowledged being called "a duck" (*gus*). Shchedrin concretized it in a later article, making him a "pintail duck." Then, in July 1864, they were all martins. "Kosatka" is a kind of martin; this may be a pun on Strakhov's pen name, Kositsa. There is a translation called "The Swallows" in Fyodor Dostoevsky, *Notes from Underground*, ed. Ralph E. Matlaw (New York, 1960), pp. 201–209.

implications of *What Is to Be Done?*[84] Dostoevsky was delighted
that Shchedrin on *Sovremennik* found himself being attacked by
Pisarev and Varfolomei Zaitsev on *Russkoe slovo* over revolutionary principles, and he entitled his parody "Mr. Shchedrin, or
the *Raskol* Among the Nihilists." Part of the parody was a "novel
in four chapters" about a certain Mr. Shchedrodarov (open-
handed), who wrote for a journal called *Svoevremennyi,* (the
name suggests "The Opportunist") which was involved in a polemic with a certain Mr. Krolichkov (rabbit: Zaitsev) and a certain
Mr. Skribov (scribe: Pisarev).[85]

The mutual insults were soon hopelessly tangled by the intervention of Antonovich, who in the July issue of *Sovremennik*
claimed that *he,* in his role of "the casual satirist" (his occasional
pen name), had written "The Martins," thus confusing both contemporaries and future scholars. Dostoevsky, who was convinced
that Shchedrin had written "The Martins," was only partly taken
in; he merely assumed that "the casual satirist" was *also* Shchedrin.[86] Antonovich's peculiar claim appeared in the form of a letter,
"To the Martins (an Epistle to the Ober-Martin, Mr. Dostoevsky)."
He parodied various articles from *Vremia* and *Epokha* and wrote
a new satire: In the editorial offices of the journal *Iupka* are gathered Mr. Sysoevsky, holding a manuscript; Triapitsa (the rag:
Kositsa); and a drunken Belvedersky (Grigorev; the Apollo Belve-
dere was a favorite symbol used by the radicals for "pure art"),
who in the course of the scene burps twenty-four times, with
"that obscene kind of burp which can only be produced in the ex-
tremes of poetic rapture." Sysoevsky reads from his manuscript,
and asks for comments.

84. The best account of the quarrel is in B. P. Kozmin, "Raskol v nigilistakh"
(The *raskol* in the nihilist camp), *Literatura i marksizm.* no. 2 (1928), pp. 51–107.
Matlaw has translated part of Dostoevsky's parody as *Munificent,* in Dostoevsky,
Notes from Underground, pp. 213–229.

85. Borshchevsky (*Shchedrin i Dostoevskii,* pp. 111–127) tries humorlessly to
prove that, while Shchedrin's "The Martins" was absolutely fair, Dostoevsky's
"Shchedrodarov" was vicious and untrue.

86. "Neobkhodimoe zaiavlenie" (A necessary explanation), *Epokha* (July 1864).
Volynsky, in *Russkie kritiki,* took Dostoevsky's assumption as a fact.

"Have I displayed the rage of Jupiter?"

"Oh good, very good," answers Triapitsa, "but haven't you gone a little too far, my friend?"

"What! Shouldn't I be very angry? Do you expect me to bow to them?"

"Oh yes, angry, of course, but all the same—"

"But they have trampled on our slogan 'the soil,' which we dreamed up with such effort in order to have a program! Don't you remember?"

"I remember, but still—"

"Quiet!" shouts Sysoevsky. "Let me bask in memories—"

Sysoevsky then begins to muse about the sacred soil, about Pushkin, about going to Europe to write winter notes in the summer on spring impressions, and so on. With a final wail, he shouts, "And now the robbers are taking my soil away from me!" Then he begins to quarrel with Triapitsa about who used the word "soil" more often; hysterics ensue. Belvedersky is awakened; he and Triapitsa put their heads together to figure out a new slogan to replace "the soil." "How about 'organic?'" suggests Belvedersky; joyously, they decide on "organic," and proceed to celebrate. Triapitsa begins to shout like a lion, promising to fill his next article with burning rage. They all begin to drink, and, while they sit around the vodka bottle, the word "martins" appears emblazoned on their foreheads.

This was not the last of the quarrel; Antonovich wrote ten articles in all directed at *Epokha* in 1864, each one answered by Strakhov or Dostoevsky. But, if he was trying to divert attention away from the *Sovremennik-Russkoe slovo* polemic, he was unsuccessful; the Chronicler kept a running commentary on it in his monthly column.

The final episode in the polemic was a satire by Shchedrin which was censored at the time and appeared only in part, in altered form, in *Otechestvennye zapiski* in 1868. The satire was origi-

nally inspired by a ballet performance, which Shchedrin ridiculed
as sentimental nonsense that might appeal to *Epokha's* readers.
He himself decided to write an even more appealing ballet:

Self-Styled Enemies

or

Lie, Don't be Afraid!

A contemporary-patriotic-fantastic ballet in three acts
and four scenes; written by the Chronicler of *Sovremennik;*
music by Serov; scenery and choreography by Iurkevich,
Kositsa, and F. M. Dostoevsky; costumes by the same tailor
who outfitted the staff of *Epokha*.[87]

Such arguments determined the dominant tone of *Epokha;*
the polemics were often funny, but they had a tendency to drag
on too long. "The Notes of a Chronicler" at least had the virtue
of being short. However, Strakhov wrote under his own name in
Epokha also, and his most interesting article was devoted to
Grigorev.

In September 1864 Grigorev died after an accumulation of
illnesses, depression, and liquor. It was a personal tragedy for
Strakhov, who had found in him inspiration and understanding
for his own work. Strakhov wrote a memorial for *Epokha*, to
which he appended Grigorev's letters from Orenburg.[88] Strakhov's
commentary on the letters reveals both the deep affection and the
deep gulf between them.

87. Saltykov-Shchedrin, "Mnimye vragi" (Self-styled enemies), reprinted in
Literaturnoe nasledstvo, XI–XII (1933), 87–112. The polemic then shifted to
the novels of Dostoevsky and Shchedrin, which were a more productive arena—
although literary scholars are in disagreement about the literary effects of Dostoevsky's polemical passages in his novels. (It seems to matter less in the case of
Shchedrin.) Borshchevsky has analyzed Shchedrin's work to underline his attacks
on Strakhov, Dostoevsky, and Grigorev. Dostoevsky sometimes answered the attacks specifically, in *The Possessed, The Idiot, The Brothers Karamazov* and, of
course, "The Diary of a Writer."
88. "Memoirs of Grigorev."

It is obvious that Strakhov saw Grigorev as a mad genius, and himself as the faithful, sober follower. He took his epigram from Hamlet:

> *O good Horatio, what a wounded name,*
> *Things standing thus unknown, shall leave behind me!*
> *If thou didst ever hold me in thy heart*
> *Absent thee from felicity awhile*
>   · · · · ·
> *To tell my story.*

Grigorev indeed liked to think of himself as Hamlet. Strakhov claimed in his memoir that their relationship was purely "literary," and he denied any knowledge of Grigorev's personal life.[89] This was a device to avoid discussing the lurid details in public; the original version of Grigorev's letters shows that Strakhov was well acquainted with them. However, in a sense Strakhov was quite honest when he claimed a limitation to their relationship. Grigorev's personal characteristics were so alien to Strakhov that they could never have been really intimate. Grigorev was a wild man; his alcoholism, his love affairs, his bohemianism were all very far from the reserve of the seminarist. This did not make Strakhov any less sympathetic; but Strakhov's services to him were somewhat impersonal. "Geh und bete, geh und bete," Grigorev once asked of him in a mood of severe depression.[90]

It is an interesting psychological fact that Strakhov throughout his life seems to have been attracted to wild creatures; Grigorev was only one example. Dostoevsky was certainly beset with women, debts, and passionate insecurities. A similar man was I. G. Dolgomostev, a young writer whom Strakhov had known in the 1850's and who had later worked on *Vremia* and *Epokha*. Grigorev and Dolgomostev shared the qualities which Strakhov once characterized as belonging to Dostoevsky's intimate circle:

89. Strakhov, "Memoirs of Grigorev," p. 439.
90. Strakhov, "Memoirs of Grigorev," p. 494.

"I was surprised, despite their professed humanitarian spirituality, to notice their laxity in physical matters . . . they condemned spiritual ugliness but not carnal ugliness . . . some came to a bad end because of this carnality, often to insanity and death."[91] Strakhov was always complaining to Dostoevsky about the drinking habits of the two men. In 1867 Dolgomostev went mad, literally in Strakhov's arms, "a mind unhinged by excesses" and muttering for hours on end about "a new policy for the pochvenniki."[92] This combination of moral weakness and intellectual commitment was to be a familiar pattern in Strakhov's future friends also: it recurred at the very end of his life in V. V. Rozanov, who—to complete the circle—married Dostoevsky's former "infernal mistress," Polina Suslova.

Strakhov said at the end of his memoir that "no writer had less *sochinenie* and more *zhizn* than Grigorev." The difference in personality between the two men can be understood very well if one recalls Dostoevsky's remark that Strakhov always wrote as if for his own Collected Works. Grigorev had retired to Orenburg with Maria Fedorovna, whom he had encountered in a brothel and intended to reform. (He was already married at the time.) It seems that she was not worthy of his efforts; she finally left him, and he returned to St. Petersburg.[93] Grigorev came back at the end of 1862 and began another cycle of drinking, debts, and breakdown. He wrote for *Epokha* but also spent much of his time in debtors' prison. In the midst of this personal chaos, Grigorev managed to produce some splendid literary criticism, including his autobiographical masterpiece, *My Literary and Moral Wanderings*. This impassioned outburst was written for *Epokha,* and partially addressed to Strakhov: "Not longer than yesterday, oh my dear Horatio Pig-

91. Miller and Strakhov, *Biografiia,* pp. 173–174.
92. Strakhov to Dostoevsky, March 1868, in *Shestidesiatye gody.*
93. We can clearly see here the outline for the story of the redemption of the prostitute, Liza, in *Notes from Underground,* which is obviously as much a reflection of Grigorev's experience as a parody of the redemption of the prostitute in *What Is to Be Done?*

tail, while talking with you after the concert . . . " [94] With Strakhov he sneers at Friedrich Beneke's physiological psychology
and eulogizes Hegel:

And truly, what kind of a passion has developed in you and
me, what kind of an irregular vein throbs in us, people of a
"transcendental" disposition, that we find it so terribly
boring to read Beneke, who is completely clear and proceeds
by the method of the natural sciences, and do not find it
boring to break one's head over *The Phenomenology of the
Spirit*. And in reality, it is not that we find it boring to read
Beneke, but simply that it would cost us an unbelievable
effort; if it would not cost you, who wrote a master's dissertation on certain infusoria bones unknown to anyone
except a microscope, or something just as unlikely, — than
I, after all an insolent humanist . . .[95]

Grigorev's themes are those of Strakhov and Dostoevsky, and
the recurrence of anecdotes and symbols in the writings of all
three illustrates how important their mutual contact was. Grigorev had matured as a critic before the other two men; his influence on Strakhov was greater than on Dostoevsky, whose
fiery brilliance was of too similar a kind and who profited much
more from Strakhov's logic.

Grigorev's death was only the last in a series of blows to *Epokha*.
The journal began with ill omens: the censor did not approve the
first issue until March, and the censor's tardiness plagued the
journal for the duration of its short lifetime. The March issue
was not approved until April 23; the September issue came out
in November. This was a serious problem for a journal which
featured such items as the "Notes of a Chronicler"; they must
have seemed very stale two months later.

Moreover, Dostoevsky's wife was ill, and he spent much of his

94. My quotations are from A. A. Grigorev, *My Literary and Moral Wanderings*,
trans. Ralph E. Matlaw (New York, 1962), p. 59.
95. Grigorev, *My Literary and Moral Wanderings*, p. 62.

time in Moscow with her; she died in April. Three months later, Mikhail Dostoevsky died, also. (Grigorev died in September.) It took two months to find another editor (Fedor Dostoevsky and Strakhov were still under a censor's ban). They finally chose Aleksandr Ustinovich Poretsky, a sincere young man from the Forestry Department who was obviously no substitute for Mikhail Dostoevsky as a business man. During the year 1864 *Epokha* collected only thirteen hundred subscribers, which was not enough to cover costs. Without money or vitality, the journal closed down after the February 1865 issue and barely a year of publication.[96]

When *Epokha* closed, Dostoevsky and Strakhov quarreled. The bad feeling was partly over the demise of *Epokha*, for which each blamed the other. But there were other issues between them; Strakhov was loath to define them because they were personal, but they were no doubt related to Dostoevsky's gambling fever.[97] The friendship resumed in 1867, when Dostoevsky married the admirable Anna Grigorevna; Strakhov was a witness at the wedding. Then Dostoevsky went abroad, and the two men corresponded for four years with an exchange of letters "perhaps warmer than it would have been in person."[98] Dostoevsky returned to St. Petersburg in 1871, and the relationship resumed in a cool atmosphere. "I was often offended by Fedor Mikhailovich, the more so the closer we became."[99] Although Strakhov saw less and less of Dostoevsky in the 1870's, he was with him the day before he died, and he was chosen, along with Orest Miller, to edit the posthumous *Collected Works*. When Strakhov

---

96. About 2,500 subscribers would have done it, according to Strakhov in Miller and Strakhov, *Biografiia*, p. 221. *Vremia* had sold 4,000 subscriptions by the time it was closed in April 1863. Most journals were in difficulties at the time. *Russkoe slovo* and *Sovremennik* (the latter with only 2,100 subscribers) were closed by the censor in May 1865. *Biblioteka dlia Chteniia* also folded in 1865. *Otechestvennye zapiski* was on its last legs; only Katkov seemed to be financially secure.
97. Miller and Strakhov, *Biografiia*, p. 284.
98. Miller and Strakhov, *Biografiia*, p. 294.
99. Miller and Strakhov, *Biografiia*, p. 317.

was asked to give a memorial speech to the Slavic Benevolent
Committee, he emphasized the symbolic significance of Dostoevsky's Pushkin Day speech and saw Dostoevsky's triumph on that
occasion as a victory for pochvennichestvo; in fact, he interpreted
all of Dostoevsky's work in terms of *Vremia* and *Epokha*.[100]

Epokha was a much less successful enterprise than *Vremia*.
Most commentators, following Strakhov's own analysis in 1883,[101]
have attributed the failure to the unambiguous Slavophilism of
the journal: thus, they confirm Mikhail Dostoevsky's supposed
suspicions about the journalistic dangers of a Slavophile editorial
policy. The implication behind this theory is that *Epokha* was
ruined by a drastic "turning to the right," by its hostility to *Sovremennik* and its sympathy for conservative journals such as
Aksakov's *Den*. As in the scholarly quarrel over the program
of *Vremia,* one's conclusions depend entirely upon how one
chooses to emphasize the various pieces of contradictory evidence.
Certainly the quarrels with the radical journals began long before
Epokha was on the scene, and quarrels tended to boost, rather
than damage, *Vremia*'s circulation.

The real change was not in the journal but in the reading public.
When *Vremia* began its publishing career in 1861, Russian
journalism was a lively phenomenon. The variety was enormous;

100. In view of the depth of their intellectual relationship, it is absurd that Dostoevsky's later biographers have paid so much outraged attention to Strakhov's
responsibility for identifying Dostoevsky himself as the original model for Stavrogin's moral excesses in *The Possessed*. In several letters to Leo Tolstoy—in particular, those of February 3, 1881 and November 28, 1883, in the midst of writing
the memoir—Strakhov expressed distaste for Dostoevsky's sexual habits. In one
letter, Strakhov transmitted a story told him by a third party: Dostoevsky had
boasted of having had relations with a young girl in a bathhouse, and he drew on
this incident for Stavrogin's "confession." Strakhov also pointed out that Dostoevsky had drawn on his own personality for the portrait of Svidrigailov in *Crime and
Punishment*. The story of the bathhouse may or may not have been true; Strakhov
merely repeated it. He certainly did not invent it out of malice, as has been claimed.
The fact that he related it to his closest friend, Tolstoy, was surely not malicious.
What is interesting about the story, from the point of view of Dostoevsky's psychological portrait, is not its veracity (which would be very hard to establish),
but the fact that Strakhov, who knew Dostoevsky so well, gave it credibility.

101. Miller and Strakhov, *Biografiia,* p. 275.

every shade of opinion, radical to orthodox, was represented. Within each journal there was substantial literary variety. They all published Turgenev, Ostrovsky, Shchedrin, Nekrasov, and Dostoevsky; they made and broke alliances from issue to issue; they excommunicated each other from time to time; but none of it was very serious. Journals prospered despite mutual attacks, and the subscription figures indicate successful competition on the open market.[102]

The year 1863, which produced such a change on Russia's political horizon, affected journalism also. Society became less benevolent when the state became less benevolent. Toleration became a luxury which people felt that they could not longer afford. The "era of good feeling," inaugurated by Alexander II's promise of reform, was over. The more difficulties the government raised in the expression of liberal opinions, the more difficult the liberals made it for the expression of anything less than their definition of "liberal" in print. For certain segments of society, which included a large part of the reading public, it seemed that the time had come for commitment; the pressure of commitment necessarily eliminated tolerance. This was as true in Russian journalism as it was in the history of Russian social thought in general. It was not so much a change in *Epokha* as a change in the mood of the public that brought the journal down.

The closing of *Epokha* was the beginning of a long period of dislocation for Strakhov. The hopes with which he had abandoned teaching for the excitement of St. Petersburg journalism were disappointed. With the removal of the protective shield of Dostoevsky's resourcefulness, he found himself in a very precarious personal position.

The next ten years of Strakhov's life were haunted by uncertainty. He was to live through the *Vremia-Epokha* experience twice more and was finally reduced to writing for journals of

102. The figures (very roughly) for 1862 are as follows: *Sovremennik*, 7,000; *Russkii vestnik*, 5,700; *Russkoe slovo*, 4,000; *Vremia*, 4,300.

which he did not basically approve. He was forced to supplement his earnings from journalism with money earned through translations. His letters of this period reveal the disappointment and bitterness of a man in his early forties who feels the weight of total failure; despite a prodigious intellectual output, he was denied the recognition and outward signs of success that a man of his age and talents might well expect. Fortunately, the end of the story is happier, and Strakhov came out of the decade of the 1870's in a much more secure position than he could ever have predicted. This was the result of both personal luck and a change on the Russian intellectual scene, which made a career on the journals less uniquely important for intellectual success than before.

But the security of 1878 was not at all apparent in 1866. Strakhov's first endeavor after the closing of *Epokha* was, in retrospect, the most bizarre of his career. For over a year he acted as unofficial editor-in-chief (still under the censor's ban for "A Fatal Question" in 1863) of *Otechestvennye zapiski,* the journal which, as soon as it left his hands, became the leading organ of the radical populists. The journal itself was an old and established enterprise, a moderate journal which had fallen victim to the sharpening of journalistic tempers after 1863. It is not surprising that Strakhov was unable to effect any startling change in the decline of its fortunes; in fact, *Otechestvennye zapiski* looked very much like *Vremia* and *Epokha* under Strakhov's tutelage. By 1867 it had only two thousand subscribers, and Pisarev could describe it as "a decaying corpse in which the worms will soon have nothing left to eat."[103] The publisher Andrei Kraevsky finally saved himself by turning it over to the radicals in 1868; Nekrasov became its editor, *Sovremennik* having been closed by the censors for good. A "respectable literary journal" had become a "faculty of whistlers and nihilists."[104]

103. J. H. Billington, *Mikhailovsky and Russian Populism* (Oxford, 1958), p. 61.
104. Strakhov to Dostoevsky, March 1868, in *Shestidesiatye gody.*

The winter of 1867–1868 was a particularly hard one for Strakhov. His young colleague and good friend Dolgomostev died during this time; Strakhov often referred to the torment of that deathbed scene, the crazed Dolgomostev churning over and over about "political programs for *Vremia*." E. N. Edelson, for many years a close friend and co-recipient of Pisarev's attacks, also died that winter at the early age of forty-four. Strakhov, who had himself just turned forty, felt these deaths with all the pain of a man who is beginning to realize that his youth, with all its hopes, is over. At such a time the loss of his journal was doubly crippling. "I'm in bad shape," he confessed to Dostoevsky, "I'm not far from a complete breakdown." [105]

There were frantic efforts to start another journal. By November 1868 they seem to have paid off. Strakhov wrote jubilantly to Dostoevsky: "*Zaria* has begun!" The money behind *Zaria* (Dawn) belonged to V. V. Kashpirev, whose idea was to found a journal that would be clearly Slavophile and yet in no way connected to the older Slavophile movement.[106] The idea was curiously like Dostoevsky's in 1860, and Kashpirev also turned to Strakhov. Strakhov was again optimistic. "Kashpirev was brought up on *Vremia* and *Epokha* as others were on *Sovremennik* and *Russkoe slovo;* these are the fruits . . . of our work." [107]

Kashpirev was apparently a rather strange character, who sat in his rooms all day like Oblomov and refused to move; he let his wife manage all the details.[108] The editorial offices were filled with Strakhov's former associates; Dostoevsky was missing only because he was abroad. Kashpirev even took on Strakhov's latest protege (discovered when Strakhov was editing *Otechestvennye zapiski*), Aleksandr Ilich Nezelenov. "Nezelenov cherishes

105. Strakhov to Dostoevsky, March 1868, in *Shestidesiatye gody.*
106. V. G. Avseenko, "Kruzhok" (The circle: memoirs), *Istoricheskii vestnik* (May 1909), p. 442. Aksakov's *Moskva* and *Moskvich* had been born and had died, all in the previous year.
107. Strakhov to Dostoevsky, November 24, 1868, in *Shestidesiatye gody.*
108. Avseenko, "The Circle," p. 439; Strakhov to Dostoevsky, January 29, 1869, in *Shestidesiatye gody.*

Epokha, and he feels that its demise was the end of Russian literature, until its awakening in *Zaria*."[109] Strakhov thought of him as typical of the freshness of the new journal. "We have the youngest and the best section of the university with us . . . I have great hopes for *Zaria*!"[110]

Zaria did indeed make a place in Russian intellectual history, somewhat obliquely, because it created several new literary reputations. But it was hardly a new phenomenon. As Strakhov had predicted, it followed a familiar intellectual path. Although its polemics with *Otechestvennye zapiski* and *Delo* (Affairs), the successor to Pisarev's *Russkoe slovo*, were less intense and less personal, they revolved around the old issues of the 1860's. Strakhov had complained of his opponents in 1868: "The new journals are poor; like emigrés, they have forgotten nothing and learned nothing since 1860."[111] The same observation could be made about *Zaria*. A typical illustration of the level of the polemics is Shchedrin's lampooning; under the pretext of a review of a pamphlet by a former pochvennik, Nikolai Solovev, in 1869, he re-evokes the image of the "martins" on *Epokha*.

They are well-intentioned birds, who—as observer-
empiricists note—have the gift of predicting which way
the wind blows . . . the public was attending to their
oracles about the soil and "a new word" and "the force of
love" and was already thinking that all these oracles were
about to be topped off by one general oracle about the
influence of [a certain novel] on the force of Russian
humility, when suddenly *Epokha* ceased and the martins
flew away, carrying with them all their secrets. For a
certain time, however, one could still hear an inarticulate
muttering escaping from "bachelor" martins, who
continued to make oracles even after the destruction of

109. Strakhov to Dostoevsky, November 24, 1868, in *Shestidesiatye gody*. Nezelenov later became a professor of literature, whose lectures extolled Apollon Grigorev and resembled in spirit those of O. F. Miller and A. D. Galakhov. See Strakhov, *Vospominaniia i otryvki*, p. 251.
110. Strakhov to Dostoevsky, November 24, 1868, in *Shestidesiatye gody*.
111. Strakhov to Dostoevsky, March, 1868, in *Shestidesiatye gody*.

their home nest; the public good-naturedly listened to their noises, trying to make sense of them, but it turned out that both before and after the destruction of the nest the oracles were one and the same vinaigrette, consisting of all possible scraps of things. There were scraps of slavophilism, scraps of nihilism, scraps of spiritualism, and even some homemade stuff. Thanks to this latter, the martins could mask their imitations . . . It seems, however, that the flight of the martins was only apparent and not real, and that these interesting birds have not flown away but only suffered a temporary eclipse. At this very minute, as we write these lines, their whole camp is in a flurry trying to organize themselves and make out of [whatever martins are on hand] a strong and unified chorus of martins.[112]

But *Zaria* had a short lifetime, because of both general inefficiency and a certain deadening seriousness which seems to have plagued the journal. The supreme irony came in a poem printed by the slow-witted editorial board itself (signed "Fet," but actually written by a radical populist V. P. Burenin). The poem was an acrostic, spelling out "Zaria Kashpireva umiraet."[113] The demise of the journal did not hurt Strakhov, however, because by this time he had already ceased, for obscure reasons, to have any influence on *Zaria*, and was not even receiving a salary from it any longer.[114]

112. Borshchevsky, *Shchedrin i Dostoevskii*, pp. 197–198.
113. "Kashpirev's Zaria is dying." Avseenko, "The Circle," p. 451. Burenin was still a radical on *Otechestvennye zapiski* at this time. His metamorphosis into a conservative did not occur until later in the 1870's when he joined the staff of Suvorin's *Novoe vremia*. Only at this later point did he begin to write of Dostoevsky, for instance, with adulation. He wrote a highly flattering review of Strakhov's *Iz istorii literaturnogo nigilizma* in 1890.
114. When Dostoevsky wrote to Strakhov to complain that *Zaria* was slighting him (February 1871), Strakhov disclaimed responsibility and said that he himself had been slighted. "Imagine, they took away both my editorial functions and my salary; they decided that I charged too much per page and that my articles were too long. Instead they plan to use me only in every other issue and as much as announced that there would be no room for me in March and April at all." Strakhov to Dostoevsky, February 22, 1871, in *Shestidesiatye gody*.

Thus, Strakhov's financial situation was once again desperate. In the first flush of enthusiasm about *Zaria,* he had expanded his style of life in the form of an apartment of his own; he now had to return to furnished rooms. As in earlier years, he turned to translations for money, this time translating Renan, Taine, and Schopenhauer. By the end of 1871 he had reached a crisis. Finally, "I began to write for the new *Grazhdanin,* that nasty journal . . . although my heart was ill-disposed toward the editor, the publisher, and the whole circle."[115]

Grazhdanin (The citizen) was Prince Meshchersky's weekly, which began to appear about the time of *Zaria'*s collapse at the beginning of 1872. It was Apollon Maikov who brought Strakhov into contact with the *Grazhdanin* circle, and Strakhov had enough doubts about his reception among these political extremists to submit an article only anonymously, through Maikov. He started to work for Meshchersky with hesitation and under great financial pressure. "They are already quite a mangy group; I fear for their honesty (in a negative sense) and I am rather rude to them."[116] He was always to be apologetic about his association with this journal, which became more and more openly reactionary. Konstantin Pobedonostsev's connections with it helped to insure its financial invulnerability; although it had a very small subscription list, it in fact lasted as a weekly until 1914.

Strakhov was at least physically close to *Grazhdanin* for a short time through Dostoevsky, who became its editor in 1873. Nevertheless, Strakhov and Dostoevsky were no longer the like-minded colleagues of the past; Strakhov grew increasingly more alarmed at the development of Dostoevsky's political extremism. "I am worried about Dostoevsky . . . he is getting old. *Grazhdanin* wearies him . . . he writes strange articles."[117] Only financial need kept him writing for the journal, that "and Dostoevsky, who as an old friend would call it treason if I didn't write for him . . . I hope

115. Strakhov to Leo Tolstoy, March 10, 1872, in *Perepiska L. N. Tolstogo s N. N. Strakhovym,* ed. B. L. Modzalevsky (St. Petersburg, 1913).
116. Strakhov to Tolstoy, March 10, 1872, in *Perepiska.*
117. Strakhov to Tolstoy, March 15, 1873, in *Perepiska.*

however to be completely free by the new year . . . My debts will be paid . . . Dostoevsky can hardly remain as editor; he is ill and the doctors recommend Italy."[118] Finally, in March 1874, Dostoevsky resigned as a result of both his ill health and the excesses of his germanophobia (which alarmed the Foreign Ministry, although not Meshchersky). Strakhov had written in February: "When Dostoevsky is finished I shall stop writing for the journals entirely."[119]

This is an entirely new tone for Strakhov; by the mid-1870's one begins to notice in Strakhov's letters a new casualness toward journals and editors, a certain freedom that was never there before. In one respect the explanation is quite simple: in 1873, he finally acquired a job that made him financially independent. He became a librarian in the section of Juridical and Social Science in the Imperial Library in St. Petersburg and, if not rich, at least solvent. "Before 1873 I was always tossed by the waves; now I was in a safe harbor."[120] He had at last a bit of personal luck, after a lifetime with a singular lack of that gift.

The appointment came just in time, because he was once again in debt. Now, at the age of forty-six, after fifteen years of freelance journalism, Strakhov had a job with a salary of fifteen hundred rubles a year. It was enough to live on without too much hoarding; he felt, for instance, that he could afford his own apartment again.

Then, soon after his move to the Library, he had another pleasant surprise. "A. I. Georgievsky himself[121] came to see me in the

118. Strakhov to Tolstoy, Fall 1873, in *Perepiska.*
119. Strakhov to Tolstoy, February 22, 1874, in *Perepiska.* Meshchersky sensed Strakhov's distance. He listed Strakhov in his memoirs as a colleague, along with Pobedonostsev, Maikov, Dostoevsky, and Tiutchev, but he admitted that, although he got help with the censors from Pobedonostsev, gay spirits from Maikov, and passion from Dostoevsky, from Strakhov there came "only the fear [a pun on his name] of falling a victim to his irony." V. P. Meshchersky, *Moi Vospominaniia* (St. Petersburg, 1898), II, 165.
120. Quoted by Nikolsky in "Strakhov," p. 261.
121. He was the editor of *Zhurnal Ministerstva Narodnogo Prosveshcheniia;* Strakhov had written for this journal from 1857 to 1860, and again in 1868 before *Zaria* appeared.

Library and asked if I would like to become a member of the Academic Committee [in the Ministry of Education] to choose scientific textbooks for state schools at a yearly salary of one thousand rubles. I agreed ... although if I hadn't debts ... and if apartments weren't so expensive, I would have refused it."[122] The following month he wrote to his friend Tolstoy: "Now I am rich! ... They are the easiest jobs in the world; I have been dreaming about such jobs for ten years; I am ashamed that I had to borrow one hundred rubles from you ... After three months I am sure that all my debts will be discharged, and I'll have my own furniture and no worries ... After fifteen years of a 'literary livelihood,' now I can simply live."[123] It was respectability that he had found. "I see now how useful it is to have a 'position' ... That old librarian at the Public Library that you see is now actually an honored personage, not just some old 'scribbler Strakhov!' "[124]

However to explain this new jubilation at ceasing to be a jour nalist in terms of financial security is not enough. Why was it that he was so willing to leave a career he had sought avidly in 1860 and had held on to for so long despite the many setbacks? Was it merely because it had been unsuccessful? I think not. Strakhov's personal transition from "journalist" to "honored personage" mirrored a change on the Russian intellectual scene itself. Strakhov was willing to leave the world of St. Petersburg journalism in the mid-1870's because that world no longer held an exclusive monopoly on intellectual expression. Although he was naturally quite unaware of it, Strakhov had been living through a period of transition in Russian life; his period in journalism covered both the most exciting period and the *last* period of its domination of literary life.

122. Strakhov to N. Ia. Danilevsky, January 6, 1874, in *Russkii vestnik* (January 1901).
123. Strakhov to Tolstoy, February 22, 1874, in *Perepiska.*
124. Strakhov to N. Ia. Danilevsky, January 6, 1874, in *Russkii vestnik* (January 1901). Stiva Oblonsky, in *Anna Karenina,* had a "well-paid" post as head of a government Board which brought him 6000 rubles a year; the salary was merely a supplement to his wife's substantial dowry, "necessary" because his tastes were so extravagant.

The 1870's saw the beginning of Russia's modernization in intellectual as well as social terms. The universities took the first steps along the path of independence and intellectual respectability. The liberal professions were born in the wake of the reforms of Alexander II, allowing for the first time in Russia a context for political action in the *zemstvos* and the law courts. This intellectual expansion helped relieve the "fat journals" of some of the functions which they had served, by default, for so long. In the course of the next few decades, the journals acquired a much more defined character; they became either professional journals, organs of specific political groups, or mass-audience magazines devoted to amusement rather than enlightenment. Daily newspapers and illustrated magazines began to appear to supplement the journals. It is only from the 1870's on that the Russian *zhurnal* really begins to resemble a twentieth-century "journal."

Strakhov's hopes for a career in journalism in 1860 were not based on a love for the medium, after all, but rather on a desire for an intellectual forum. By 1880 the possibility of other kinds of platforms existed. The publishing of books made a tremendous leap in these years, and Strakhov began to utilize that outlet. University argumentation began to intersect with public literary life in general, and the printed polemics took on a more directly intellectual tone. Strakhov did not *need* the journals any more. He never ceased to write articles, but he appeared in these polemics as a well-known figure whose words were attended to because he had a serious interest in a specific problem.

By the 1880's then, Strakhov had an established literary reputation. He had become a "man of letters" in a society that was more able to tolerate the open play of intellect. He was frequently present at the more exclusive literary and academic gatherings. The days when the closing of a journal such as *Vremia* or *Epokha* had literally thrown him out on the streets and on his own were long passed. This was the result of a steady production of important articles and books which earned him the respect of his audience.

III

Idealism and Literary Criticism

Strakhov's contribution to *Zaria's* first issue was in many ways the most significant article of his career. His analysis of Tolstoy's *War and Peace* led to an emotional and intellectual relationship with the writer that would dominate the rest of his life; it was undoubtedly his most influential piece of literary criticism.

Although Strakhov had already turned his attention to literature in the 1860's in his reviews of Turgenev's novels in *Vremia*,[1] he would make a literary reputation with his understanding of Tolstoy. When his friends in the 1890's referred to him as a literary critic, it was primarily the essays on Tolstoy that they had in mind. Indeed, for some modern scholars this label seems to represent Strakhov's unique contribution to Russian intellectual life.

In fact, however, "literary critic" is a misnomer for Strakhov, especially when used by twentieth-century scholars. His approach to art was limited by the characteristics of his intellectual era. He did indeed object to the narrow use which his radical opponents made of literature, and for this reason he argued for an autonomy in the literary experience which appealed to later generations of "pure" critics; yet his own use of literature, as a weapon in the fight for philosophical idealism, was itself as utilitarian as Chernyshevsky's.

We have already referred to the deviousness into which Russian intellectual life was forced by the exigencies of the political regime. Forbidden by restrictive censorship to discuss political issues openly, and kept from active political and intellectual careers by an undeveloped social system, Russian intellectuals found indirect and, on the surface, unpolitical methods of political argumentation. Literature was the arena in which political positions were most often delineated; even when creative artists themselves declined to produce a socially-conscious body of writing, the literary critics after Belinsky made up the deficit with a socially-conscious literary criticism, which either lamented the

---

1. These essays will be discussed later in this chapter.

absence of a social message or created one out of thin air. Hence, the 1860's expressed its radicalism more in the literary criticism of Chernyshevsky, Dobroliubov, and Pisarev than in directly political writings.

Strakhov's reaction to radical criticism was negative, but he did not totally reject it. There were basically two hostile approaches to the criticism Dobroliubov produced. Some poets and critics, known in the 1860's as "the aesthetes," (Annenkov, Botkin, Druzhinin), preached an "art for art's sake" doctrine which maintained that art is an autonomous phenomenon unrelated to social and political concerns. Other writers, known to their opponents as "reactionaries," criticized Dobroliubov's criteria but not his method; they agreed that art has, above all, a high moral purpose, but they looked for the message in politically conservative, or completely unpolitical, terms. One must be careful to distinguish between these two varieties of "anti-nihilism" in the 1860's. Most contemporary Western students of Russian literature in the last three decades, under the influence of the Russian Formalists and the New Critics, tend to identify themselves with "art for art's sake" in some form or other; regretting the inheritance of Russian social criticism in its current guise as Socialist Realism, they hastily assume that all opponents of the "proto-Socialist Realists" in the 1860's advocated "art for art's sake" themselves. In fact, this position was a rare one.

Strakhov was by no means an "aesthete," although many of his supporters and critics misunderstood him in this respect. It is certainly true that he fought with all his intellectual power the type of criticism which accepted art merely as a vehicle for social protest: this was the meaning of his polemic with Antonovich over Pushkin. But Strakhov was as much involved in a search for the total commitment as the radicals. This is very apparent from an attentive reading of his analysis of *War and Peace*.

Strakhov begins with an almost purely aesthetic attack on nihilist literary criticism and its disastrous influence on Russian literature. "Who really understands Tolstoy's genius?" he asks. Russian critics are only interested in their own ideas; they find it disturbing to confront another dimension to life, in which beauty alone exists. Strakhov's remarks are quite obviously a reaction to the hostile reception that *War and Peace* received in the radical press. Nikolai Shelgunov had condemned it as "the philosophy of stagnation" and S. Navalikhin had mocked its "elegance."[2]

Like most critics after him, Strakhov saw an important aspect of Tolstoy's genius in the simplicity of his realism. Tolstoy portrays nature only as it appears to his characters; the consistency of his point of view is an artistic miracle. If one wanted to approach literature from Dobroliubov's point of view, Tolstoy's novel could be taken as a perfect revelation of the emptiness of the Alexandrine epoch; as Ostrovsky "exposes" the merchant class, Tolstoy "exposes" the military elite.

But for Strakhov realism was hardly the essential element in the novel. "There are realisms and realisms."[3] A good realist is more than a photographer; he sees beyond his material into the realm of the ideal.[4] "[Tolstoy's] artistry is not in vain; let no one think it can exist apart from profound thoughts and feelings, that it can be an unserious thing."[5] Tolstoy's realism is neither an ex-

2. S. Navalikhin, "Iziashchnyi romanist i ego iziashchnye kritiki" (An elegant novelist and his elegant critics), *Delo* (June 1868). S. Navalikhin was the pen name of Wilhelm (or Vasily) Vasilevich-Bervi, who was in exile in Vologda at the time. The following year he used his more famous pen name, F. Flerovsky, to publish *The Position of the Working Class in Russia*, under the obvious influence of Engels' book. *Zaria* noted this second book with a sarcastic review by the pseudonymous D. Anfovsky, whose pen name was a Greek pun on the derivation of "Flerovsky" from "fleur." Anfovsky has been identified by Boris Eikhenbaum ("Tolstoi posle 'Voiny i mira'" [Tolstoy after *War and Peace*], *Literaturnoe nasledstvo*, XXXV–XXXVI [1939], p. 223) as F. N. Berg, Strakhov's colleague from *Vremia*. Berg-Anfovsky's devastating review was published in the same issue of *Zaria* as the last of Strakhov's essays on *War and Peace*. Strakhov later attacked Flerovsky's book as a perfect example of "diseased Westernism." Thus, Tolstoy had the final word, by proxy, against his first and most acid critic.

3. N. N. Strakhov, *Kriticheskie stati ob I. Turgeneve i L. Tolstom* (St. Petersburg, 1895), p. 244. Hereafter referred to as *Turgenev i Tolstoi*.

4. Strakhov had already noted this about Tolstoy in "Tolstoi, 'Sobranie Sochinenii,' 1864" *Otechestvennye zapiski* (December 1866), pp. 184–224, in reference to a somewhat prematurely published *Collected Works of Tolstoy*. The article is reprinted in Strakhov's *Turgenev i Tolstoi*.

5. Strakhov, *Turgenev i Tolstoi*, pp. 236–237.

posé nor a photograph. He is a psychological realist; he depicts the reality of the human soul in its search for the ideal.

It is in Tolstoy's concern with this metaphysical search that Strakhov finds the center of the novel. "Current opinion has it that *War and Peace* shows much artistry but little profundity. This is a travesty on artistry! Some people represent me as an aesthete who says that artistic beauty can exist in the absence of internal meaningfulness; this is nonsense!"[6] "The artist is a free soul . . . but freedom is a dangerous gift . . . It cannot itself distract us from the real path . . . It is only an expanse in which to perform, a necessary condition . . . The poet, completely free and pure, inevitably finds himself involved in the search for God."[7] As Strakhov later wrote to Tolstoy: "You are not a moralist, you are a true artist; but a moral position is always latent in a work of art. I penetrate beneath your forms with fascination and joy, tracing this moral position."[8]

There is a certain inconsistency in Strakhov's views, which he maintained by avoiding a confrontation with the essential problem of his aesthetics. He interpreted the moral ideal in very broad terms. At times, it seems as if the ideal might be synonymous with beauty; his criticism tolerates pure lyricism, whereas Chernyshevsky's aesthetics could not. Strakhov was later, for instance, to praise Fedor Tiutchev merely for the beauty of his lines.[9] Thus, he contradicted himself.

Strakhov was not the first to be confronted with this problem. In a sense it is the basic issue of literary criticism. Strakhov confused the issue by avoiding it; Vladimir Solovev, faced with the same issue, attempted a philosophical solution by vindicating the idea of the reality of beauty as an ethical concept.[10] In "A First

6. The articles on *War and Peace* were published separately as a book (N. N. Strakhov, *Kriticheskii razbor "Voiny i mira"* [St. Petersburg, 1871]); this quotation is from the introduction.

7. Introduction to the first edition of *Turgenev i Tolstoi* (1885), p. viii.

8. Strakhov to Tolstoy, November 16–23, 1875, in *Perepiska.*

9. N. N. Strakhov, *Zametki o Pushkine i drugikh poetakh*, 2nd ed. (Kiev, 1897), pp. 269–271.

10. Heinrich Stammler, "Vladimir Solovev as a Literary Critic," *Russian Review* (January 1963), pp. 69–81 passim.

Step Toward a Positive Aesthetics" (1894), Solovev argued that art has a cognitive objective as well as a moral value; he rejected the phenomenalism of idealist aesthetics and argued, in a sense, for the reality of the beauty in Chernyshevsky's hypothetical picture of a real apple.[11] As a result of this philosophical solution, Solovev passes as severe a moral judgment on a work of art as Chernyshevsky, rejecting the frivolity of the "decadent" art of Valery Briusov as the earlier critic had rejected Annenkov. In his commitment to a vision of unity, he rejected the irrelevant and the amoral.

Strakhov never came to such a complete rejection of "mere lyricism," however, and he is therefore more liable to misinterpretation by partisan critics. He emphasized his disapproval of utilitarian aesthetics without realizing how much he himself shared its premises. Because he was historically in the center of the utilitarian epoch in Russian intellectual history, an epoch which he found distasteful in every way, he well appreciated the dangers of the viewpoint. Solovev, a generation later, was writing in a new atmosphere: the utilitarian critics had been routed (partly due to Strakhov's efforts); he saw the greatest danger to be in an irresponsible worship of art. Faced with the beginning of Formalist aesthetics, Solovev was forced to consolidate his instincts into a doctrine which reacted to the present danger as he saw it. His task was more rigorous than Strakhov's. He lived in a generation which took for granted the abstract value of beauty; it no longer sufficed for the literary critic merely to establish the truth of the position of the Fathers in Turgenev's novel. But if Strakhov's problem was simpler, it had the advantage of allowing him more flexibility. He was able to appreciate both form and content; it was, in fact, precisely the juxtaposition of these two in *War and Peace* that made him hail Tolstoy as "the great Russian knight."

The message of the novel, as Strakhov saw it, was that the search for an ideal has to be conducted not in heroic terms but in

11. Chernyshevsky, in "The Aesthetic Relationship of Art to Reality," in *Selected Philosophical Essays* (Moscow, 1953), pp. 281–381.

the dimensions of everyday life. War, usually considered a heroic milieu, is stripped by Tolstoy to reveal to us the ordinary reality beneath; true heroism is in the actions of the ordinary men, the Kutuzovs and Bagrations rather than the Speranskys and the Napoleons. The basic drama of the novel, then, is between heroics and life. "Tolstoy's theory of history is that all human life, not only history, is controlled not by the mind or the will but by *Nature;* the sources of life are deeper than consciousness." [12] Tolstoy made use of the War of 1812 not because he was a historian but because he saw that this was the era in which the forces of life took over in Russia. Tolstoy equated life with the concrete reality of the Russian soil. "The French burned down my house and hence are my enemies": the Russian battle against the French became a popular national battle against cosmopolitan ruthlessness and abstractness. The Russians were the first to understand the national idea at Borodino.

Strakhov's unqualified moral enthusiasm for *War and Peace* was followed by an attempt to understand the novel within the context of the history of Russian literature in general. It is in this endeavor that the distinct qualities of Strakhov as a critic appear. He saw that the immediate ancestor of *War and Peace* was Pushkin's *A Captain's Daughter,* which both is and is not a historical novel in exactly the same sense. Pushkin had really written a chronicle of the Grinev family, in which Catherine the Great and Pugachev make token appearances; similarly Tolstoy had written a chronicle of the Rostovs and the Bolkonskys. In this sense both novels resemble Aksakov's *A Family Chronicle* and the third chapter of Pushkin's *Eugene Onegin* ("The devotion of a Russian family").

Strakhov regretted that this aspect of Pushkin's genius—his Russianness—had been so neglected by the two major Pushkin critics, Belinsky and Annenkov, because both were such convinced Westernizers. They were indifferent to *A Captain's Daughter,* to the *Belkin Tales,* to *Dubrovsky,* to *The Chronicle of the*

12. Strakhov, *Turgenev i Tolstoi,* p. 271.

Village of Gorokhino, because they appreciated only the cosmopolitan side of Pushkin. It took another age, ushered in by Apollon Grigorev in *Russkoe slovo* in 1859, to appreciate the Russian aspect of Pushkin's art.

Strakhov devoted many pages of his essay on Tolstoy to an exposition of Grigorev's ideas about Pushkin before he himself picked up the theme of Tolstoy as Pushkin's successor. It is here that we can first understand the extent of Grigorev's intellectual influence over Strakhov. Moreover, Strakhov's analysis was the first real appreciation of Grigorev as a great Russian critic.[13]

Grigorev had interpreted Pushkin's creativity as a successive struggle against various foreign literary ideals, which appeared in historical form as the classic, the romantic, and the Byronic hero. Pushkin assimilated these three types in turn, but he eventually created his own special type, which was completely original; he described the ideal Russian as a reconciliation of all previous Western ideals. Pushkin was able to sympathize with alien ideals, but he reconciled them in a love for his own soil. The symbol of this uniquely Russian reconciliation is the character Belkin. "Bel-

13. Strakhov later attempted an edition of Grigorev's collected works; only the first volume appeared, in 1876, but it did not sell well. Strakhov thought of writing a long memoir about him (Strakhov to Dostoevsky, February 22, 1871, in *Shestidesiatye gody*), but he never wrote it. Grigorev was not to find general appreciation in Russia until the 1890's when Strakhov himself began to attract attention as a literary critic. A Grigorev jubilee in 1914 – fifty years after his death – rediscovered him as a great and original thinker. Alexander Blok began a biography; Leonid Grossman wrote a long essay on his work as a precursor of Bergsonian philosophy (*Tri sovremennika* [*Dostoevskii, Tiutchev, Grigorev*], Moscow, 1922); and scholars began once more assembling his "collected works." But the Revolution again restored Grigorev to that esoteric position he had enjoyed before the 1890's. Up to that point, Strakhov had been almost the sole admirer, playing his missionary role with great understanding; his own literary criticism continued the work that Grigorev had begun. When Dostoevsky read Strakhov's essay on *War and Peace,* he wrote: "Each critic is associated with some great writer: Belinsky with Gogol, Grigorev with Ostrovsky. You, as I see, with Tolstoy. You have had a sympathy for him ever since I've known you . . . I consider you, *in fine,* to be our only true representative of the literary criticism which belongs to the future" (Dostoevsky to Strakhov, February 26, 1869, in *Shestidesiatye gody*). In 1871 Dostoevsky wrote to Maikov, "He [Strakhov] is the only real critic of our times" (Dostoevsky, *Pisma,* II, 333).

kin is the voice for simplicity and goodness, a voice raised in our souls in protest to falsity."[14] Belkin is *smirennyi* (humble) in contrast to the *khishchnyi* (predatory) Western type.[15]

Strakhov, under the impetus of Tolstoy's novel, actually completed Grigorev's scheme. He postulated that the task of Russian literature was to reconcile these two types, Russian and Western, to produce a new type of hero: a strong man with traces of Belkin's humility. That strength was a Russian characteristic also, he had no doubts. "After all, Russia has had its Pugachevs and Stenka Razins."[16] This Strakhovian synthesis corresponds to that synthesis of traditional Slavophilism and progressive Westernism that the pochvenniki claimed in their earliest statements in *Vremia*. Strakhov interpreted *War and Peace* as the apotheosis of the Russian type in the figure of Platon Karataev. Pierre represents the germ of the future, the possibility for the strong hero: he combines in himself the passion of his old father the Count ("a dying lion," as Strakhov said) and the peacefulness of Platon Karataev.

Thus, the analysis of Tolstoy's novel on the basis of Grigorev's suggestions can be taken as Strakhov's literary credo. All his other criticism derives from this essay; some later essays present the points in greater detail, but none with more persuasiveness.

It is obvious from Strakhov's treatment of Grigorev that he recognized not only his own debt to Grigorev, but also Grigorev's debt to other writers, particularly to Slavophiles like Kireevsky and the German idealists. Grigorev's major tenet was that art is an expression of the age and the nation in which it originates. As Strakhov summarized it: "Art is not a simple expression of life; it is also a judgment on life, based on the highest principles; and

14. Strakhov, *Kriticheskie stati*, p. 353.
15. Strakhov appreciated the tragic flaw in Grigorev's reasoning, however. "Grigorev's analyses are all the more acute when one realizes that he himself was a romantic; this disquieting principle found in him ready soil for development" (*Kriticheskie stati*, p. 355).
16. Strakhov, *Turgenev i Tolstoi*, p. 325. Grigorev suggested the same synthesis.

not in abstractions . . . but in the very form in which life presents them . . . Hence we get expressions of the truth only in particular, national forms . . . in the creation of [national] types . . . The relationship which art has to life is called by Grigorev 'organic' in opposition to 'aesthetic' criticism (which is too abstract) and 'historical' criticism (in which art is seen only as a *result* of life, and not as an expression of that ideal toward which life is directed.)"[17]

Strakhov's vocabulary is a bit involuted, but his idea can be stated more clearly to reveal the nature of the Grigorev-Strakhov synthesis. Art exists neither for its own sake, nor as a reflection of the concrete conditions of life which have produced it;[18] it is, rather, a moral endeavor which seeks to illuminate the search for an ideal within a Hegelian universe of continually evolving ideals. Art is the repository of the process of understanding social reality by the social organism; hence, criticism must take into account the historical ramifications of the social organism, especially the national context. The critical task is best described, then, by the term "organic."

Far from being a Formalist aesthetics, "organic criticism" depended heavily on a historical approach to literature. Strakhov wrote several studies of literary history which refined Grigorev's notion that Russian literature is in conflict with alien types. In "The Course of Our Literature Since Lomonosov," he pointed out that the eighteenth century was by no means as derivative an epoch as had been claimed. In fact, he found it much less imitative than the "civic poetry" of the nineteenth century, which, with the example of Pushkin before it, has much less justification for existence. Lomonosov was highly Westernized, but he considered himself equal to any Western genius; he was perhaps a student, but not a copier.

Catherine's time was one of an astounding reconciliation of two opposing principles . . . the influx of Catherine's

17. Strakhov, *Kriticheskie stati*, p. 350.
18. Strakhov was referring not so much to Marxist aesthetics as to the work of Taine on English literature.

enlightenment, and the jealous guarding of Russia's own distinctiveness . . . Cosmopolitanism in principle and *narodnost* in practice—these two principles, almost incomprehensibly, got along together . . . Karamzin was fully a son of the Eighteenth Century, was imbued with all the best aspects of the enlightenment of that time . . . but at the same time he was a Russian, was proud of his Empress . . . sincerely loved his people.[19]

Strakhov discerned a progressive alienation in Russian literature after Pushkin. Gogol was hounded, Ostrovsky misunderstood, and Turgenev ostracized by the radical critics. The miracle occurred only with Tolstoy. *"War and Peace* shows us the only possible *free* stance toward Europe, one based on faith in Russia."[20] *Anna Karenina* made the same point. "Levin's older brother is a Slavophile, the second brother a nihilist; only Levin himself is the pure Russian man without theories!"[21]

In a broad perspective, "organic criticism" is only one instance of the nineteenth century's interest in the historical and biological metaphor, and it parallels developments in other intellectual disciplines as part of the general reaction to the rationalism of the eighteenth century. There is an obvious relationship between Grigorev's ideas and those of the German idealists. Herder's messianic hopes for a truly Germanic literature is the prototype for Grigorev's search for the Russian type. They both saw in Shakespeare the example of a perfect English literature and hoped to find a similar figure for their own national cultures: Grigorev found Pushkin.

Schiller's aesthetic views also had a great influence on Grigorev's prophetic hopes. Schiller has often been misinterpreted as a "pure" aesthete, and indeed there is little question that his use

---

19. N. N. Strakhov, *Borba s zapadom v nashei literature*, 2nd ed. (St. Petersburg, 1890), II, 38–39.

20. Strakhov, *Kriticheskie stati,* "Zametki o tekushchei literature" (Remarks about current literature), p. 89.

21. Strakhov, *Turgenev i Tolstoi*, p. 450.

of the Kantian idea of aesthetic autonomy was the fountainhead of German idealist aesthetics. But to read Schiller only as an aesthete would be a mistake. More significant is his insistence on the civilizing role that art plays as the mediator between the world of nature and the world of man. Hence, from Schiller, Grigorev derived the notion that art is the locus of man's progressing self-awareness. The specific conception of organic evolution from one type to another through progressive stages was refined into a total philosophy of organic aestheticism by Schelling. Grigorev learned most directly of all from Schelling: "Poetry is the teacher of mankind"; therefore, we must look to poetic genius for enlightenment.[22]

Although it is a much used device in Russian intellectual history to search for progenitors among the German idealists, it must be pointed out that the tie is by no means very direct for the generation after 1840. It is legitimate to speak of the influence of Schelling on the young Alexander Herzen or Belinsky without any explanatory apologies. But, by the 1840's, the idealists were out of fashion in Germany (symbolized, one might say, by Wolfgang Menzel's influential attack on Goethe). Russian fondness for the Germans was partly a matter of fashionableness, and the fashion had run its course in Germany. It is therefore necessary to explain Grigorev's enthusiasm for Schelling.

The renascence of German idealist aesthetics in the 1850's in Russia (with Grigorev, Annenkov, Botkin, and others) is due more than anything else to the fact that these German ideas had been taken over by other Europeans after they fell into disrepute in Germany itself. The energetic patronage of Thomas Carlyle, Victor Cousin, Ralph Waldo Emerson, and Edgar Allan Poe gave

---

22. Here one notes that Strakhov differed from Grigorev in a characteristic way. True to his seminarist training, and in the positivist spirit of the 1860's, he justifies his interest in literature on empirical grounds: Russia's literature has already demonstrated that it contains the greatest educational potential for Russian life. "We are more committed to literature than other countries" (*Turgenev i Tolstoi*, p. 435). Of course, Strakhov had lived longer than Grigorev to witness the genius of Tolstoy and Dostoevsky.

German idealism a reincarnation on other soils. Carlyle's writings, I would argue, are as important to an understanding of Grigorev as Schiller's.[23] Strakhov, who was biographically even further removed from the generation of the 1830's than Grigorev, was even more directly influenced by Carlyle.

Although it has been customary to separate Carlyle's literary criticism from his social prophecy, the dichotomy is a misreading of both phases of Carlyle's development. Carlyle was a critic and a prophet at the same time. His criticism reflected just those elements of Schiller's credo which have often been slighted; Carlyle and Schiller never suggested that art could be divorced from life. Carlyle did not desert the idealists when he turned to social criticism, and his literary work was permeated with social concerns.

A sample from Carlyle's *Life of Friedrich Schiller* (1825), I would argue, shows that he was more than anything interested in the moral core of a work of art and was convinced that he had learned this lesson from Schiller.

In a poet worthy of that name, the powers of the
intellect are indissolubly interwoven with the moral
feelings; and the exercise of his art depends not more on
the perfection of the one than of the other. The poet who
does not feel nobly and justly, as well as passionately,
will never permanently succeed in making others feel: the
forms of error and falseness, infinite in number, are
transitory in duration; truth . . . alone is eternal and
unchangeable.

As Schiller viewed it, genuine Literature includes the
essence of philosophy, religion, art; whatever speaks to
the immortal part of man. The daughter, she is likewise
the nurse of all that is spiritual and exalted in our
character. The boon she bestows is truth; truth not merely
physical, political, economical . . . but truth of moral

23. P. V. Annenkov, in his *Literaturnye vospominaniia* (Moscow, 1960), p. 331, says that Botkin read Carlyle with great interest.

feeling, truth of taste, that inward truth in its thousand
modifications, which only the most ethereal portion of our
nature can discern, but without which that portion
languishes and dies, and we are left divested of our
birthright, henceforth of the earth earthy, machines for
earning and enjoying, no longer worthy to be called Sons of
Heaven.

Genius . . . is the inspired gift of God! a solemn mandate
to its owner to go forth and labour in his sphere, to keep
alive "the sacred fire" among his brethren which the heavy
and polluted atmosphere of this world is forever
threatening to extinguish.[24]

Schiller represented for Carlyle the virtues of truth, honesty, and
sincerity, as he many times tells us in the biography. Schiller as
poet is Carlyle's Affirmer, shouting the Everlasting Yea to purify
his age.

When Grigorev suggested Carlyle as an example of an "organic"
writer, he meant it in exactly the way that Carlyle meant his praise
of Schiller.

After all, it would appear that you [Strakhov] do believe
in art? You do believe in it, isn't that right? Well, just how
do you believe in it? Of course, not as Mr. Druzhinin and
the advocates of the aesthetic point of view do, that is,
not as a gastronomic enjoyment. You believe in its living
significance, in its seriousness, isn't that so? And what
does that mean? You believe that art, concentrating in one
place the variegated manifestations of life, gives them
significance . . .[25]

24. Quotations are from *Thomas Carlyle's Collected Works*, 30 vols. (London:
"Library Edition," 1869–71), V, 228 and 234.

25. Grigorev, *My Literary and Moral Wanderings*, p. 151. Carlyle, being no
aesthete himself, amended Goethe's lines, "Im Ganzen, Guten, Schönen, Resolut
zu leben" to "Im Ganzen, Guten, Wahren, Resolut zu leben" (Eric R. Bentley, *A
Century of Hero Worship* [Philadelphia, 1944], p. 154). One is reminded of
Carlyle's platonic triad for Schiller (truth, honesty, and sincerity) and Strakhov's
for Tolstoy (*prostota, dobro, i pravda*).

Strakhov's strong interest in Carlyle is apparent from his letters, in which he is continually recommending Carlyle to Tolstoy. The social critic is as appealing as the literary critic: Carlyle, who shouted the Everlasting Yea in the face of eighteenth century skepticism; Carlyle, whose "Signs of the Times" attacked utilitarianism in the name of moral perfection; Carlyle, who called for a new transcendentalism to supplement the materialistic science of the superficial phenomenal world; Carlyle, who rejected the mechanistic view of nature as "Being" for the organic view of nature as "Becoming." The essence of Carlyle's diagnosis of the ills of the nineteenth century coincided with Strakhov's views. It was primarily this moral agreement that attracted Strakhov to Carlyle's criticism.

Strakhov promised his readers a complete analysis of the style of *War and Peace*. It is very significant that, although he recognized the need for such an article, it was in fact never written. He appreciated the purely formal aspects of a work of art without being able to analyze them. The few attempts at such an analysis, for example, his discussion of Afanasy Fet and Tiutchev, end with a mere collection of passages, a string of quotations. Strakhov could analyze symbols; in fact, his entire discussion of Tolstoy is really an iconography. But this was an intellectual abstraction of the novel; the niceties of style, while very much within his perception, were beyond his abilities to discuss.[26]

There are indications that Strakhov was not aware of his deficiency. The introduction to his *Remarks on Pushkin and Other Poets* promises to provide a discussion of formal elements. "We are now experiencing a great decline of taste in the matter of poetic form; they seize on content and say that form is unimportant . . . The level of the new poetry is very low and public taste is even lower; people have forgotten what good poetry is . . . The

---

26. H. Stammler, "Vladimir Solovev as a Literary Critic," points out that Vladimir Solovev suffered from a similar inability to discuss style. In Solovev's case, however, the weakness was more justified; his "positive aesthetics" postulated an interest in ethics rather than strophes.

gift of form is the *sine qua non* of poetry ... Our present versifiers do not have it."[27]

Nevertheless, in the essays Strakhov was most of all concerned with pursuing Grigorev's image of Pushkin as a "national organic poet." Only in one essay did the promised stylistic analysis appear.[28] But the very subject — Pushkin's parodies — is itself a denigration of the importance of formal elements. Pushkin was not original in a formal sense, as Strakhov liked to point out; he was a skeptic, one form being as good as another for him. Strakhov assiduously traced examples in Pushkin's poetry of imitations from Zhukovsky, Iazykov, Derzhavin, Batiushkov, Chenier; he showed how Pushkin imitated Dante, the Koran, and Latin verse ("Tsesar' puteshestvoval; my s Titom Petroniem sledovali za nim izdali"). In *Eugene Onegin* he even lifted three lines directly from Lomonosov.[29] Strakhov applied himself to an analysis of style in the same spirit that Pushkin applied himself to a parody of style: in order to show that style itself was insignificant in comparison to the meaning of a work of art. "For Pushkin, form was an instrument for expressing thoughts and feelings; he took many forms ... from his colleagues Baratynsky, Delvig, and Iazykov. For these men, form was the prime concern, and beauty of form more important than beauty of content."[30] This was not so for Pushkin; hence, Strakhov's analysis of Pushkin's style is paradoxical.

The confusion of Strakhov's ideas about form and content is most striking in a long essay he wrote on Nekrasov and Iakov Polonsky. Why has Nekrasov had five editions and Polonsky only two? he asked. The answer is that Nekrasov, with his "civic

27. Strakhov, *Zametki o Pushkine*, p. xiv–xv.
28. "Remarks about Pushkin" for the *Skladchina* collection in 1874; it appears in *Zametki o Pushkine*, pp. 35–66.
29. Strakhov made this point in another essay, first printed in *Grazhdanin* in 1873 and later in *Bor ba s zapadom*, 2nd ed., II, 35.
30. Strakhov, "Khod nashei literatury, nachinaia ot Lomonosova," *Zametki o Pushkine*, p. 55.

poetry," and with his narrow Muse, is easy to understand. The critics are simple-minded and unable to understand the sources of inspiration of a poet such as Polonsky. The goal of *real* criticism is sympathy with the poet, in an attempt to define and characterize the nature of his muse.

It is interesting, however, that Strakhov felt compelled to illustrate his notion of "real" criticism with a quotation from another critic, Turgenev. *Otechestvennye zapiski* (Nekrasov's journal) had criticized Polonsky's verses as trivial. Turgenev wrote a letter of protest which explicated the formal genius of Polonsky's verse. Strakhov reprinted Turgenev's letter in full in his own article. Rather than analyze Polonsky's muse himself, he left the task to Turgenev.

What is more, Strakhov elaborated on Turgenev's comments with a characteristic claim: the most significant element in Polonsky's verses is his *pravda*. He rejected the notion that art can exist in its own realm. "God preserve us from that German theory according to which a man develops compartments and can consider religion *qua* religion, government *qua* government, poetry *qua* poetry, and life *qua* life."[31] "Faith in art means that art is connected with all the higher interests of the human soul and for this reason should be freely subordinated to these interests. Faith in art leads to a rejection of the temporary, the false . . . *Pravda* is the highest law of art."[32] Thus, Strakhov criticizes Nekrasov for his utilitarian poetry, and he rejects an analysis of Polonsky based on his politics, but he completely confuses the issue between the two poets himself by subordinating Polonsky's muse to his *pravda*.

In a similar manner, Strakhov applied himself to a study of Fet's versification with dubious results. The result was merely lyricism on Strakhov's part about the beauty of Fet's poetry, accompanied by elucidating quotations. Although he praised Tiut-

31. Strakhov, *Zametki o Pushkine*, p. 175.
32. Strakhov, *Zametki o Pushkine*, p. 176.

chev for being a "pure" poet, he in fact analyzed only his Slavophilism.[33]

Strakhov's response to Turgenev's art was curiously ambivalent,
because of the ambiguity of Strakhov's own aesthetic demands.
He appreciated the artist but rejected the social critic and was
unable to admit the dichotomy openly. Strakhov admired Turgenev; his very first attempt at a complete literary analysis was
a review of *Fathers and Sons*.[34] He praised Turgenev as a prophet
of his generation who had created an authentic hero in Bazarov;
he defended Bazarov as a genuine "Russian" character, and then
he ruled out a discussion of the novel in political terms. (Both
radicals and conservatives at the time were exhausting themselves with attacks and defenses of Bazarov's social philosophy.)
Instead, Strakhov allowed himself a lyrical apotheosis of the
poetry of Turgenev's novel and especially of the manner in which
the beauties of the world of nature were described. Strakhov
ended his essay with the thought that, being true poetry, *Fathers
and Sons* is its own justification and can be discussed in no other
terms.

Strakhov never again felt that sympathy for Turgenev which
he admitted to be necessary for good literary criticism. The loss
of response on his part was a moral rather than an aesthetic one.
Although Strakhov disapproved of Turgenev's rather obvious

33. There is an exception to my generalization about Strakhov as a critic. His
analysis of Maikov's "Two Worlds" is a gem of formalistic analysis. The poem was
written in 1873 and largely ignored. In 1882 Strakhov recommended the Maikov
poem to the academy in connection with a prize competition. He was, it is true,
also highly attracted to the theme of the poem, which concerned the transition
from the pagan world of Rome to the Christian era. It was in some ways an elaboration of Danilevsky's idea of the progression of cultural-historical types. (See the
following chapter.) But Strakhov devoted his energy to a close analysis of the
characterizations in the poem, as they illustrated the struggle between ancient
naturalism and the new spiritualism: the pagans speak in loud clear tones, the
imperial decrees are couched in the language of the chancelleries, the Christians
speak in the soft tones of the catacombs, etc. The essay was both sensitive and precise. As in the case of Tolstoy's novels, the closeness of theme and style was felici-
tous.

34. Turgenev's "Fathers and Sons" was published in *Russkii vestnik* (February
1862) and Strakhov's review, "Ottsy i deti," in *Vremia* (April 1862).

Europeanization, he presumably would have been willing to ignore his politics in the interests of his genius had Turgenev not ruled out such a possibility. It must be admitted that in this case Turgenev made himself vulnerable to Strakhov's scorn (whether he cared or not is another matter) and allowed Strakhov to get away with something less than critical consistency. Strakhov had made a great show of defending Turgenev as a poet when he was attacked by the radicals for his ideology. "Inasmuch as he is a poet, to that extent he is right in all things."[35] But Turgenev, later on in his memoirs, bragged about his own politics and tried to defend himself in these terms. Turgenev apologized to the radicals for any unfairness in this portrait of Bazarov; he claimed that he had always been not only a Westernizer but also a nihilist himself, thus making the Strakhov of 1862 seem foolish for having defended him. Faced with this Strakhov complained with irony, "Imagine how I feel now! There I was, crediting Turgenev with all sorts of poetic insights into the nature of skepticism, and now he says that this was all an illusion."[36] Strakhov could now only say that he, Strakhov, understood Turgenev better than Turgenev himself (as he had once said that Turgenev understood the nihilists better than they themselves). Paradoxically, we find Strakhov claiming that Turgenev is a poet while Turgenev protests that he is really a nihilist! "In order to save Turgenev's reputation as an artist, we must separate his thoughts from his art . . . he is a poor thinker."[37]

Strakhov consequently had little sympathy for Turgenev when he began to lose popularity with the public; having taken popularity as a valid criterion, Turgenev had invited his own fate. But Strakhov never failed to note the contrast between Turgenev's intellectual commitments and his poetic gifts. "The intolerance from which Turgenev now suffers is temporary; it is a result of hot tempers among our parties . . . It would be a shame if we re-

35. Strakhov, *Turgenev i Tolstoi,* pp. 101–102.
36. Strakhov, *Turgenev i Tolstoi,* p. 104. See above, chap. II.
37. Strakhov, *Turgenev i Tolstoi,* pp. 119–120.

quired all our writers to be harnassed to some sort of government (or any other) yoke, if it were the rule that, as among the Greeks, everyone belongs to a certain accepted party or else is considered not only useless, but harmful."[38] Strakhov's obituary on Turgenev in 1883 expresses all his ambivalence in striking terms. "He had culture, good taste, talent; how can we not love a writer who was so close to us?"[39] Despite his exile, he was somehow truly Russian; but his thoughts were borrowed, unassimilated European ideas. Strakhov ended on a note borrowed from Grigorev: Turgenev had been frozen in the second Pushkinian stage; his struggle against the "predatory" types of western European culture was unsuccessful.[40]

It was not surprising that Strakhov was one of the earliest champions of Dostoevsky's novels. His insight into the philosophical problems with which Dostoevsky was concerned is most natural, since Strakhov himself provided the philosophical inspiration; hence his iconography of Dostoevsky is still repeated by all students of the Russian novel.

Strakhov's review of *Crime and Punishment* was so enthusias-

---

38. Strakhov, *Turgenev i Tolstoi*, p. 132.
39. Strakhov, *Turgenev i Tolstoi*, p. 173.
40. Turgenev in his memoirs had condescended to Belinsky as a critic; Strakhov objected. He quoted at length Grigorev's positive evaluation of Belinsky, with his combination of social and literary concerns. Grigorev was sure that Belinsky would have become a Slavophile if he had lived into the 1850's because Belinsky had always been so susceptible to current manifestations of the spirit of truth. The contradictions in Belinsky were the contradictions of his time. In quoting Grigorev on Belinsky, whose writings inspired the radical criticism of the 1860's, Strakhov was being curiously faithful to the organic literary approach. Dostoevsky was far less sympathetic to the man who had given him his earliest literary encouragement. He criticized Strakhov for being too "soft" on Belinsky. V. la. Kirpotin has written a book (*Dostoevskii i Belinskii*, [Moscow, 1960]) in which he tries to make Strakhov responsible for most of Dostoevsky's reactionary ideas after *Notes from Underground;* he grudgingly admits that Strakhov was easy on Belinsky, but he does not understand the reason, and he manages to insinuate (p. 153) that there was something dishonest about Strakhov's attitude. Kirpotin to the contrary, we must admit that Strakhov had a respect for Belinsky's love for literature and for Belinsky as Russia's first literary critic.

tic that he ran into difficulties with his publisher about it. He praised the book as the most successful of the antinihilist novels, successful because the hero is a real man instead of a grotesque. Raskolnikov was a theoretician, held prisoner by his own ideas. His crime was not so much murder, as murder on principle; he tried to put into practice his philosophy of intellectual superiority, enlightened despotism, and egotism. Only after his crime did he begin to identify himself with other human beings; ironically, life had the final victory over theory.

Strakhov interpreted most of Dostoevsky's major characters as portrayals of the Russian nihilist or his Europeanized predecessor in the 1840's, both similarly cut off from Russian roots and the soil on which they exist. He saw *The Brothers Karamazov* as the epitome of Dostoevsky's work, a supreme fulfillment of *Crime and Punishment*. Ivan Karamazov is another Raskolnikov on a higher level, with Smerdiakov and Fedor Karamazov as cruder doubles. The story of the Grand Inquisitor prefigures another kind of nihilism, the excess of rationalism. The monastic background is the hope for a final victory—a victory of life; Alesha preaches Slavophilism in its most idealistic form. Alesha's counterpart is Dmitry, the ordinary Russian man, composed of both good and evil and willing to accept on his shoulders the sins of others. Dmitry truly symbolizes the Russian spirit; the essential point of the novel is that Dmitry, despite all provocations, *does not* murder his father; he does not commit murder because he believes in God and in the immortality of the human soul. For Strakhov, as for many others later on, Dostoevsky's novels saved the writer from the opprobrium due to him for his political journalism.[41]

Strakhov was cautious about Gogol; he felt that Gogol's ironic stance had been responsible for much of the bitterness of later Russian "accusatory" literature and, in particular, the writings of

41. He was, incidentally, very critical of Dostoevsky as a stylist. He found his writing too verbose and complicated, filled with journalistic irrelevancies. He continually advised pruning in his letters to Dostoevsky.

Saltykov-Shchedrin. Gogol himself had moved from irony to seriousness even in the first part of *Dead Souls;*[42] but later writers, without Gogol's love and skill, moved from irony only to cynicism.

Gogol became the focus of a small debate between Strakhov and the older Slavophiles in the late 1860's, because the Slavophiles had made a national hero of Gogol. Grigorev (who was also ambivalent about Gogol) had held up Ostrovsky as a countermodel, but Strakhov championed Pushkin. One of his earliest pieces of literary criticism was a small defense of Pushkin's literary reputation. The obvious surface target was the nihilists; Bazarov in *Fathers and Sons* had deliberately rejected Pushkin as a symbol of "pure" art; Pisarev in *Russkoe slovo* had developed the theme at great length. But the more subtle target of Strakhov's defense was the Moscow Slavophiles: "It is sad that the Slavophiles, who so deeply understand the failures of Russian life, should forget Pushkin and be hostile to him."[43] They chide Pushkin for his alienation from his milieu; but they do not seem to realize that he was more a victim of the romantic conception of isolation from the world than a willing seeker of it. In his heart he desired synthesis, as his poem "A Monument" illustrates. It was out of this polemical interpretation of Pushkin that Strakhov, under the influence of Grigorev, would then turn to Tolstoy as the true successor of Pushkin in Russian literature, and in this make his own contribution to Russian literary criticism.

As a literary critic Strakhov displayed no great originality; he was the first to admit his debt to Grigorev and Carlyle for his theory. But one could argue that this is not a significant criterion, that neither originality nor theory is very important to literary criticism after all. Like Charles Augustin Sainte-Beuve in his time, and Edmund Wilson in ours, Strakhov wrote with grace, and he

42. N. N. Strakhov, "Ob ironii v russkoi literature" (About irony in Russian literature), *Russkii vestnik* (June 1875); cited here from Strakhov, *Zametki o Pushkine*, p. 184.

43. Strakhov, *Zametki o Pushkine*, p. 4. The attack against the Slavophiles' blind worship of Gogol was pursued in Strakhov's *Bednost nashei literatury* (St. Petersburg, 1868), this time also in defense of Ostrovsky.

had good taste. At times, when he was able to respond with that intuitive sympathy which Schiller recognized as necessary for good criticism, he even approached greatness. But even in the best of his work, about *Fathers and Sons* and *War and Peace,* Strakhov's technique was polemic in the name of Russianness and philosophical idealism. Hence, attractive as he is, as an unusual literary talent in an era remarkable for lack of talent in the field of criticism, he hardly achieved real distinction. If Strakhov were to be limited to the category of "literary critic," we would miss much of his intellectual power.

IV

The Struggle with the West

If a contemporary in the 1880's had been asked to define Strakhov as a thinker, he would probably first have answered "Strakhov is a Slavophile." The readiness to apply such a label would reflect the fact that the vast questions raised by Peter the Great had been by no means settled for Russian minds. The relationship between Russia and Europe, the nature of Russian national identity, the balance between learning from and dependence upon the West were issues faced even more sharply by the nineteenth century than by Peter's century; the tempo of "catching up" was frantic, the defensive reaction against it equally great. Every thinking Russian had to take a position on the issue, and the answers covered the entire intellectual spectrum. There was a Slavophile Right (Aksakov) and a Slavophile Left (populism), a Westernizing Right (Sergei Witte) and a Westernizing Left (Chernyshevsky). Consequently, the label "Slavophile" itself is singularly uninformative.

To be sure, Strakhov himself accepted the categorization. His most famous book (which appeared in three volumes between 1882 and 1895 and contained nearly all his articles after 1870 except the purely scientific and philosophical essays) was called *The Struggle with the West in Our Literature*. The title reveals the Slavophile influence of Apollon Grigorev; that evolution from "alien" to "native" type which Grigorev saw as the essence of Pushkin's literary development was taken by Strakhov as emblematic of Russia as a whole. His major theme as a writer was that Russia must emancipate herself from the cultural domination of the West in order to discover her own personality.

Nevertheless, to admit this concern for national identity on Strakhov's part is not to be satisfied with the label "Slavophile." There are so many aspects of Strakhov's thought that set him apart from the Slavophile movement that in the end the term is simply inadequate. He was separated from a thinker such as Khomiakov not only by his social background, as we have seen, but also because he saw Russia's uniqueness more as a *potential* than as an actualized fact. Much as he admired Khomiakov's enthusiasms, he himself had no interest in (and indeed was skeptical about) the exploration of the particulars of the Russian soul. Strakhov's fascination with, and expert knowledge of, the current European intellectual milieu went far beyond that enthusiasm for Schiller which characterized the respect for "the land of holy miracles" in Dostoevsky; this is most obvious in Strakhov's interest in the natural sciences. But more than anything it was his total alienation from politics that separated him from the Slavophilism which was contemporary to him; on almost every specific issue he took a position very far away from the current Slavophile orthodoxy.

This can be illustrated nicely by a somewhat scandalous incident early in Strakhov's career which I have already touched upon. Pochvennichestvo as a slogan for *Vremia* was certainly understood in a Slavophile context. Nevertheless, *Vremia* was abused by Aksakov and closed down by the government because of a supposedly "unpatriotic" article written by Strakhov.

Historians have often noted the polarizing effect on Russian national consciousness of the Polish revolt and the "drift to the right" which resulted. In the spring of 1863, Aksakov and Katkov began a journalistic attack on both the Poles and Herzen's pro-Polish *Kolokol* (The bell). The radical press in general was silent; given stringent censorship, silence was not only discreet but was in itself a form of protest. Nevertheless, *Vremia,* with its usual prickliness, produced "A Fatal Question," written by Strakhov and defiantly signed "A Russian."

Strakhov asserted that the whole Polish affair was being discussed in terms that were irrelevant. The issue was not one of territory or political control, but of self-image — both of Poles and of Russians.

The Poles have risen against us as an educated people rises
against a less developed, or completely undeveloped one.
Whatever the details, the struggle is inspired by the fact
that one side is a civilized nation and the other, barbarians

. . . The Poles look at themselves as a fully Europeanized
nation, a part of the "land of holy miracles," of the great
West, which expresses the summit of humanity and the
main current of human history. And we? What are we?
Let us not deceive ourselves about the way in which Poles
and even Europeans look at us . . . We have developed
apart, and we do not share Europe's destiny . . . We cannot
congratulate ourselves on our development, and we can
hardly put ourselves on a level with other more fortunate
peoples. *This* is how *they* see us, and *we* ourselves agree
with them.[1]

To the claim that the Russian government was strong enough to
overcome this "disadvantage," Strakhov answered that a government is simply an external phenomenon which may or may not
give hope for moral greatness. Russia *may* have a civilized future,
but no one will believe it without proof.

Only we, Russians, can take this seriously. Only we can
accept our faith in our future. In order to preserve our
honor we must recognize that the same people which created the great body of our government has preserved in
itself its own spirit, and that its spiritual life is strong and
will develop as greatly as the strength of its government.
    The essential point is that we must recognize ourselves
as independent. In the context of European civilization, an
alien and dependent context, we bow to the Poles; but we
wish to believe in an indigenous civilization, with healthy
roots, and in this we need not bow to anyone.
    It is an obvious point. If we measure ourselves with the
common European yardstick . . . the Poles come out better.
Only if we recognize that each people has its own greater
or lesser independent development do we perhaps come out
better. The Poles have no right to Russian territory only if

1. N. N. Strakhov, "Rokovoi vopros" (A Fatal Question), *Vremia* (April 1863);
here quoted from *Borba s zapadom v nashei literature*, 3rd ed. (Kiev, 1897),
II, 92–94.

Russia has its own destiny . . . We are not speaking of ex-
ternals now, or about apportioning rights and territories
between Poles and Russians. We are speaking only of the
inner temper of the two peoples and trying as hard as possible to find the source of the internal pain which leads
them to their mutual struggle . . . For us, Russians, it is
obvious that we must turn with great hope and faith to our
own national principles.[2]

In order to appreciate the effect of Strakhov's article, one has to
be conscious of the heat of patriotic passion in the spring of 1863.
Katkov's *Moskovskie vedomosti* (The Moscow gazette) immediately denounced the article as vicious anti-Russian treason,
heaped scorn on the author for his deceitful pen name, and demanded a public revelation and confrontation. Aksakov's *Den,*
which for the first time found its Slavophilism a truly popular
cause, made a similar attack.[3] Strakhov tried to explain himself
to Katkov, and to protest his innocence, but Katkov was adamant.
"How could you write such a thing? It all sounded very ironical
to me. I don't doubt your sincerity in trying to explain it to me,
because I respect you; but all the same, I can't see how you wrote
it."[4] Katkov was careful to point out that Strakhov's Hegelianism
had *always* been suspect; all those searchings for roots and principles shows that the pochvenniki wanted Russians to be Russians
"not in the Russian way, but in accord with some sort of German
metaphysics."[5]

Strakhov tried to appease Aksakov and others also, but all in
vain. All his "explanations" make the assumption that he had
expressed himself poorly as "Russkii" and only thus was misunderstood. Indirectness, after all, was Kositsa's characteristic

2. Strakhov, *Borba s zapadom,* 3rd ed., II, 102–103.

3. Iury Samarin wrote it: "Zametki" (Remarks), *Den,* no. 22, (1863).

4. Strakhov's article, his explanatory letters, and Katkov's letter are all in Strakhov, *Borba s zapadom,* II. This quotation is from a letter from Katkov to Strakhov,
June 18, 1863, quoted in *Borba s zapadom,* 2nd ed. II, p. 134.

5. Katkov's article in *Russkii Vestnik* (June 1863) is quoted in Nikolai Barsu-
kov, *Zhizn i trudy M. P. Pogodina,* (St. Petersburg, 1906), XX, 321.

stylistic device. But in fact there is nothing particularly vague about "Russkii's" article, and his explanations are disingenuous. His point was that Russia, by the criteria which she herself accepts, did not *deserve* to dominate Poland; she would have to earn this by developing a civilized future, on spiritual rather than political terms. It could not be a popular point of view in 1863. In the midst of inflamed patriotic passions and the Russian national humiliation resulting from general European pro-Polonism, Strakhov preached humility, pacifism, and moral self-improvement.

There is something absurd — almost perverse — about Strakhov's approach to the Polish revolt. Poles rose in revolt in 1863 against a century of Russian imperialism, and yet "Russkii" suggests that it is the Russians who are the victims — victims of a Westernizing cultural affront whose terms they themselves accept. Such an interpretation is possible only within the context of a peculiar historical vision, an abstractness from the concrete political issues which allows one to overlook the unpleasant details — not the least of which was the deliberate policy of Russification practiced by the Russian administration in Poland. This was to be Strakhov's characteristic stand on most political issues, particularly Slavophile ones.

It is this quality of abstraction which emerges most clearly from his response to N. Ia. Danilevsky's *Russia and Europe,* in whose defense he wrote many articles, those which most clearly labeled him a Slavophile. *Russia and Europe* appeared in installments in *Zaria* at the same time as Strakhov's essays on *War and Peace.* Although it had much less intellectual significance for Strakhov, it was to have important ramifications for his career; it was largely through Strakhov's efforts that the book acquired a reputation, and his association with it went a long way toward identifying him as a Slavophile.

Strakhov once called Danilevsky's book "the complete catechism of Slavophilism."[6] He found in it a historical foundation for the

6. In the introduction to the fourth edition, 1889. He defined the "catechism of Westernism" as the belief that "the history of the West is the model for the rest of the world."

uniqueness of the Russian cultural tradition. He was interested in the book largely for its dissection of the dangers of European cultural imperialism. Although hardly original, the book was a coherent codification of much of the ideology hitherto expressed by such writers as Katkov, Tiutchev and others who were responsible for the growing significance of the Pan-Slav movement in Russia. Robert MacMaster has demonstrated how much more than a Slavophile or Pan-Slav tract the book really was.[7] Nevertheless, it was this aspect that appealed to Strakhov.

Danilevsky was writing a political essay in reaction to the Russian defeat in the Crimean War; from Russia's humiliation he drew the conclusion that Russia must sever the connection which linked her political fortunes to that of a Europe which had rejected her. Danilevsky developed his idea of Russian separateness into a universal historical scheme in which he postulated that each cultural group evolves in isolation and with its own characteristics (as what he called "cultural-historical types"); at each stage of history, one or another of these types represents the dominant group. Danilevsky supposed that the Slavic type was now in an ascendant position; soon it would have to fight for its right to mature against the hostility of the Romano-Germanic type. Slavdom's mission (the success of which he did not doubt) was not so much universal salvation as the preservation of the right of separate cultural-historical types to mature in their own individuality.

One can immediately see what Strakhov would find in Danilevsky's book to praise. Although the book was written in isolation from the St. Petersburg literary world, there was more than a casual resemblance to the views expressed in *Vremia*. Dostoevsky's very first article had been a protest against Europe's influence and a plea for Russia to return to her cultural roots. The basic argument between Kositsa and Antonovich about the meaning of pochvennichestvo had revolved about the relevancy, or lack of relevancy, of Europe's experience for Russian problems. Danilev-

7. Robert E. MacMaster, *Danilevsky, a Russian Totalitarian Philosopher* (Cambridge, Mass., 1967).

sky's very conception of cultural-historical types was couched in
that organic terminology which the pochvenniki had made their
trademark; Grigorev's literary criticism had emphasized the role
of the Russian poet as a discoverer of the Russian cultural type
through struggle against Europe's model, and this was precisely
the process which Danilevsky prescribed in the political sphere.
Hence it was fitting that Strakhov's adulation of Tolstoy as the
archetypal Russian writer should appear coincidentally in *Zaria*
with Danilevsky's predictions of Russian political self-fulfillment.

Strakhov had actually known Danilevsky since his days at the
university, but they did not become friends until 1868 when Danilevsky was in St. Petersburg trying to find a publisher. Strakhov
was working for the *Zhurnal Ministerstva Narodnogo Provesh-
cheniia* when Danilevsky's manuscript was turned down; he was
very much impressed with it, nevertheless, and, as soon as *Zaria*
was conceived, he prevailed upon Kashpirev to publish it. Strakhov wrote to Dostoevsky with great enthusiasm about the book,[8]
and Dostoevsky was overwhelmed when he read the first install-
ment. "It so coincides with my own views that I am amazed . . . I
wanted to write an article with practically the same conclusions
and even the same title . . . I am so eager for further installments
that I rush every day to the post office for the next issue of *Zaria*."[9]

Despite such enthusisam, Danilevsky's book did not attract
much attention when it first appeared in 1869; it was merely
another item in the growing collection of Pan-Slav literature
that followed the Slavic Exposition of 1867. Strakhov tried to
arouse some interest in it by defending its originality. He outlined those points in which he thought the book differed from earlier ones of the genre: it was "a scientific theory, based on observation and experiment, in contrast to former 'artistic' theories
which put all phenomena into the mold of an a priori formula";
it rejected the idea of a universal world culture, and hence of a
universally significant messianic role for the Slavs. Thus, Stra-

8. Strakhov to Dostoevsky, November 24, 1868, in *Shestidesiatye gody*.
9. Dostoevsky to Strakhov, March 18, 1869, in *Shestidesiatye gody*.

khov carefully distinguished Danilevsky's treatise from early Slavophilism.[10]

It was in its details that the difference lay. The idea of cultural-historical types which always retain their separate identities is one of the major concepts of the book. This is a specifically pluralistic notion of cultures which ran counter to Slavophile assumptions on the whole. This conception was by no means original with Danilevsky; as Strakhov himself would later point out, other writers such as Vico and Heinrich Rückert had had such an idea.[11] But Strakhov was interested not in Danilevsky's originality as such, but in his originality within the context of his Slavophile predecessors. He noted that Danilevsky also rejected any simplistic romantic notion of "the rotting of the West." Although Strakhov indeed called *Russia and Europe* a catechism of Slavophilism, he meant it as a "Slavophilism in an abstract, ideal sense, for there is much that is original and purely Danilevsky in the book."[12]

Thus, the term "Slavophile" is not very useful as a description of either the book or Strakhov's reaction to it; one might ask whether the term "Pan-Slav" is any more helpful. It is fitting enough as an adjective for *Russia and Europe,* but very poor as a label for Strakhov's appreciation of the book. In fact, Danilevsky's book was not even appreciated by those who called themselves Pan-Slavs; it tended to get lost in a growing morass of such literature at the end of the 1860's.

The apparent early success of *Zaria* as a journal was merely one of many signs that the Slavic Exposition of 1867 had inaugurated a new social movement in Russia. The Moscow Slavic Benevolent Committee as a cultural organization had been formed as early as 1858, but the St. Petersburg Committee held its first meeting only in January of 1869, coincident with the first issue of *Zaria.* The president of the committee, Aleksandr Fedorovich Hilferding, a noted Slavist, was also connected with *Zaria.*

10. Strakhov, *Kriticheskie stati,* p. 163. Strakhov's articles appeared in *Zaria* in 1869 and 1871.
11. In Strakhov's introduction to the third edition, 1888.
12. Strakhov, *Kriticheskie stati,* p. 161.

Strakhov wrote to Dostoevsky in November of 1868: "It's a pity we had to leave out of the subscription announcement your name and Hilferding's, since you are both abroad now."

Many scholars have hastened to identify *Zaria*, and Strakhov personally, with "reactionary Pan-Salvism" by association with the Slavic Benevolent Committees. It would be a mistake, however, to draw any simple conclusions about *Zaria*'s, or Strakhov's, Pan-Slavism. One must not exaggerate the cohesion of this movement. The committees were less homogeneous than common historical opinion has painted them. They were the only official groups in existence that maintained relations with other Slavs at the time; later on, in the 1870's, they were the only legal instrument for aid to the anti-Turkish rebellions in the Balkans. Consequently, many people who were interested in the Slavic cause were associated with the movement without in any way accepting the conservative political views of Ivan Aksakov (who in any case dominated the committees only in the last phase). The most famous example of dissident association is that of A. N. Pypin, Chernyshevsky's cousin and Strakhov's literary opponent on *Vestnik evropy* (European Messenger). In 1873 he wrote *Panslavism, Past and Present,* which professed a liberal humanitarian Pan-Slavism that bore no relationship to Aksakov's nationalism.[13]

Pypin had attacked the committees, at least, as "obscurantist"; other liberals, however, actually joined them. Kraevsky, publisher of *Otechestvennye zapiski* and the liberal *Golos* (The Voice) in the 1870's, was one of the organizers of the 1867 exposition.[14] G. K. Gradovsky, a Westernizer whose interest in Pan-Slavism reflected more than anything else a reaction to German nationalism under Bismarck, joined the St. Petersburg Committee in 1871; he even acted as editor of *Grazhdanin* for its first year, although he left (and was succeeded by Dostoevsky) when Meshch-

13. Robert E. MacMaster, "Danilevsky, Scientist and Panslavist" (Ph.D. disertation, Harvard, 1952), p. 20.
14. S. A. Nikitin, *Slavianskie komitety v Rossii v 1858–1876 gg.* (Moscow, 1960), pp. 202–208.

ersky began to insist on a more nationalistic editorial policy.[15]

Even as late as 1876, enthusiasm for the Slavic cause could be identified with left-wing movements. This was the year of the height of radical populist passion to join their Slavic brethren fighting for freedom against Turkish despotism in the Balkans. Nekrasov wrote articles about the Balkan martyrs and many young Russians went off to die for liberty in Bosnia and Herzegovina. It was not until A. S. Suvorin and N. P. Ignatev began to take over the movement in 1877 that Pan-Slavism acquired a singularly reactionary label.[16]

There was, then, a basic dichotomy between liberal and conservative in the Pan-Slav movement from the very beginning; only at the end did the liberals leave the movement entirely in the hands of the nationalists. *Zaria,* however, was associated with the early years of Pan-Slavism; its endorsement of *Russia and Europe* was combined with a moderate political liberalism. In this respect the journal resembled *Vremia,* which had also combined liberalism with Slavophilism in a unique formulation.

The best example of *Zaria*'s complex physiognomy was the presence of Aleksandr Dmitrievich Gradovsky on the editorial board. Gradovsky was a prominent legal historian at the University of St. Petersburg who despite his Slavophilism was considered a liberal. His friend Strakhov even made fun of "the liberal jabbering" at his dinner parties.[17] In time Gradovsky outgrew his Pan-Slavism, and he tried to turn his back on Strakhov also. When the first volume of *The Struggle with the West in Our Literature* appeared in 1882, Gradovsky wrote a review of it which reveals much about *Zaria*'s position a decade earlier.[18] Strakhov's book was a compilation of articles he had written

15. G. K. Gradovsky, "Iz minuvshego" (Memoirs from the past), *Russkaia starina* (October 1908), pp. 57–74.

16. Billington, *Mikhailovsky and Russian Populism,* pp. 99–100.

17. Strakhov to Danilevsky, March and September, 1882. Strakhov's correspondence with Danilevsky was published in *Russkii vestnik* (1901), January, pp. 127–142; February, pp. 453–469; March, pp. 125–141.

18. A. D. Gradovsky, "Po povodu odnogo predisloviia" (On the subject of an introduction), *Vestnik evropy* (March 1882), 271–288.

for *Zaria,* with a new introduction. Gradovsky, from the point of view of his new attitude, criticized both Strakhov's title and his introduction; he asserted that Strakhov was trying to force a point by making a series of excellent articles quite illegitimately into a ten-year xenophobic struggle against Europe. Gradovsky pleaded for more appreciation of the European heritage and a more conscious effort at a synthesis of Russia and Europe. His review was the first in a long series of misunderstandings of Strakhov's position.

Actually, Gradovsky was not attacking Strakhov at all. At no point in his review did he make a statement with which Strakhov would have disagreed. He merely revoiced the pochvennichestvo of *Vremia.* Despite the somewhat strident tone of the introduction to *The Struggle with the West* (written in the wake of the assassination of Alexander II), Strakhov was as good a European as Gradovsky. Gradovsky exaggerated the implications of Strakhov's preface.

The real villian for Gradovsky was not Strakhov but Dostoevsky, who had abandoned the moderation of pochvennichestvo for the more rabid nationalism of "The Diary of a Writer." Gradovsky's attack on Strakhov was merely a disguised attack on Dostoevsky, with whom he had been engaged in a polemic for some time. Dostoevsky's recent Pushkin speech, and subsequent death, had provoked an orgy of adulation for the writer which could only be attacked obliquely. Strakhov was justly annoyed at the use which Gradovsky made of his book.[19]

Strakhov's presence on the editorial board of *Zaria* thus can hardly be used as evidence for reactionary Pan-Slav convictions, as some commentators have been so quick to assume. But he did continue to associate himself with the St. Petersburg Slavic Benevolent Committee long after most liberals had left. He was asked to join in October 1873 and almost immediately was invited to be editor of the proposed *Slavianskii sbornik* (Slavic Miscellany); Strakhov was reluctant, but he finally agreed, mainly

19. Strakhov to Danilevsky, March 29, 1882, in *Russkii vestnik.*

because he needed the proposed salary.[20] Nevertheless, Strakhov's connection with the committee is not a significant biographical fact. He joined because most of his friends had joined, and he merely acted as a literary adviser. His most important activity on the committee was the writing of a biography of Dostoevsky which he undertook in connection with the posthumous *Collected Works*. Strakhov was certainly no germanophobe, and he was not interested in "the Eastern question" or indeed in any political question. Although, as literary executor of Danilevsky's estate, he published Danilevsky's political essays (*Sbornik politicheskikh i ekonomicheskikh statei*, 1890) and professed agreement with them in the preface, there is no evidence of any interest in such subjects in his own writings. Moreover, it is difficult to reconcile any putative Pan-Slavism with his defense of Tolstoy's *Anna Karenina;* Strakhov arranged for the publication of the epilogue, with its heavy satire of the Pan-Slav movement after Katkov had refused to print it with the rest of the novel.

If the evidence about Strakhov's political nationalism is ambiguous, this is because the question is almost meaningless for him; it reflects his general lack of interest in actual political matters. This is illuminated no more poignantly than in his defense of Danilevsky's extremely political and nationalistic book. If the term "Pan-Slavism" has any meaning it is a political one. It is distinguished from its Slavophile progenitor by the acute sense of political reality to which it pretended to adhere. Even Herder, whose emphasis on linguistic affinities was the seedbed for all later nationalisms, had suggested what would later be the ideology of the Pan-Slav movement: the future *political* domination of the Slavs. German nationalism, the Crimean defeat, and increasing tension with the Austrian and Turkish empires, were the catalysts for Russian Pan-Slavism. Danilevsky's *Russia and Europe* accurately reflected this political orientation; Strakhov's essays on Danilevsky's book, however, did not. His indifference to these issues gave his defense of Danilevsky a very dry and academic

20. Strakhov to Danilevsky, January 6, 1874, in *Russkii vestnik*.

quality. He supported him on many points, but he never endorsed the book as a whole. Paradoxically, at no point does Strakhov appear more of an old-fashioned Slavophile, than in his defense of *Russia and Europe*. It is hard to recognize the book from Strakhov's words; he defends it as Denis Fonvizin might have a century before. He ignored the germanophobia and the violent solution to the Slavic dilemma and stressed instead the idealization of the Slavic cultural-historical type.

Leo Tolstoy once said, "Danilevsky is Strakhov's weak point"; he was implying that his defense of the book was an anomaly and that Strakhov's loyalty was personal rather than intellectual.[21] And indeed, Strakhov spent many summers after 1869 at Mshatka, Danilevsky's Crimean estate. The warmth of the summer sun and the family life there provided emotional resuscitation after the hard and lonely winters in St. Petersburg. It was this emotional attachment, rather than intellectual commitment, that led Strakhov into the most famous of all his polemics, that with Vladimir Solovev over *Russia and Europe*.

Russia and Europe did not have a startling debut in 1869, and it was not even popular among Pan-Slavs during the Russo-Turkish war. Strakhov decided to bring out a new edition of the book in 1888, only because he was left executor of Danilevsky's papers at the latter's death. It was at this point that the anti-Slavophile Solovev attacked the book; Strakhov's answer, and the ensuing debate, gave the book the *succès du scandale* it had missed on its first appearance.

Strakhov and Solovev had first met in the 1870's, and Strakhov was very sympathetic toward the young philospher who had taken on the positivists with such fervor. He attended his public lectures and wrote a favorable review of his *The Crisis in Western Philosophy*. Solovev wrote to him in 1877: "I look upon you as my most intimate friend in St. Petersburg and you are like an

21. V. F. Lazursky, ("Diary,") *Literaturnoe nasledstvo*, XXXVII–XXXVIII (1939), p. 459.

uncle to me."[22] Solovev used Strakhov's apartment and his books in 1875 to prepare for his defense of his doctoral dissertation.

There were, however, always undercurrents of philosophical disagreement between the two men which threatened to explode the friendship. Eventually the quarrels erupted into the public domain on the subject of *Russia and Europe*. In the late 1880's when Alexander III's reactionary policies deprived Solovev of a philosophical platform, he turned to journalism for his audience. He issued a warning to Strakhov in a letter in the winter of 1887. "Apparently the theological journals are forever closed to me now . . . Only the negative, critical side of my thoughts is left to me; hence Slavophilism, and Danilevsky in particular, will be my target. Can you understand my position? . . . I would even take up arms against your *Struggle with the West* had you suggested any definite 'Eastern' counter-model to that of the West . . . You, of course, are more lucid and profound than your deceased friend; but *he* erected a structure which happens to stand right across my path . . . Please take my forthcoming article in the proper spirit."[23] Later in the month he wrote: "My criticism is not at all disrespectful . . . Out of friendship for you I have tried to tone it down . . . I will send you the proofs and you can make suggestions."

Strakhov never did see the proofs, and so it came as something of a shock when he read Solovev's article in the press in the form of a joint review of *Russia and Europe* and *The Struggle with the West*. (Strakhov's book had just had a second edition.) Solovev attacked both the Pan-Slav interpretation of history and the assumption that war with Europe was inevitable. He denied that Russians were a separate historical type and insisted that history proves them a mere derivative of European culture. He attacked Danilevsky's advocacy of violence as un-Christian and pointed out how much a deterioration it was of early Slavophilism.

22. Solovev to Strakhov, 1877. Solevev's letters to Strakhov were published in *Pisma V. S. Soloveva*, ed. E. L. Radlov, (St. Petersburg, 1908), I.
23. Solovev to Strakhov, December 5, 1887, in Radlov, *Pisma*.

"The most essential question for a true Russian patriot is not Force or Mission, but the question of Russia's sins." [24]

Strakhov's answer defended the basic idea of nationalism on the grounds that it had been since Napoleon a liberal historical force. He claimed that Solovev had misunderstood Danilevsky, who never suggested that violence was a preferred mode of social action but only a necessary one. Solovev, in trying to illustrate the ever-present tendency toward world unity in history, had brought forth Cyrus and Alexander the Great as examples of positive forces. Strakhov was quick to point out that Solovev's vision of unity ("the submission of narrow and personal elements to broader and more universal principles") is merely a euphemism for conquest by force of one people by another. [25]

These first two articles are really the essential ones in the polemic. The intellectual and moral arguments are clearly stated; later articles were only variations on the theme. Solovev reacted instinctively and totally against Danilevsky because he associated him with Katkov and those advocates of an aggressive foreign policy who were becoming more vociferous in the late 1880's. His own vision of a universal Christian culture made the notion of a "Russian" or "Slavic" culture meaningless.

Strakhov saw Solovev as just another victim of the prevailing European cultural dominance over Russia. To Strakhov, Solovev's "universal unity" was a synonym for cultural imperialism. He by no means idealized the nature of Russian culture; indeed, he emphasized its illness. But he saw the difficulty precisely in the fact that Russians had been too little resistant to Western influences, and this had created a generation "cut off from the Russian soil." Diversity is the natural condition of man; individual nations must fight to retain their individuality. Strakhov saw

24. Vladimir Solovev, *Sobranie sochinenii V. S. Soloveva* (St. Petersburg, 1901–1907), V, "Rossiia i Evropa" (Russia and Europe), pp. 82–147.
25. N. N. Strakhov, "Nasha kultura i vsemirnoe edinstvo" (Our culture and universal unity), *Russkii vestnik* (June 1888), 200–256. In fact, both Solovev and Danilevsky had a tendency to speak as if they were merely stating the sad, but true, facts of history when talking about violence.

Russia's problem as a defensive, rather than an aggressive, one.

It was only natural that, as the polemic progressed, Danilevsky's book tended to get lost in the argument. Insofar as the discussion was restricted to general issues it was intellectually fruitful; whenever *Russia and Europe* was dragged into the discussion, the argumentation became trivial and, in the long run, tiresome.

Solovev tried to keep the polemic impersonal. "They tell me that you are angry," he wrote to Strakhov in September 1888. "Please don't be . . . friendship is friendship." But as the months passed, each with its bitter reply and counterreply, Strakhov became more and more pessimistic about their relationship. Strakhov's hostility, which Solovev refused to recognize, had deeper roots than Danilevsky's book. He was extremely sensitive about insults to his deceased friend, whose family he had nursed through the depression which followed Danilevsky's death. (Tolstoy, who also did not think very highly of Danilevsky, displayed more sensitivity by not revealing his feelings to Strakhov at this time.) More important than personal hostility, however, was Strakhov's conviction that Solovev had become an adulator of authoritarianism. Solovev's praises of Alexander the Great repelled him. In the final analysis, Solovev's respect for harmony in this polemic was part of the same instinct that led him eventually to espouse the cause of ecumenicalism under the authority of the Pope. Strakhov perceived this immediately. "I'm sending you a copy of Solovev's *L'Idée russe*," he wrote to Tolstoy. "Oh, the French will love it! It's Solovev in a nutshell . . . We should all submit ourselves to the Pope, who is infallible . . . He argues from analogies and from the beauty of formulae." [26]

Strakhov, however, was ambivalent about the polemic; he was both bored and disturbed by what he considered Solovev's hypocrisy, but he recognized the value of a public discussion of the issue. "The polemic with Solovev of course pleases *me* least of all. It is more a difference of opinion than an argument . . . But in

26. Strakhov to Tolstoy, September 13, 1888, in *Perepiska*.

the first forty days since it has appeared on the market, the new edition of *Russia and Europe* has sold five hundred copies ... Since most reviewers are silent, this is a miracle!"²⁷

Solovev kept writing to Strakhov to complain about the latter's coldness to him, but all the while he persevered with his attack. "The last word in this business will be with me, *golubchik,* it's in the stars ... Don't be angry ... I never understood your praise for *Russia and Europe;* now it has become the Koran for all those idiots who wish to ruin Russia and make way for the anti-Christ ... When an enemy sits in the forest, one cannot question the value of individual trees; one simply takes the matter in hand and burns down the whole forest."²⁸ The burning was another article against Strakhov.

"Solovev has been courting me again in Moscow ... You can imagine, then, how surprised I was to discover today that he had written another bitter article ... What a Judas!"²⁹ Tolstoy advised Strakhov not to answer him, but Strakhov could not resist. "Here we have Solovev acting as Inquisitor, burning me and all copies of *Russia and Europe!*"³⁰ One sees how much Solovev's authoritarianism bothered him; the image recalls the superb figure of the Grand Inquisitor of *The Brothers Karamazov,* who also burned men and books in the name of the social utility.

The polemic had a tendency to run in circles after 1889. Solovev indeed had the last word, in fact several last words, and the polemic eventually deteriorated into an argument between personalities. There was one final flare-up in 1894 when Solovev reprinted all his articles in *The National Question in Russia* and found himself in an argument with V. V. Rozanov, Strakhov's disciple. During the peace of a quiet holiday at Iasnaia Poliana, Strakhov again sat down to answer Solovev's accusations. The postscript

27. Strakhov to Tolstoy, April 13, 1889, in *Perepiska.* This was the third edition; the fourth sold out immediately, also (see Strakhov to Tolstoy, April 24, 1890); Strakhov brought out a fifth edition in 1895, shortly before his own death.
28. Solovev to Strakhov, August 1890, in Radlov, *Pisma.*
29. Strakhov to Tolstoy, August 22, 1890, in *Perepiska.*
30. Strakhov to Tolstoy, September 20, 1890, in *Perepiska.*

to the polemic was no better and no worse, in tone or argumentation, than previous installments. A visitor to Tolstoy's house tells us that "the good-natured Nikolai Nikolaevich admitted that he was again indulging in malice at Solovev's expense."[31] Tolstoy again intervened to stop the polemic, and, finally, Solovev wrote to Tolstoy: "I am going to make peace with Strakhov on the basis of the Gospel, and without having come to any intellectual agreement—which seems impossible between us. Your advice to end the quarrel comes to me as advice that I have already given myself."[32] Tolstoy noted in his diary: "Strakhov just read me his last article. Its great defect is that it is completely and absolutely unnecessary." Tolstoy's remark can serve as a footnote to the entire polemic.

Russia and Europe provided for Strakhov a historical justification for a generally Slavophile attitude toward the West, but unlike most Slavophiles, Strakhov was much more interested in the European tradition than in the Russian one. He was a severe critic of the European intellectual scene after Hegel, especially in its materialist guise, but he took most of his ammunition from disenchanted Europeans themselves, such as Carlyle and Ernest Renan, or from former Westernizers such as Herzen.

Even if the current European tradition had been a more vital one, however, Strakhov still would have considered it irrelevant for Russia. He took as his special problem the spiritual emptiness which results from an unresisting subordination to an alien cultural domination. Russia in the nineteenth century was living on borrowed dreams. "[Russian] people are blind to [their own] reality; they waste their time on the pursuit of imaginary goals and on a battle against imaginary evils; their aspirations arise from no real need, and hence they cannot find satisfaction within

31. Lazursky, "Diary," p. 466.
32. Solovev to Tolstoy, in *Literaturnoe Nasledstvo*, XXXVII–XXXCIII (1939), pp. 275–276.

the context of their own environment; thus they destroy themselves." [33]

Strakhov at one point wrote to Tolstoy:

> I was once sitting on a train. When the sun began to pour
> in through the windows on one side of the aisle, the
> passengers there lowered their shades. Seeing this, a
> passenger on the other side of the aisle immediately
> lowered his shade also. Only when he let it down did he
> realize that the sun was not shining through the window
> on that side, and only then did he raise his shade again. I
> think that our intelligentsia is like that.[34]

Nothing illustrates Strakhov's point more than his own polemic
with John Stuart Mill over "the female question." This was one of
the most characteristic social issues of the nineteenth century.
For those struggling to liberate man from the arbitrary restraints
of the existing social and political order, it seemed only humane
that attention be paid to that one half of mankind in such obvious
need of emancipation. It was the novels of George Sand which
first brought "the female question" into prominence in Russia;
Herzen's memoirs, among others, suggest the enthusiasm with
which the issue was raised. In one sense feminism was a "safe"
cause; it was tolerated as a diversion from political reform by the
authorities, and it was used in some cases by radicals in an
Aesopian way.

One must note that "the female question" was not a question
at all; it was a position. One did not raise "the female question";
one supported it. Every self-respecting radical at one time or
another became involved in the fight for female emancipation.
Sensitivity to the issue is well illustrated by the scandal over
"Egyptian Nights" which aroused Dostoevsky and *Vremia*
against Katkov in the early 1860's. Mikhailov was only voicing
the feelings of all his friends when he protested against the insult

33. Strakhov, *Borba s zapadom*, 2nd ed., I, ii.
34. Strakhov to Tolstoy, May 4, 1881, in *Perepiska*.

to the lady from Perm who had read aloud Pushkin's "Egyptian Nights."[35] Mikhailov conducted his personal life as a concrete illustration of his views; the fact that his wife had had a child by his friend Shelgunov in no way hindered the collaboration between the two men.[36] But it was not the actual example in life of such men as much as the *literary* expostulation of these views that made feminism such a popular issue in the 1860's. Mikhailov wrote a long series of articles in *Sovremennik*,[37] and these were the theoretical foundation for the widely admired life style of Chernyshevsky's "new people" in *What Is to Be Done?*[38]

Strakhov's approach to Chernyshevsky's novel was in part a critique of this answer to "the female question."[39] He criticized the radical ideology for excessive abstraction; much as he admired the good intentions of the theory, he found that it had little to do with the realities of life. The "new people," said Strakhov, assume that they can conduct their life on the basis of rationality, but they do it only by ignoring the real problems. They completely ignore the problem raised by differences between the sexes in considering relations between them; they do not seem to realize that children often result from such relationships. Such a theoretical approach leads only to fantasy.

Moreover, abstraction can have dangerous and absurd moral conclusions. "The Remarks of a Chronicler" in *Epokha* drew attention to the charter of a new Society for Female Labor, which had proclaimed both the dignity of labor and woman's right to

35. See chapter II.
36. Franco Venturi, *Roots of Revolution* (London, 1960), p. 244.
37. They have been collected in *Zhenshchiny, ikh vospitanie, i znachenie v seme i obshchestve* (St. Petersburg, 1903). See also, T. A. Bogdanovich, *Liubov liudei shestidesiatykh godov* (Leningrad, 1929). Both cited in Venturi, *Roots of Revolution*, p. 757.
38. The very opposite position on the female question was proposed by Proudhon, for which he lost the support of many young radicals. Herzen reacted to his *De La Justice dans la revolution et dans l'église* (1858) with anger and disappointment, calling it the "testament d'un vieillard" for its patriarchalism and its attack on George Sand. In *Poliarnaia Zvezda*, Herzen blasted Proudhon's book as "the resurrection of the Pater Familias."
39. See above, chapter II.

engage in it as equal to man.[40] The radicals justify their feminism on the grounds that women are potentially as productive as men. This rationalist-materialist argument alarms Strakhov. "As a worker and an achiever of [material] value, woman will always be inferior to man, and hence such a view of her [as a commodity of labor] condemns her to perpetual economic subordination." The only solution to the dilemma is to abandon the materialist scaffolding. "Fortunately, the worth of a human being is not judged by economic criteria; hence a woman can claim complete *spiritual* equality as a wife, a mother, and a warm link between other human beings." The real significance of the role which women have to play is a moral one; we need not look on women as members of the labor force in order to respect them.

So energetically did Russians treat the issue that immediately after John Stuart Mill's *The Subjection of Women* appeared in 1869 there were two Russian translations.[41] Mill's book was a classic liberal treatment of a social question. Women find themselves in an inferior social position now because the legal system had promulgated conditions which made this inevitable; if we remove the legal barriers we shall see that there is in fact no natural difference between women and men.

The laudatory introductions to the Russian translations by Mikhailovsky and Blagosvetlov were a natural target for Strakhov's satire. A long essay appeared in *Zaria* in 1870.[42]

These hordes of contemporary skeptics are illumined by
joy; clearly they are not governed by grief over lost truth,
but on the contrary, by a deep faith, a strong conviction.
This faith is easy to name; this is a faith in *human reason*,

40. N. N. Strakhov, "Zametki letopistsa" (The remarks of a chronicler), *Epokha* (April 1864).

41. With introductions by Mikhailovsky (*Podchinenost zhenshchiny*) and Blagosvetlov (*O podchinenii zhenshchiny*). Mill had been writing about feminism since the early 1850's and *Sovremennik* had often repeated his views on the subject.

42. N. N. Strakhov, "Mill (zhenskii vopros)" (Mill [On the Female Question]), *Zaria* (February 1870).

blind and fanatical like many other faiths. These skeptics firmly believe that human reason can solve everything, and that there are no secrets from them, neither on earth nor in the heavens . . . The new solution to the ancient questions, boldly put forth, amounts to the following:

There is no difference between God and nature (God is merely nature personified) . . . between spirit and matter (spirit results from the behavior of matter) . . . between human beings and animals (a human being is simply an upright animal) . . . or between man and woman (a woman is some kind of beardless man, only shorter).[43]

Such an attitude is a normal correlative to that which makes no distinction between morality and happiness (morality is simply that which leads to happiness) or between beauty and utility (that is beautiful which is useful). But *true* wisdom, the article continues, lies in the ability to differentiate; one must distinguish the essential from the unessential, the essence from the mere form. The "new people," far from being bearers of a new enlightenment, "are really prophets of a world of gray chaos, in which beauty and variety and form is a lie; everything will be colorless and gray."[44]

For Strakhov, a woman's capacity to work is irrelevant to the question of female emancipation. He raised no objections to the removal of juridical restraints (he belittled this "typically English" approach), but he did not think that this would change the basic female character. The fact that women *are* allowed to own property in Russia, in contrast to England, indicates how irrelevant the legal situation is. As for granting political rights to women, this is surely foolish in the Russian situation, when even men do not have them. Mill's formulation of "the female question" can have little meaning for Russia; but of course Russians read him anyway, because he is an Englishman. "The issues are borrowed from Europe; not only the principles for

43. Strakhov, *Borba s zapadom*, 2nd ed., I, 172 and 176.
44. Strakhov, *Borba s zapadom*, I, 180.

their solutions, but the very issues themselves . . . In a similar way one hears of 'the war against Capital!' when we have no capitalists . . . and 'the Factory Question' when we have no factories."[45]

Strakhov saw a moral rather than a legal issue for Russia in the female question. The real question is: what should woman *do* with her freedom? To ignore this question is to ignore the fact that a woman has special qualities which distinguish her from men. When Mill suggests that women turn to politics instead of housekeeping, he is suggesting a new race of sexless women; all we will have left will be old maids and loose women. Politics and business will do for women in an emergency, such as spinsterhood or widowhood; but they will hardly do as a feminine ideal. Mill talks about marriage entirely in terms of "marital comradeship," as if love never entered the picture. After all, he concluded, "the female question" arises simply because there are sexual relationships between men and women based on sexual differences; one cannot eliminate this fact by eliminating the institution of marriage.

Strakhov had moved, at the end of his article, from a historical to a moral position; basing his argument on what he took to be the psychological (he calls them "spiritual") immutables, he resolved that a woman's only true role is in the family. His position is not as simplistic as it may appear on the surface. The fact that "the female question" is still debated today, when many of the legal and social disabilities of women have been removed, is a vindication at least of Strakhov's objections to Mill's argument, if not his conclusions. The fact is that most contemporary women have not taken advantage of the removal of restrictions to become emancipated from their familial roles.

Strakhov's remarks on Mill of course drew rejoinders from the radical press. Mikhailovsky called him "a comical and tragic Don Quixote . . . who dares to joust with the knight John Stuart Mill, and actually calls him stupid."[46] Mikhailovsky retaliated to the

45. Strakhov, *Borba s zapadom*, I, 215.
46. Mikhailovsky, "Literary and Journalistic Remarks for 1872," *Polnoe sobranie sochinenii* I, 706.

charge of irrelevancy by countercharging that the real irrelevancies in Russian life are on the side of the reactionary Aksakovs and the Katkovs (from whom, however, he carefully distinguished Strakhov).[47] Shelgunov, speaking for Blagosvetlov in *Delo*, also responded to Strakhov's remarks.[48]

The most interesting reaction to Strakhov's article on Mill was a silent one, of which Strakhov was unaware at the time but which was indirectly to have a profound influence on his later life. Leo Tolstoy was so impressed by the article that he wrote a long letter to Strakhov (which, however, he never posted). He praised Strakhov's perception of the issue very highly. He took exception to one point only. Although there is no room for women in business or politics, he said, there is ample need for housemaids and governesses, a role which would bring women into proximity with the family life to which they are by nature suited. He bettered Strakhov also on another, related, point; far from condemning "loose women," he asserted that the existence of prostitutes was vital to the preservation of the institution of the family. "What would London be without its eighty thousand prostitutes?"[49]

Tolstoy's letter to Strakhov has more than anecdotal significance. It reveals again the natural attraction which the work of one had for the other. The theme of The Family played a central role in Tolstoy's art; as early as *Family Happiness* (1859) he had set himself the task of exploding the George Sand image of the emancipated woman. He wrote his own response to *What Is to Be Done?* in the form of a satirical play called *A Contaminated Family,* in which the main target is an emancipated *nigilistka*. When confronted by a young man trying to steal a kiss, she exclaims "Stop! Do you know what you are doing? Isn't this merely animal passion? . . . It is not my womanhood but my humanity that you insult!" She infects her younger brother with dreams of communal living, and he decides to run away from home. He leaves

47. In a later article, in response to the republication of Strakhov's article in *Borba s zapadom* in 1882. Mikhailovsky, V, 614.

48. N. V. Shelgunov, "Suemudrie metafiziki" (Metaphysical sophistries), *Delo* (June 1870), pp. 155–180.

49. Tolstoy to Strakhov, March 19, 1870, in *Perepiska*.

his father the following note: "Father! I have reflected long and seriously upon the problems of our age, and have come to the conclusion that it is the family which checks and disturbs individual development; now I cannot see why I should sink and perish in an environment that is hostile to all progress . . . I am going to St. Petersburg to study . . . If you are not an unnatural father, you will send me money . . . Farewell, Father, perhaps the time will come when we can meet as men and equals."[50]

As Strakhov himself pointed out, *War and Peace* is also primarily a family chronicle. Tolstoy's epilogue, centered around Natasha and the dirty diapers, makes the author's intent quite clear.[51]

At the time of Strakhov's article on Mill, Tolstoy himself was planning another novel as a statement on "the female question"; it was to be a tragic story of an unfaithful wife. Tolstoy was bolstered in his plans not only by Strakhov but also by Arthur Schopenhauer's views on women in *The World as Will and Idea*. He even took from Schopenhauer the figure of the eighty thousand prostitutes in London.[52] A variant chapter of this projected novel (which of course later evolved into *Anna Karenina*) contains a detailed discussion at a dinner party at the Oblonskys' in which both Strakhov's article and Tolstoy's unposted letter to him are utilized in the text.[53]

Although Strakhov did not know about Tolstoy's admiration of the article, he did write to him on behalf of *Zaria* asking for a

50. Translated in Rene Fulop-Miller, *Tolstoy: Literary Fragments* (New York, 1931), pp. 203–204.
51. There is a variant of the epilogue in which Tolstoy is even more outspoken. In it, he conducts a polemic with Turgenev, who was an admirer of Berthold Auerbach's *The Villa on the Rhine,* a popular romantic novel about free love. Strakhov reviewed this very novel with sneers (*Borba s zapadom,* 1st ed., III, 328–338) in 1870. This is discussed in Boris Eikhenbaum, *Lev Tolstoi: Semidesiatye gody* (Leningrad, 1960), p. 131.
52. Eikhenbaum, *Lev Tolstoi,* p. 138.
53. Strakhov shared with Tolstoy his admiration for Schopenhauer. He translated *Grundprobleme der Ethik* in 1870, and wrote a long article on Schopenhauer and Hartmann in 1875 (in *Filosofskie ocherki,* pp. 374–427). Strakhov encouraged the poet Afanasy Fet, whom he had met through Tolstoy and who had been Grigorev's mentor in the 1840's, to translate *Die Welt als Wille und Vorstellung* in 1881 and wrote an admiring preface.

literary contribution. Tolstoy responded with an invitation to visit his home, Iasnaia Poliana. When in 1871 Strakhov had a windfall in the form of four hundred rubles in back wages paid by *Zaria,* he accepted, and from that June on he was never without the warmth of Tolstoy's influence and affection.

Strakhov had criticized both Mill's overly optimistic and legalistic solutions to social questions and the sycophantic adoption of his entire philosophical apparatus by Russian intellectuals. He was bolstered in his sense of urgency about "the struggle with the West" by the fact that Europe itself had begun in these years to lose self-confidence. John Stuart Mill aside, that optimism characteristic of the years before 1848 was no longer so prevalent among European social thinkers. This was a very helpful situation for a Russian Slavophile. "It is for Russians to complete the critique of prevailing European trends and thus to discover our own, better principles."[54] Strakhov was particularly sensitive to admissions of moral weakness and appreciation of Russian potential by European critics such as Carlyle and Renan. He was even more receptive to such admissions from Russian Westernizers, and to none more than that archetype Westernizer, Alexander Herzen.

Strakhov saw Herzen's Westernism as a result of despair of a philosophical kind.[55] His philosophical evolution from Hegel to Feuerbach was itself a Western pattern. Herzen's Westernism was the most complete possible, and, because he was so completely identified with Europe, Herzen felt free to criticize it (as the more Russian Vissarion Belinsky and Timofei Granovsky could not). Eventually, Herzen met philosophical despair in Europe, also; his disenchantment led him slowly back to Russia; hence Strakhov's great interest in Herzen. Strakhov was the first to point to the singificance of *From the Other Shore* as a confession of despair about the West. Herzen's disappointment with

54. Strakhov, *Borba s zapadom,* 2nd ed., I, iv.
55. N. N. Strakhov, "Herzen," *Zaria* (March, April, and December 1870).

European socialism in the *Letters from France and Italy* pushed him into a severe form of nihilism.

Strakhov made Herzen's nihilism into an abstraction. He saw it as an expression of a soul engaged in an idealistic search, like Tolstoy's heroes, frustrated at every turn. He felt that Herzen's nihilism was a uniquely Russian phenomenon, an emblem, as it were, of Russian idealism. His rejection of Europe was, finally, based on faith in the human personality, in individualism, which he found violated by the European idol of progress. In his final despair the disenchanted Westerner became a nihilistic Slavophile. Herzen's development shows that the Russian cultural-historical type will eventually realize itself despite all influences, and by using everything, including the Western heritage, for its own purposes. Thus, Herzen is the perfect model for the Russian "struggle with the West."

Although Herzen's new faith in Russia was a consequence of his loss of faith in Europe, his return was one without hope and with a great sense of irony. "The thinking Russian is the most completely free man in the world," he wrote to Jules Michelet. This is pure nihilism, a sacrifice of self without hope, a truly Russian irony. It bears no relation to the "golden era" optimism of the so-called Russian nihilists of the 1860's; a pure freethinker, Herzen rejected all systems whatsoever. He moved from Europe to Russia in the organic Russian way, just as Pushkin had.

Strakhov was the first to see this Slavophile side of Herzen. He saw in him a total negation of the old ways and a religious devotion to the new way, which might have led to a completely independent intellectual posture, a Hegelian reversal on an enormous scale. Nihilism could have turned into the most sophisticated of all "struggles with the West." It could have evolved into a new Russian way, much as Pushkin's Eugene Onegin had evolved into the Russian Belkin.

It must be pointed out that Strakhov's notion of nihilism was highly theoretical and selective. It would not fit in with the usual definition of the term, which comes from the mouth of Turgenev's "nihilistic" Bazarov. The February 1862 issue of *Russkii vestnik* which contained *Fathers and Sons* was a landmark in Russian literary history. Almost everyone, including Katkov who published it, attacked either the novel or its nihilist hero Bazarov. Antonovich reflected the consensus on *Sovremennik* when he accused Turgenev of a libel against the younger generation.[56] Only Pisarev[57] and Strakhov[58] came to Bazarov's defense.

Pisarev accepted Bazarov's extremism with enthusiasm. Strakhov was also eager to see Bazarov as an authentic and positive figure; far from being an insult, Bazarov is really an ideal type, and his negativism is only a logical culmination of the negativism of his time. Bazarov is indeed overcome by two unexpected accidents whose existence he had refused to recognize—love and death—but Bazarov dies a hero nonetheless. He is broken but not vanquished. Like all the "superfluous men" in Russian literary history, he finds action impossible, but in Bazarov there lies real hope for the first time. It would seem from Strakhov's attraction to Bazarov that he expected a vast positive upsurge to arise from the negativism. Six years later he would say, "Negation is the distinguishing mark of nihilism . . . This skepticism and lack of naiveté is a good sign, a sign of hope."[59]

Strakhov's approval was very limited, however. He had only disdain for what we would say were the essential elements of nihilism as a Russian phenomenon and which are best exemplified in the writings of Chernyshevsky: philosophical materialism and hope for social revolution. In fact, Strakhov was the leading opponent of *this* form of nihilism in the 1860's; he himself admitted the confusion in the term by calling his collected essays from that period *Pages from the History of Literary Nihilism.*[60] If Strakhov's analysis of Herzen seems one-sided, it is precisely

56. M. A. Antonovich, "Asmodei nashego vremeni" (An Asmodeus of our time), *Sovremennik* (March 1862).

57. D. I. Pisarev, "Bazarov," *Russkoe slovo* (March 1862). He accepted all of Bazarov's extremism as an accurate reflection of the legitimate desire of his generation.

58. N. N. Strakhov, "Fathers and Sons," in *Vremia* (April 1862). Also, in Strakhov, *Turgenev i Tolstoi.*

59. Strakhov, *Bednost nashei literatury*, pp. 51–52.

60. He published Kositsa's letters in book form as *Iz istorii literaturnogo nigilizma.*

because Strakhov was not interested in the political aspects of life, whereas Herzen, for all his nihilism, was a very political man.

Strakhov indeed pointed to an important part of Herzen's thought, a part which had tended to disappear from the critical interpretations of Herzen's life which centered on *The Bell;* on the other hand, when he ignored the fact that Herzen remained a socialist in his return to Russia, he was missing an important point. Herzen in practice was not a pure nihilist at all, and Strakhov's image of him as a noble Denier is more applicable to the fictional nihilist Bazarov. But his desire to place Herzen in this purely literary company led him to ignore the real political factors.

If one does take a look at the Russian socialist movement of Herzen's day, one can say that in part Strakhov's hopes for Russian nihilism were justified. The Slavophile elements of Russian populism are very much tied up with Herzen; it was precisely these elements that gave the "movement to the people" its unique Russian quality. When the populist Mikhail Protopopov reviewed the first volume of Strakhov's *The Struggle with the West,* containing the essay on Herzen, he specifically included populism on the side of "the struggle." He rebuked Strakhov for saying that all Russians are imitators. "I am an independent . . . For example, the economic order of the West – the most significant and important element of Western life – has been picked to pieces and rejected precisely by us so-called Westerners, a fact of which Strakhov cannot be ignorant . . . V. V. [a populist economist, Vorontsov] says that . . . [the *kulak* and the journeyman farmer] are not necessary for us, that we have our *own* path, which Europe herself will sooner or later follow."[61]

Nevertheless, populism was more than intellectual rebellion; it was also a revolutionary movement eventually bent on terrorism, and it was in this sense that nihilism's progeny disappointed Strakhov. He had failed to see that these political ramifications

61. Mikhail Protopopov, "Kladbishchenskaia filosofiia" (A cemetery philosophy), *Delo* (June 1882), pp. 16–17.

existed already in Herzen's thought. As intellectual attitudes became transformed into action, Strakhov disavowed them. What he had half admired in the abstract he soon hated in the concrete.

The histories of the Reform Era in Russian history make a great deal of the significance of the student riots of 1862 and the Polish revolt of 1863 in solidifying a conservative reaction. We have seen that Strakhov's attitude toward the Polish affair was, at the least, "detached." With respect to the student riots, he was even considered by them as a moral supporter. One of the student leaders, Mikhail Pavlovich Pokrovsky, was a close friend, and Strakhov was well liked by Pokrovsky's student circle.[62] When the students were imprisoned after the riots, *Vremia* sent roast beef, wine, and cognac. When many, including Pokrovsky, were sentenced to exile, they held a last carousal in Strakhov's apartment.

In later years, though, Pokrovsky lost his radicalism; and Strakhov also, under the influence of later events, changed his evaluation of the riots. The Paris Commune was an intellectual shock for many of those liberals who had cherished the ideals of 1789. Strakhov, too, was unpleasantly surprised by an absence of idealism that he saw in the events of 1871.[63] He sensed only naked class struggle, a hatred of the "have-nots" against the "haves"; of all European revolutions, this seemed to him the first real class revolt. The blood, hatred, and greed stirred up by the revolt could only lead to a regime founded on those very principles. Herzen had also foreseen this: *Letters from France and Italy* had predicted the coming of a socialism based entirely on vengeance and despotism.

Strakhov's attitude toward the nihilists had reached a midpoint. He still admired their purity but he was becoming more alarmed by their political activities. Our nihilists, he said, live like monks, but they deny themselves ideals. They want to destroy prejudice but they have no positive substitute for it. They speak of educa-

---

62. Panteleev, *Iz vospominanii proshlogo*, p. 193.
63. N. N. Strakhov, "Parizhskaia Kommuna" (The Paris commune), *Zaria* (October and November 1871).

tion but they do not know what they want to teach. They speak of freedom but they do not know what they want to do with it. They despair of sickness but they do not know the meaning of a healthy life. They speak of material well-being as a goal, but by their own self-sacrifices they indicate that they realize that man does not live by bread alone. Hence they confuse their ends with their means.[64]

The trial of Vera Zasulich, the young radical who had shot General Trepov, was a sensational event which led to many Russian quarrels among friends. Strakhov was appalled by the acquittal, and he quarreled with Tolstoy about it. "They treated her with honor; the whole trial was a justification of her action, an incredible justification. It seems to me a sacrilege."[65] Tolstoy answered indignantly, warning Strakhov that this was only the beginning of a vast revolutionary upheaval that had to come.[66]

When Alexander II was assassinated, the differences between Tolstoy and Strakhov over the terrorists became more open. Strakhov was outraged. "They have killed an old man who was perhaps the most liberal and well-intentioned tsar in the whole world!"[67] Tolstoy, however, saved his outrage for the brutality of the execution of the terrorists; he wrote a letter pleading for mercy for the young people.[68] The events aroused Strakhov to a new effort of journalism, after a four-year silence.

The "Letters on Nihilism" appeared in Aksakov's new journal *Rus*. Strakhov had considered nihilism his "specialty" ever since the 1860's, but in fact the articles did not turn out very well; he was ambivalent, under Tolstoy's influence, and very diffuse in his writing. He explained his views much more clearly in a personal letter to Tolstoy:

64. "Something about the Character of our Times," in Strakhov, *Kriticheskie stati.*
65. Strakhov to Tolstoy, April 2, 1878, in *Perepiska.*
66. Eikhenbaum, by judiciously selected quotations, tries to make Tolstoy far more sympathetic to the terrorists than his letters—even to Strakhov—indicate (*Lev Tolstoi*).
67. Strakhov to Tolstoy, March 6, 1881, in *Perepiska.*
68. Strakhov, incidentally, used his official connections to transmit the letter to the tsar.

This theme has attracted me since I first encountered it
at the university in 1845. The St. Petersburg type, with
its intellectual and emotional framework and its seminary
atmosphere, gave us Chernyshevsky, Antonovich,
Dobroliubov, Blagosvetlov, Eliseev, and the rest—the chief
proponents of nihilism. All this I know very well, I watched
them develop and followed their literature. For thirty-six
years I have been studying these people, their society,
their thoughts—and I have always been searching for
some sign of real thought, real feeling, real activities . . .
And I did not find it, and my revulsion grew stronger,
and I was overcome by grief and horror when I saw that,
after thirty-six years, *THIS* had been the only result! . . .
You well understand the joy I felt at coming upon *War
and Peace;* but life in general flowed on past *War and
Peace* and continued as before . . . Of course the good and
honest nihilist is a thousand times better than the
mediocre society surrounding him . . . But I can't just sit
back and contemplate the perversity and destruction. It
is as if a man tore off his head or his foot, imagining that
thus he would give mankind some great gift and win
fame and fortune.[69]

Strakhov repeated, in his articles, some of the arguments he
had put forward a decade before about the Paris Commune. "Nihilism is a transcendental sin, a sin of inhuman pride . . . It is
madness because it allows a man to act like a beast and think he
is a saint."[70] However, he still felt that Russia was strong enough
to overcome and outlive nihilism. In the face of this betrayal of
Russia by the Westernized intelligentsia, Strakhov—like Herzen
—returned to the Slavophile verities, to the purely Russian reality. "In one thing I believe with all my heart, one firm hope con-
soles me: whatever threatens us, we will always have at least the
Russian people (*narod*)."[71]

Tolstoy did not like Strakhov's articles for several reasons, some

69. Strakhov to Tolstoy, May 25, 1881, in *Perepiska.*
70. Strakhov, *Borba s zapadom,* 2nd ed., II, 75.
71. Strakhov, *Borba s zapadom,* II, 64.

rather perverse. He objected to the Slavophilism. "Chto takoe narod?" he asked him.[72] This was an odd question from a man who had created Platon Karataev as the apotheosis of the Russian peasant type. Strakhov himself was puzzled by Tolstoy's reaction, by his accusations of callousness and coldness to the sacrifices which the terrorists had made. It was probably the fact that Strakhov published in Aksakov's journal that angered Tolstoy; it was surely Aksakov's definition of the "narod" to which he objected, rather than Strakhov's, who never defined the "narod" at all except in reference to Platon Karataev.

It is clear, moreover, that Tolstoy's real objections to Strakhov's articles came out of his sympathy with political causes. "You condemn the revolutionary struggle because evil comes from it, and you say that you don't want to hear any more of it . . . But you must hear to understand . . . From what you say I would suppose that you value the existing Russian system very highly . . . You make a mistake in not wanting to hear about the struggle and yet judging its outcome so harshly . . . They sacrificed their lives for a political goal . . . Man is basically good; if he does evil, the cause lies in the evil surrounding him . . . such as exile in Siberia, prisons, war, poverty, corruption."[73]

Nevertheless, Tolstoy ended his criticism on a positive note. "In the last article you judge from the point of view of Christ, and the *narod* is beside the point; this is the only correct way."[74] This was, indeed, the point from which Strakhov made his final judgment of the nihilists, returning to the mood of complete abstraction with which he had started the evaluation of Bazarov. In 1894 the French President Sadi-Carnot was assassinated by an anarchist. Strakhov was moved to write about "A Special Kind of Villainy,"[75] in which he repeated the same argument which Dostoevsky had

72. Tolstoy to Strakhov, May 28, 1881, in *Perepiska.*
73. Tolstoy to Strakhov, May 1881; this letter appears in V. G. Chertkov and N. N. Gusev, *Tolstoi i o Tolstom* (Moscow, 1926), vol. II.
74. Tolstoy to Strakhov, May 28, 1881, in *Perepiska.*
75. N. N. Strakhov, "Zlodeistva osobogo roda" (A special kind of villainy), *Russkoe obozrenie* (October 1894).

elaborated in *Crime and Punishment*. As long as men condone revolutionary violence in the name of progress they have no right to condemn political assassins of any kind; such men all act in the name of what they call human good. When we abandon the old-fashioned rules of good and evil, we are left entirely without moral principles. Political crimes have had a long history of historical idealization: Cicero praised Brutus and Cassius, and Charlotte Corday is beloved of the poets. But Dante had the more correct idea; in the lowest depths of hell he placed a three-headed Satan, clutching Judas, Brutus, and Cassius, one in each of his jaws. Strakhov's Christianity in this last article was the final stage of his disassociation from nihilism as a specifically Russian phenomenon.

Strakhov was simply not interested in politics as a real issue. It was part of the domain of the "temporary" and "casual" which he so often advised Dostoevsky to abandon. His abstractness made him a poor journalist; he did not have that sense of "the moment" which Dostoevsky had to such a brilliant degree. Strakhov's sensibility was of the kind to make men powerless to act against the political obstacles which well-intentioned men faced in nineteenth-century Russia. His quietism or indifference or abstraction from life kept him from taking political stands.

Because of his excessively theoretical attitude, then, it would seem foolish to label Strakhov as a "liberal" or a "reactionary." On specific issues he took no recognizable "line," sometimes sympathizing with right and sometimes with left. He condemned the assassination of 1881 but joined Tolstoy and Solovev in asking for mercy for the murderers. He continued to sympathize with rebellious students;[76] he bitterly complained about censorship. But like so many intellectuals, he always saw the "larger" issues. In 1895 he refused to sign a petition condemning censorship: "I wish to sign; I cherish freedom of the press more than anything . . . But this whole affair is alien to me; the people involved are

76. See, for instance, his letter to N. Ia. Grot, February 1895, in *N. Ia. Grot v ocherkakh, vospominaniiakh i pismakh*, ed. K. Ia. Grot (St. Petersburg, 1911).

not those with whom I sympathize . . . The signers all represent only one side." [77]

He was very sensitive about being taken for a conservative like Katkov. He wrote to Ia. K. Grot in 1894, in connection with a laudatory article about Strakhov which the latter had written: "Only one point, unfortunately, you did not raise in my defense, and I shall raise it. Every Slavophile is accused of sympathizing with despotism and hating foreigners . . . I myself, whatever my sins, am free from these . . . I have never written an antiliberal page, and I have no hatred for Jews and Catholics." [78] And his opponents always *did* distinguish him from such men. "Strakhov merely plays into the hands of obscurantists, with whom he has nothing in common in terms of instincts, feelings, wishes . . . Such is the fate of people who are not quite of this world." [79] Strakhov once quarreled with his friend Rozanov, on the occasion of a monarchist pamphlet written by the latter. "You understand very well that with true Christianity political life is an impossibility . . . But you do not see that Monarchy can be founded no more on the Bible than Republicanism . . . Monarchy is dictatorship and at the very least an inevitable evil . . . What you write in praise of Ivan the Terrible and the French kings is awful . . . Our ideal is high, very high: we can only cry out with impatience about its failure and nourish our tender dreams." [80]

Strakhov was attracted by Herzen's nihilism principally because he saw it as a critical reaction to Western ideas. But he did not have to seek these critiques only in Russia; Europe had her own critics, and in a sense they served as better examples for Strakhov. He was as fascinated with the appurtenances of Western culture as he was with Russia's potential to overcome its temptations. It was the breadth of his knowledge that impressed his

77. Strakhov to L. F. Panteleev, January 8, 1895, in *Sovremennik* (April 1913), p. 259.
78. Strakhov to Grot, March 13, 1894, in *N. Ia. Grot.*
79. M. Protopopov, "A Cemetery Philosophy," p. 9.
80. Strakhov to Rozanov, February 23, 1893, in V. V. Rozanov, *Literaturnye izgnanniki* (St. Petersburg, 1913).

contemporaries; he not only had great respect for "the holy miracle" of the West, he was completely familiar with it. An example of its influence on him is seen in the respect he had for Ernest Renan.

It would be difficult to explain Renan's attraction for Strakhov if one followed his contemporaries in calling Renan a "positivist." Renan acquired such a reputation largely because of his "objectification" of historical study and his belief that the future would be built around progress in the sciences. But reading Renan today without prejudgments, one is struck most by the metaphysical elements of his writing despite the "positivist" label. It was exactly this aspect of Renan's work that attracted Strakhov; he read him eagerly and translated two of his books.

His personal identification with Renan lies partly in the similarity in biography. Renan's birthplace in Brittany recalled the Ukrainian backwater and northern provincial town in which Strakhov was born and raised. Renan's early education at the ecclesiastical school at Tréguier bore a striking resemblance to the seminary at Kostroma:

I was educated at a small school by honest priests who
taught me Latin in the ancient way (the good way), which
is to say with wretched books, without method, almost
without grammar, just as Erasmus and the humanists
of the sixteenth century learned it . . . These worthy
priests were the salt of the earth . . . They tried most of
all to create men of honor. Their moral lessons, which
seemed to me the very personification of virtue, were
inseparable from the dogma they taught. Their historical
teaching consisted solely of reading Rollin. Of criticism,
natural science, philosophy there was not a word. As for
the nineteenth century . . . my good masters knew nothing.
One could not imagine a more complete isolation from
the contemporary atmosphere . . . There was never a word
of modern French literature; French literature ended
with Delille . . . One would have to be very ignorant about
human nature not to understand the hold which these

simple, strong, and honest disciplines had on the better
students. The basis of this primitive education was a
stringent morality, inseparable from religious practice,
a way of taking life as something which implied severe
duties toward the truth.[81]

. . .

The education which these good priests gave me was
as unliterary as possible. We wrote innumerable Latin
verses, but they did not admit the existence of any French
poetry later than the *Religion* of Racine the younger. The
name of Lamartine was never pronounced without a
sneer; Victor Hugo was unknown completely. To write
French verse was considered a dangerous occupation and
could lead to expulsion.[82]

A fortunate accident brought Renan to the attention of a certain
M. Doupanloup, who ran an exclusive seminary in Paris and took
on a few scholarship students every year. Like Strakhov, at the
age of sixteen Renan came from the provinces to the big city:

Yes, a Buddhist Lama or a Muslim Fakir, transported
in a twinkling from Asia to the boulevards of Paris, would
have been no less astounded than I on suddenly finding
myself in a setting so different from that of my good
Brittany . . . My arrival in Paris was a passage from one
religion to another. My Breton Christianity resembled what
I now found as little as an old piece of stiff cloth resembles
fine percale . . . Now I found myself presented with printed
cotton and calico, a musky and beribboned piety, a devotion
of delicate tapers and petite flower pots, a theology of
young ladies, with no solidity.[83]

81. From *Souvenirs d 'enfance et de jeunesse,* the last book whith Strakhov
translated. I have used the Calmann-Levy edition of Ernest Renan's *Oeuvres
complètes,* ed. Hcnriette Psichari (Paris, 1947–61), II, 787–789.
82. Renan, *Oeuvres complètes,* II, 732.
83. Renan, *Oeuvres complètes,* II, 807–808.

When Renan left Saint-Sulpice and the ministry altogether, he, like Strakhov, turned to teaching and finally to journalism. He wrote for the journal of the Ministry of Education (*Journal de l'instruction publique*) as Strakhov had for *Zhurnal Minister-stva Narodnogo Prosveshcheniia*.[84] His *Vremia* was Jules Simon's *La Liberté de penser;* later he joined the more traditional *Revue des deux mondes* and *Journal des débats*. It was from articles in these later journals, in the 1850's, that Renan's first two published books were assembled, *Études d'histoire réligieuse* (1857) and *Essais de morale et de critique* (1859). Strakhov translated the first book in 1871 and found in it both a religious reverence and a sensitivity to the need for faith, despite Renan's skepticism about biblical scholarship. But it was the second book which had the greater influence on Strakhov.

Essais de morale et de critique heralded Renan as a literary critic. The article best known today is "The Poetry of the Celtic Races," in part because Matthew Arnold's enthusiasm gave it a European reputation. This is Renan's apotheosis of his Breton heritage and his idealization of the spirit of Brittany as reflected in its literature.[85] Renan writes of the Celtic spirit as Carlyle wrote of the Scots and Grigorev of the Russian type.

The Celtic race has used itself up in resisting the march
of time and in defending desperate causes. It does not
seem to have had any aptitude for politics at any time: the
strength of its family life has stifled any more extended
loyalties. It does not seem as if its people are susceptible
to Progress. Life appears to them as a fixed condition,
which it is beyond human power to change. Gifted with
little active initiative, too inclined to see themselves as
minors and tutees, they willingly believe in Fate and
resign themselves to it.[86]

84. H. W. Wardman, *Ernest Renan, A Critical Biography* (London, 1964), p. 40.
85. For a detailed analysis, see René Galand, *L' Âme celtique de Renan* (Paris, 1959).
86. *Essais de morale et de critique, Oeuvres complètes*, II, p. 257.

One can say that the Celtic races were predestined to
Christianity by the sweetness of their manners and their
exquisite sensibility, together with an absence of any
previous organized religion. Christianity, which in effect
addresses itself to the humble sentiments of human
nature, found admirably prepared disciples here; no race so
delicately understood the charms of smallness or placed
the simple man, the Innocent, so close to God.[87]

The primitive German hero repels with his purposeless
cruelty, his love of evil, which gives him ingenuity only
to hate and to hurt. But the Celtic hero, even in his
wildest flights, seems overcome by habits of goodness and
empathy for the weak. The sentiment is one of the
deepest of the Celtic people.[88]

If one could assign sex to nations, as to individuals, one
could say without hesitation that the Celtic race . . . is
essentially a feminine one. No human family has carried
such mystery into the act of love.[89]

This race seeks the infinite; it thirsts for it, it pursues it
at all cost, even beyond the grave and hell. The essential
Breton defect, the penchant for drunkenness, a defect
which — according to sixth-century tradition — was
responsible for all their disasters, is due to their
unconquerable need for illusion. Do not say that this is a
vulgar appetite for pleasure, for there has never been a
people more sober and detached from sensuality; no, the
Bretons seek in liquor what Owen, St. Brendan, and
Peredur sought each in his own way: a vision of the
invisible world.[90]

Or, as Renan later said in his memoirs, "The chief trait of the
Breton race is Idealism, the pursuit of a moral or intellectual
goal, often in error but always disinterested . . . Religion is the

87. Renan, *Ouevres complètes*, II, 288–289.
88. Renan, *Ouevres complètes*, II, 263–264.
89. Renan, *Ouevres complètes*, II, 258.
90. Renan, *Ouevres complètes*, II, 259.

form behind which the Celtic races hide their thirst for the Ideal."[91]

What are Renan's words if not a match to Grigorev's picture of "the Russian physiognomy" and to Strakhov's elucidation of the pure and simple Belkin as the apotheosis of the *smirennyi russkii chelovek* (the humble Russian man)? In fact, it is in Strakhov's article on *War and Peace* that we first find his admiration of Renan as the perfect example of German idealism in literary criticism.[92]

In the year of Renan's death, 1892, Strakhov found occasion to remark specifically about the identity between the Celtic and the Slavic peoples.[93] It was not Renan who made the analogy so much as Strakhov, although Strakhov confuses the reader by adopting Renan's categories for his own. Strakhov noted that the Slavs, too, have often been called "feminine, receptive, passive."[94] In other essays, Strakhov characterized Pushkin as "feminine" and "idealistic"[95] and the Russians as idealistic in their drunkenness. "Our inclination toward idealism is a Russian trait: we usually rescue ourselves from indecision by 'the good old faith' or by absolute submissiveness . . . We cannot be objective because of this inclination toward idealism."[96]

But the Breton trait which most appealed to Strakhov was their resistance to modernization. "At the present they are still resisting a dangerous invasion, that of modern civilization, because it destroys local varieties and national types."[97] Renan, like Carlyle and Dostoevsky and many of his nineteenth-century contemporaries, had a distaste for the vulgarities and mediocrities of the age of industrialization. He expressed it most vividly in an essay on the Paris Exposition of 1855, whose paeans to industrial prog-

---

91. *Souvenirs de l'enfance et de jeunesse*, in *Ouevres complètes*, II, 761–762.
92. Strakhov, *Turgenev i Tolstoi*, p. 304.
93. "Otzyvy Renana o slavianskom mire" (Renan's remarks about the Slavic world), in *Borba s zapadom*, 1st ed., III, pp. 81–92.
94. *Borba s zapadom*, III, 91.
95. "Towards a Portrait of Pushkin," in Strakhov, *Zametki o Pushkine*, p. 69.
96. "A View of Current Literature," in Strakhov, *Turgenev i Tolstoi*, p. 424.
97. Renan, *Essais de morale et de critique*, in *Ouevres complètes*, II, p. 255.

ress seemed as ironical to Renan as the Crystal Palace to Dostoevsky. Renan found a refuge from modernity in rural Brittany.

Strakhov, also, reacted against the characteristic facts of the
nineteenth century. But, in sympathy with the basic Slavophile
messianism, Strakhov also had faith in Russia's ability to overcome them. He found that same hope, although less overt, in
Renan.

In the condition of an ever-invading Progress, without
a nationality and only classified as "Modern" or "European,"
it would be childish to hope that the Celtic race will
retain in the future the isolated expression of its originality.
And yet we are far from assuming that this race has said
its last word . . . Who knows what will come out of it in
the intellectual realm if it assimilates its own profoundly
rich nature with modern thought? It seems to me that
this combination would produce highly original results, a
fine and discreet way of life, a singular mixture of strength
and weakness, coarseness and sweetness. Few races have
a poetic infancy as well-rounded as the Celtic race:
mythology, lyricism, epic poetry, romantic imagination,
religious enthusiasm — nothing is lacking. Why then should
Reflection fail them? Germany, which began with science
and criticism, has ended with poetry; why should the
Celtic race, which began with poetry, not finish with
criticism?[98]

When Renan's *Life of Jesus* appeared in 1863, it was greeted
by the French clergy as sacrilege, and he immediately lost his

98. *Ouevres complètes*, II, 300–301. Renan wrote an interesting article on Turgenev in 1883. "The honor of that great Slavic race, whose appearance on the
world's stage is the most unexpected phenomenon of our time, is that it has been
depicted at the outset by such an accomplished master . . . When the future has
given us in full measure the surprises that this extraordinary Slavic genius has in
store for us, with its fiery faith, its profound intuition, its peculiar ideas of life and
death, its need for martyrdom, its thirst for the ideal, Turgenev's portraits will be
priceless documents, in some measure like the portrait of a man of genius in his
childhood" ("Adieu a Tourguéneff," in *Ouevres complètes*, II, 870). While Renan's
view of Turgenev is not Strakhov's, it was similar to Strakhov's portrait of Tolstoy,
and Grigorev's of Pushkin, as the ideal expression of the Russian soul.

position as lecturer at the Collège de France. Strakhov was one of the few Russians to react to the book; he was cautious in his approval, stressing the attack which Renan made on Voltaire.[99] But his appreciation grew with the years. When Tolstoy asked him about certain religious questions, he recommended Renan for the answers. "Renan, for all his faults as a Catholic and a seminarist, understands . . . But I fear you will not like him."[100] Strakhov was correct; Tolstoy did not approve. Strakhov persisted in his admiration, however; "there are wonderful moments in his description of Christ's life . . . Of course, it is all spoiled by Catholicism and a French secularism which Renan, as a seminarist, overexaggerates . . . But he has a great love for his subject."[101]

Strakhov easily perceived the religious impulse which underlay Renan's writings and which his contemporaries missed to the detriment of their understanding of his work. In an appreciation after his death, Strakhov mocked those "who considered him merely a freethinker, another Voltaire . . . He really assimilated all the essence of German idealism . . . In this he bettered de Staël, Cousin, Quinet, each of whom merely copied."[102]

Renan's interest in biblical exegesis had led him many times to acknowledge his debt to David Friedrich Strauss's *Das Leben Jesu* (which first appeared in 1835). Strauss also had another, more political, significance in Renan's life. During the Franco-Prussian War the two men engaged in an open polemic. It began, on Renan's part, as a dialogue between Olympians above the battle; it ended, with Strauss's intransigence, in a rather nasty display of nationalism, which led Renan to regret that he had ever begun such a debate with "his learned master." After the war and the Commune Renan published their correspondence in book form in conjunction with his postwar analysis of France's political collapse. The book appeared in late November 1871, as

99. N. N. Strakhov, "Svalka avtoritetov" (A conflict of authorities), *Epokha* (June 1864).
100. Strakhov to Tolstoy, December 12, 1877, in *Perepiska*.
101. Strakhov to Tolstoy, April 25, 1878, in *Perepiska*.
102. N. N. Strakhov, "Neskolko slov o Renane" (Several Remarks about Renan), *Russkii vestnik* (November 1892), p. 245.

La Réforme intellectuelle et morale; Strakhov reviewed the book in *Grazhdanin* and again found in Renan a support for his own philosophical idealism.

Renan felt that France had lost the war and suffered through the Commune because of moral incapacity. The drive toward universal suffrage tended only to enshrine the acquisitiveness of the working class and the selfishness of the bourgeoisie. France's only hope was a return to aristocracy or, as this was already impossible, to certain modifications of the republican regime.

It is obvious why Renan's book outraged the liberals. In Russia, Mikhailovsky sharply criticized it for its cult of the past.[103] It appealed to critics on the right for this reason, and later, during the Dreyfus Affair, Maurice Barrès and Charles Maurras would remember this book as Renan's best. But Renan still retained a reputation for anticlericalism because of his *Life of Jesus*, and hence Strakhov met with oposition from *Grazhdanin*'s staff when he proposed to review this latest book.[104]

Strakhov's analysis focused on the ambiguities. "The truly educated European is not a Communist or a materialist or a positivist; he sees the contradictions implicit in all these deformities . . . Renan rejects neither philosophy nor religion and the spiritual world; however, the way in which he recognizes these things is so vague as to appear meaningless." [105] "Renan resembles a French Slavophile; he values the principles of the old way, but he does not really believe in it . . . just as he values religion without really believing." [106] Surely the old feudal notions of property and politics are beside the point in such a moral discussion. What is truly valuable about the ways of the past has nothing to do with either monarchy or socialism. And most assuredly it has nothing to do with the supposed Prussian system which Renan appears to admire and wish to adopt for France. It does, however, have to do

103. N. K. Mikhailovsky, "Literary and Journalistic Remarks for 1872," *Otechestvennye zapiski* (September 1872), 706–737.
104. Strakhov to Tolstoy, March 10, 1872, in *Perepiska*.
105. "Renan," in *Borba s zapadom*, 2nd ed., I, 294.
106. Strakhov, *Borba s zapadom*, I, 340.

with the *Russian* system. "Renan never mentions the simple people (*prostoi narod*), because there *are* none in Europe; the ship of Europe is still without this heavy ballast." [107] But it is in this that the past has value for the future.

Here, again, Strakhov used Renan to develop a Slavophile argument; calling Renan a French Slavophile, he modified Renan in order to make him one. [108] Renan, at the end of his book, had pleaded for a Franco-Prussian alliance against a predicted Russian threat. Far from being embarrassed (it enraged the germanophobes on *Grazhdanin*), Strakhov turned the plea to his own advantage. "Renan sounds as if he has been reading Danilevsky." [109]

Strakhov was no germanophobe in any sense; he did not indulge in racial hatreds, and he had great respect for German culture. But he did sympathize with Renan's attack on Strauss. He found Strauss turgid and his nationalism disagreeable;[110] but Strauss's rejection of religion was what really turned him against the German critic, especially as it appeared in *The Old Faith and the New* (1873). Strauss's book, like Renan's, was a conservative plea for monarchism but based on different principles. Strakhov's complete rejection of the materialism eventually saved him from condoning what was, after all, merely a preview of some of the more nasty aspects of later German nationalism. "Strauss groans at the workers' movement . . . but he does not understand the philosophical reasons behind their envy of wealth . . . Hence he has no solution but the use of force against them . . . In reality, only the promulgation of higher ideals can work against this materialism." [111] Religion is the only possible counterweight to social-

107. Strakhov, *Borba s zapadom*, I, 377.
108. Mikhailovsky wrote a favorable, if sarcastic, review of Strakhov's analysis in which he commented: "We would like in the future to paint a portrait of Strakhov to show that he is in reality a Russian Renan" (Mikhailovsky, *Polnoe sobranie sochinenii*, 736).
109. Strakhov, *Borba s zapadom*, 2nd ed., I, 388.
110. N. N. Strakhov, "Itogi sovremennogo znaniia; po povodu knigi Renana" (The sum of contemporary knowledge: On the subject of Renan's book), *Russkii vestnik* (January 1892). See also Strakhov to Tolstoy, December 12, 1877, in *Perepiska*.
111. Strakhov, *Borba s zapadom*, 2nd ed., I, 442.

ism, and Strauss in his philosophical materialism rules this out. Man in a constant state of anxiety needs faith; Strauss's offer of humanism is an empty consolation. It is meaningless either to reject socialism or to pose a morality without a belief in God. "This is no moral teaching at all; it is merely crude self-satisfaction with the current state of things . . . and in our sad and suffering century this amounts to simple moral stupidity." [112]

Although Strakhov seemed to overemphasize the religious elements in Renan's thought, he was not unaware of the ways in which Renan resembled Strauss. He criticized his "objective history." "There is no such thing as objective history, despite Renan's dreams; history is discovered by us in terms of those principles which we already think lay beneath it . . . It gives to each exactly what he can take from it." [113] He regretted a certain moral blindness in Renan as a result of his attempt at objectivity. It seemed sad to him, for instance, that Renan could think of the saying "Love thine enemies" merely as something that some Jewish rabbi said two thousand years ago, merely as a historical fact. "Renan's inconsistency is that he combines blind positivism with German idealism (a love for Kant and Hegel), and hence he searches through the history of Christianity in the spirit of German exegesis . . . If Renan *recognized* his contradictions it would not be so bad . . . But his misfortune is that he considers them wise." [114] "The historian of Christianity has not learned the really profound characteristics of the human spirit . . . He thinks that man is just a wild, good-natured gorilla who needs moral restraints in order to be kept under control." [115] Strakhov found Renan's persistent refusal to separate the worlds of matter and spirit erroneous; his stubborn monism surprised Strakhov all the more in view of Renan's religious sensibilities: Renan should have known better.

112. Strakhov, *Borba s zapadom,* I, 458.
113. N. N. Strakhov, "Istoriki bez printsipov" (Historians without principles), *Rus* (August and September 1885).
114. *Borba s zapadom,* 2nd ed., I, 417.
115. "The Sum of Contemporary Knowledge," p. 87.

V

The Defense of Science

Of all the intellectual currents flowing from Europe to Russia in the later nineteenth century, the most prestigious was a deep faith in the development of the natural sciences. It lay at the base of the materialism of the men of the sixties, and fostered their utopian dreams of a future world in which poverty and disease would be eliminated and the human personality liberated. Science, and the economic development of Russia on the European model which would follow from its pursuit, was the foundation of the aspirations of all Russian reformers whether government officials or liberal opposition.

The political conservatives, however, were in general more hostile to the sciences. Some, like Mikhail Katkov and Dmitry Tolstoy, feared the intellectual content of the study of science and tried to eliminate it from the Russian schools to the advantage of classical studies. Others, more traditionally Slavophile, viewed science as a Western importation, unsuited to the Russian way of life and therefore unnecessary.

Strakhov's attitude toward this question is the key to an understanding of his intellectual position. It cannot be described simply; at first glance it appears confusing, because he rejected both the radical faith in science and the conservative fear of it while adopting many elements of both positions. It becomes clear from a study of his position as it emerged during his lifetime that he was much more sophisticated than most of his contemporaries in his understanding of the advantages and the limits of the scientific experience.

Strakhov, after all, *was* a scientist. He had earned an advanced degree in biology and had stood for an academic post. He had spent ten years teaching science in gymnasia and had published several scientific treatises. He was later to become a member of the Academic Committee by virtue of this training; his duty was to choose scientific textbooks for the state schools. Strakhov did not, however, dedicate himself to the laboratory; there were many men in his time who did, but he was not one of them. When he took up journalism in 1860, he in some sense abandoned the scientific profession for which he had been trained. But he never ceased to think of himself as a scientist; and as it turned out, much of his journalism was concerned with scientific issues.

Three trends stand out clearly in Strakhov's many writings on the subject, and they appear in varied forms in all his polemics. (1) He believed in the value of knowledge for its own sake, and, therefore, he respected scientific truths because they *were* truths; he would tolerate no avoidance of them on the grounds of Slavophile or conservative expediency. (2) On the question of scientific method he was a rationalist, following his Hegelian instincts against the empiricists. (3) Nevertheless, respecting as he did the results of scientific inquiry, he made no further claims for these results beyond the fact that they were true in a limited sense; he did not find science a basis for a metaphysics.

Strakhov involved himself in the major scientific polemics of his time. He tackled Atomism, Vitalism, Darwinism, Mechanism; he translated many of the most famous contemporary scientific treatises. He was an early admirer of Darwin; he wrote a review of the first foreign translation of *The Origin of Species* which began with a spirited defense of scientific inquiry as "the most vital sign of our contemporary life."[1] It is clear that he thought of himself both as an expert on and a propagandizer for the scientific achievments of his era.

In 1866 Strakhov translated Claude Bernard's *An Introduction to the Study of Experimental Medicine*, with a long analytical essay as an introduction.[2] The essay touches on all the points that he would make during his career and in itself illustrates very well Strakhov's anomalous position. The casual observer might find Strakhov's respect for Claude Bernard (like his respect for Renan) curious; Bernard, after all, was the hero of the "new people" in

---

1. "Durnye priznaki" (Bad signs), in *Kriticheskie stati*, p. 385.
2. In several parts in *Otechestvennye zapiski* in September 1866, pp. 217–234; and March 1867, 148–163; later published in Strakhov, *Filosofskie ocherki*, pp. 123–173.

Chernyshevsky's *What Is to Be Done?* and a perfect symbol of scientific progress for the radicals. Nevertheless, Strakhov considered Bernard's book the revelation of modern science at its best, although for reasons with which the radicals would find little sympathy.

In the first place, Strakhov approved of Bernard's methodology. Despite the title of Bernard's book, and in contrast to many of his supposed followers, Bernard was not an empiricist. His entire experimental procedure was postulated on the a priori. "The object of experimentation is to transform an a priori conception into an a posteriori interpretation based on experimental study." Although the experiment itself is carried on in the realm of objective truths, "the greatest truths are subjective . . . like mathematics . . . They are independent of verification by experiment."[3]

Strakhov's first book, *On the Method of the Natural Sciences* (a compilation of articles written between 1858 and 1864, published in 1865) was essentially a study of the significance of the a priori. He emphasized throughout his essays that the mere collection of facts is meaningless; science is valuable because it seeks to satisfy our theoretical demands for a knowledge of basic principles. Hence he emphasized the importance of homology and classification as methodological devices, and he chose a morphological topic for his own dissertation. Strakhov found that Bernard fully shared his predisposition. "Medicine, a young science, will pass through empiricism by way of the experimental method."[4]

But another aspect of Bernard's famous book interested Strakhov even more. Bernard seemed to recognize the limitations of the scientific method; science could not answer our fundamental questions about life. Bernard was interested in the hows, rather than the whys, of behavior. "Neither spiritualism nor materialism exists for the experimenter . . . We can know neither spirit nor matter . . . First causes are outside the realm of science."[5]

3. Claude Bernard, *An Introduction to the Study of Experimental Medicine* (New York, 1927), p. 29. Originally published in Paris in 1865.
4. Bernard, *An Introduction*, p. 216.
5. Bernard, *An Introduction* p. 66.

Bernard's agnosticism developed out of his polemic with the Vitalists who had dominated early nineteenth-century biology. Vitalism postulated that the apparent spontaneity of living bodies precluded any certainty of experimental results. There seemed to be, they said, a "vital force" in organic bodies which removed them from the realm of general physical and chemical laws. Bernard maintained, on the contrary, that organic bodies behave with a regularity that can be *determined:* hence, he invented the term "determinism" to describe his philosophy. The essence of his book is a faith in determinism, and it was a faith which Strakhov shared (although he preferred to call it "the principle of the causal link").[6] Bernard suggested that the "vital force," this *quid divinum,* was an unnecessary and obstructive hypothesis. If living bodies behave erratically, he said, it is only because they seem to; we have not yet determined all the conditions which would fully explain their behavior. It is the object of experimentation to determine these conditions; the scientist must not postulate any more than he can determine.

Strakhov in his earliest work agreed that metaphysics must be banished from the scientific study of behavior. In his master's thesis, published in 1857, Strakhov maintains: "The life force cannot even be allowed as a proposition . . . All physical developments of organic bodies are unfolded according to inevitable physical laws, just as is the case for inorganic bodies." This is not to say, of course, that there are not spiritual dimensions which make a human being differ from a stone. (This latter fact had been the subject of his articles on organic life in 1860.) Surely men are not stones, but the successes of the scientific method can tell us little about those dimensions, which relate to the realm of essences. Hence, science rejects the study of first causes and restricts itself to secondary phenomena as sufficient for a scientific understanding of behavior.[7]

6. Strakhov, *Filosofskie ocherki,* p. 132.
7. In fact, as Strakhov pointed out, determinism itself is based on a priori faith in certain basic physical laws. See Strakhov, *Filosofskie ocherki,* p. 151. In a final note to his essay, Strakhov recognized that the mechanistic view of organic behavior does not answer the question of the origin and development of new forms

Both Bernard and Strakhov were making a determined case for philosophical dualism when they banished first causes from scientific study; they wished to separate the investigation of spirit and matter. Bernard was motivated by a desire to save science from what he thought of as a crippling metaphysical handicap. But Strakhov's interest in the problem came from a decided interest in metaphysics itself and in particular from the kind of attack which the scientists had sought to make on it. As both a philosophical idealist and a scientist, Strakhov was committed to proving that there was no contradiction between the two métiers because they operate in entirely separate realms.

In the vigorous exposition of this dualism, both Bernard and Strakhov eventually found themselves expounding a curious form of positivism. This does not seem strange for Bernard, but, on the surface, any connection between Strakhov and positivism would seem absurd. Comte's rejection of metaphysics was the very keystone of radical materialism, but Strakhov reinterpreted Comte in his own way. He approved of his fastidious separation of metaphysics and scientific knowledge; he deplored only his mistaken assumption that the realm of science was larger than it is in fact. Like most of Bernard's empiricist followers, Strakhov found that most of Comte's positivist followers had misunderstood Comte's real point. Strakhov makes an ingenious case for his own redefinition of positivism.

He used as his examples two of the most famous positivists of their day, Ernest Renan and Hippolyte Taine. Renan, after his

---

of life. Bernard postulated something which he called "the creative idea" to explain this; see Bernard, *An Introduction*, pp. 93–94. Bernard does not elaborate, however, and Strakhov considered this an important omission. "The significant fact lies not so much in life itself as in development" (*Filosofskie ocherki*, pp. 171–172). We recognize here the context of the "Letters on Life." Change in developing organisms is qualitative as well as quantitative. "Therefore we must study the development of organisms to that we can understand why new things happen when the old conditions remain constant." This emphasis on morphology was later to be the basis of his disagreement with the Darwinists. The idea of development is indeed a partial retraction of determinism, but it is also a preview of that holistic conception of life so common in twentieth-century biology and which is a modification of vitalism that broadens the mechanistic view. See on this, Ernst Cassirer, *The Problem of Knowledge* (New Haven, 1950), pp. 188–212.

quarrel with the church, had jumped with open arms into a kind of secular humanism very much related to the year of the book he wrote to expound it, 1848. *L'Avenir de la science* was not published, however, until 1891; Strakhov reviewed the book critically in the Russian press, using the language of his early agreement with Claude Bernard. "One cannot deny that things are improving in the world, but have we been any happier for this improvement in external conditions? Obviously not . . . In contrast to our greatly expanding knowledge about Matter, what has science given us in answer to Life's questions?"[8] He goes on to say that "we cannot but recognize that our moral condition is not consistent with our physical well-being."[9] One must never confuse spiritual and material phenomena; such a monism represents both a scientific and a philosophical heresy. Renan's early faith that scientific progress would be the salvation of the world has not been justified. Nor could it have been, but this should not lead us to abandon science.

Renan, as we have already seen, was very inconsistent. He never abandoned his monism, despite his many metaphysical tendencies. In his *Souvenirs* he placed great emphasis on calling himself a positivist. More royalist than the king, at one point he said: "The great enthusiasm I have for philosophy does not delude me as to the certainty of its results. I very soon lost all confidence in that abstract metaphysics which pretends to be a special science for the solution of the highest problems of man. Positive science remains for me the only source of truth. Later, I experienced great irritation at seeing the exaggerated reputation of Auguste Comte, who was made into a great man of the first rank for having said, in poor French, what all scientific men have said for the last two centuries more clearly than he."[10]

The label "positivist" did not frighten Strakhov at all. In fact, he chided Renan for using it incorrectly; Renan was *not* a positivist.

8. N. N. Strakhov, "On Renan's Book," *Russkii vestnik* (January 1892), p. 66.
9. Strakhov, "On Renan's Book," p. 69.
10. Renan, *Oeuvres complètes,* II, 845.

Strakhov's comment on Renan's boast was that Renan was a heretic precisely because he had gone beyond Comte into error. "Comte once said that positive science could not solve mankind's highest problems, but Renan, apparently, lacks this courage." [11]

Strakhov criticized Taine for this heresy also. Taine was known as a positivist mainly because of his claim that man's literary creations are the result of his physical conditions, his milieu. But Strakhov accused him of inconsistency. "[Positivism] is an attempt to escape from the anarchy of doubt and the negation of the eighteenth century . . . to give a firm foundation to intellect in 'les sciences' . . . Comte accepted on faith that the sciences were founded on experiment . . . He realized that science had its limits but he felt that we could not go beyond that limit . . . All other concerns were to him 'theological' or 'metaphysical' . . . Positive knowledge gives us an answer to all *practical* questions, and we should remain satisfied with these . . . Taine, however, found more than empirical laws and experiments in science; he found a certain metaphysic and, hence, went beyond the limits set by Comte . . . Taine, infected by German enthusiasm, tried to unite Hegel and Comte." [12]

Strakhov once said, "What is knowledge? There are limits to any subject . . . Positivism deserves its fame more than anything else for its appreciation that the true problems of science are only in the *laws* of phenomena and not in their essences." [13] He found a certain satisfaction in the fact that the great Dubois-Reymond supported his view of the limited nature of scientific inquiry. [14] There was a great difference, of course, between Dubois-Reymond's "Ignorabimus!" and Strakhov's assertion that science

11. Strakhov, *Borba s zapadom*, 2nd ed., I, 416.
12. N. N. Strakhov, "Zametki o Tene" (Remarks on Taine), *Russkii vestnik* (April 1893), pp. 240–246.
13. N. N. Strakhov, *Ob osnovnykh poniatiiakh psikhologii i fiziologii*, 3rd. ed. (Kiev, 1904), pp. 68–69.
14. See, for instance Strakhov to Tolstoy, April 15, 1873, in *Perepiska*. Dubois-Reymond's pamphlet, *The Limits of Science*, had just appeared, and it corroborated Strakhov's rejection of the atomic theory of matter as "metaphysical" and unnecessary and excessively teleological.

gives us no answers to moral problems. Dubois-Reymond spoke absolutely and in the future tense: "We shall *never* know"; Strakhov was certain that we *can* know such things in a metaphysical sense. Dubois-Reymond, the arch-positivist agnostic, rejected this type of knowledge entirely.

It is interesting to note that a monograph by a British historian, D. G. Charlton, defends Strakhov's thesis that Taine and Renan were positivist heretics.[15] He suggests that Taine's quest for certainty through science and Renan's attempt to derive a religion through science, both revealed debts to Hegel which in the end made them espouse a "scientism" which was a fundamental betrayal of positivism. In fact, Charlton thinks that Comte himself betrayed positivism in his attempt to derive a social science. Only Claude Bernard and Emile Littré can be called pure positivists; hence, the neo-Kantian critique of positivist scientism left Bernard and Littré untouched. Charlton pictures Bernard as the archetypal positivist, who accepts experiment and observation but admits that knowledge derived from them is limited; hence Bernard criticized Renan, Taine, and Comte for their metaphysical excursions. Thus, Strakhov and Charlton agree about Bernard, and Strakhov accepts Bernard's position. He does not suggest that we should scrap metaphysics, but he sees it as outside the bounds of science and unaffected by its results.

In Darwin, or at least in the Darwinists, Strakhov found a consistent enemy of his dualism; there is little question that Strakhov's interest in Darwinism is largely the result of a negative stimulus. He considered Darwinism the greatest scientific heresy of its day because it asked from science more than science could legitimately offer. The absolute hold which Darwinism had over contemporary liberal minds was incentive enough for Strakhov's attack against the Western authority. "How *can* you attack the great genius Darwin?" he was asked.[16] It was not so much the

15. D. G. Charlton, *Positivist Thought in France During the Second Empire* (Oxford, 1959), pp. 156 and 224.
16. In the introduction to *Borba s zapadom*, 2nd ed. II, xii.

Westernism that alarmed him; he was profoundly disturbed by the extravagant claims which some of Darwin's followers made for his scientific hypothesis.

The Origin of Species appeared in a Russian translation in 1864; in that year Pisarev wrote a long and tortuous series of articles in summary and praise of the book.[17] Strakhov also remarked upon the book; he praised it for its thoroughness and rejoiced in this further evidence that man is the final, and highest, stage of organic development.[18] However, it was immediately obvious to him that Darwin's book had a potentially sinister aspect. It was not only the hostile European critics who centered their arguments upon the moral and theological aspects of the theory of evolution by natural selection. Many of Darwin's supporters also argued along these lines. Ernst Haeckel was perhaps the most extreme example: "Evolution is henceforth the magic word by which we shall solve all the riddles that surround us."[19] Thus, the Darwinists from the beginning exceeded the limits of the scientific evidence, and it was in this tendency that Strakhov saw "Bad Signs."[20]

He praised Darwin's investigations of the laws of organic development; he objected to the vitriolic theological attack on Darwin's work; but he was very much disturbed by the attitude of the French translator, "who finds in Darwin's book the absolute basis for a distinction between good and evil, a full philosophy of humanity."[21] The translator outdid both Haeckel and Malthus in ruthlessness, praising the struggle for existence as the most fortunate factor for human perfection. "Mlle. Royer is not the first to point out that men differ zoologically . . . but surely the point is that they are equal *as men,* not as animals, and that *this* is the

17. D. I. Pisarev, "Progress in the Animal and Vegetable Worlds," *Russkoe slovo* (April–July, and September 1864), in Dmitry Pisarev, *Selected Philosophical, Social and Political Essays* (Moscow, 1958), pp. 297–496.

18. In "Chem otlichaetsia chelovek ot zhivotnykh" *Naturalist* (1865), and in N. N. Strakhov, *Mir kak tseloe* (St. Petersburg, 1872), p. 337.

19. Quoted in Cassirer, *The Problem of Knowledge*, p. 162.

20. Reprinted in Strakhov, *Kriticheskie stati*, p. 386.

21. Strakhov, *Kriticheskie stati*, p. 392.

sign of human value that makes totally insignificant any 'animal' difference between them."[22]

Strakhov's article raised two major points. The first is one that we are already familiar with, based on an interpretation of positivism that was a direct denial of the premises of Comte's sociology: One cannot draw social and moral conclusions from the discoveries of the natural sciences. Man is indeed part of nature and must be considered as such for complete understanding, but man is also something more than a part of nature. Hence, the study of nature gives us only limited knowledge. As a second point, Strakhov remarked that analogies between man and animal such as those made by Darwin's followers are not only incomplete and hence incorrect, they are also *cruel*. In Strakhov's article we see the first Russian protest against the moral implications of what would later be called Social Darwinism.

There were to be many more such protests in Russia in the following decades. In fact, it was the radical thinkers who made by far the loudest protest against Social Darwinism, even as they supported Darwinism as a satisfactory biological explanation of life which excluded the necessity for a belief in God. The epistemology of the populists remained positivist, but their ethics was personalist. Peter Kropotkin, Chernyshevsky, and Lavrov devoted many words to rejecting the predatory aspects of the struggle for existence:

Darwinism, where it is correct, is no novelty for me . . . but unfortunately for science, it was Malthus who impelled him to these conclusions . . . His ideas have taken root in the theories of Darwin; the results of evil actions are good . . . This is an absurd, disgusting confusion of words. In Darwin all these stupidities are relatively harmless, because concern with the good of plants and animals does not form a particularly important part of our human

22. Strakhov, *Kriticheskie stati*, p. 396.

consciousness. But when these stupidities are applied to
the history of human beings, then it degenerates into
bestial inhumanity.[23]

The most vociferous of these radical critics was Mikhailovsky.
The first evidence of his ambivalence toward Darwinism appeared in an essay which took as its subject, in part, Strakhov's
"Bad Signs." A new Russian translation of Malthus had appeared
with an introduction by (P. A. ?) Bibikov, who attacked Strakhov's
article as sentimental. He said that Strakhov's praise for Darwin
and attack on the translator Mlle. Royer were inconsistent because her conclusions were logical deductions from Darwin's
theories. Mikhailovsky then discussed the issue between Bibikov
and Strakhov in a long essay devoted to the question of the relationship between the natural and the social sciences.[24]

Mikhailovsky, on the surface, supported Bibikov against
Strakhov; Bibikov was a "new man" and Strakhov merely one of
the "old insinuators." But he himself was receptive to Strakhov's objections to Darwinism. "After accepting from biology
the law of the struggle for existence, sociology also ought to
study the course of this struggle under the influence of coopera-
tion, as witnessed in a beehive or in animal colonies or in a coral
reef . . . One need not only submit to the law of Nature; one may
seek other laws, a certain combination of laws which might put
people outside the influence of sulfuric acid . . . There is no
morality in Nature; morality is desirable but not inevitable . . .
Man must himself unite Nature and Morality."[25] This was later

23. Chernyshevsky, quoted in Venturi, *Roots of Revolution*, p. 185. On Kropotkin, see J. A. Rogers, "Darwinism, Scientism, and Nihilism," *Russian Review*
(January 1960) pp. 10–23; see also, G. L. Kline, "Darwinism and the Russian Orthodox Church," in E. J. Simmons, ed., *Continuity and Change in Russian and
Soviet Thought* (Cambridge, Mass., 1955), pp. 307–328.
24. N. K. Mikhailovsky, "Analogicheskii metod v obshchestvennoi nauke" (The
method of analogy in the social sciences), *Otechestvennye zapiski* (July 1869),
pp. 1–53.
25. Mikhailovsky, "The Method of Analogy," pp. 50–53.

to be the theme of Kropotkin's famous book *Mutual Aid: A Factor in Evolution* and a continual theme in radical populism. Thus, Strakhov had unusual allies in this cause.

A new Russian edition of Darwin's writings in 1871 again prompted Strakhov to turn to Darwinism. But suddenly Danilevsky arrived in St. Petersburg and announced that he, too, was engaged in writing a book about Darwin. Strakhov's reaction was characteristic: "I decided to step aside in deference to his efforts and to give up my own book; only later did I realize that he was lazy and that it would be necessary to take up the matter myself anyway."[26] Strakhov's instincts were correct; Danilevsky's book did not appear until 1885 and then only after a great deal of help from Strakhov. In the meantime, Strakhov wrote his own essay.[27]

Just as he had criticized the Russian adulation of John Stuart Mill, Strakhov now issued a warning against a similar passion for the supposed authoritativeness of Darwin's views. "Darwin expresses delight that his views have been so widely accepted . . . Darwin is obsessed with the notion of the Authority of his science."[28] Strakhov tried to show that popularity does not bestow intellectual credentials and that, moreover, many of Darwin's followers, such as Ernst Haeckel, had misunderstood him in the first place. He also drew attention to the fact that other authorities, such as the biologist Karl Ernst von Baer, opposed Darwin on purely scientific grounds.

The substantive part of Strakhov's essay was his refutation of the notion of pure chance as the single operative factor in evolution. He felt that chance was not only unproven, but also unelucidating as an explanation. "Formerly, men thought that a man who had been killed by thunder was somehow a guilty man who had been punished by the wrath of God . . . And then the eighteenth century taught us that this was not so, that both the

26. Strakhov to Tolstoy, March 10, 1872, in *Perepiska*.
27. It appeared in two parts: "Perevorot v nauke" in *Zaria* (January 1872), pp. 1–18, and "Posledovateli i protivniki" in *Grazhdanin*, no. 29 (1873), pp. 809–812.
28. Strakhov, *Borba s zapadom*, 3rd ed., II, 306.

innocent and the guilty can be killed by thunder . . . The older hypothesis was a *full* explanation, untrue but perfectly clear; the new hypothesis merely raises new questions, being true but very unclear . . . For the old one assures that there is a meaning in this death, but the new one just demonstrates that it is completely senseless." [29] Darwin tries to answer the question of a higher origin by denying that the basic question exists, "just as questions in philosophy are sometimes denied by rejecting all philosophy and questions about Pushkin by rejecting all poetry." [30] The doctrine of pure chance explains neither how species change, nor by what laws they differentiate. It does not explain either the mechanism of heredity or the laws of sexual differentiation or the variety of species. Man proceeds from the ape; but why is he *different* from the ape?

These points were later used by Danilevsky in his *Darwinism*. One could diligently search through Danilevsky's book for evidence of Strakhov's ideas, but it would be a sterile search. Neither Danilevsky nor Strakhov made any claim to originality; they were both heavily dependent on other sources, such as Albert Wigand, von Baer, and Karl Nägeli. Danilevsky worked on *Darwinism* for fifteen years in close contact with Strakhov. The book appeared under Strakhov's editorship. There was an obvious mutual influence.

However, their views were not identical despite Strakhov's association with the book. They often quarreled in their letters on specific points.[31] Danilevsky, for instance, was essentially an empiricist; he found himself meeting stubborn resistance in Strakhov's rationalism. "It seems to me that we are as far apart in our views as ever . . . You go on about empiricism until I am all confused . . . You say: 'homogeneity is proved by experiment'; but this is an impossible assertion. Experiment can prove only

29. Strakhov, *Borba s zapadom*, 3rd ed., II, 318.
30. Strakhov, *Borba s zapadom*, 3rd ed., II, 324.
31. Especially in the years between 1879 and 1885. See also, Strakhov to Tolstoy, March 18, 1884, in *Perepiska*.

things like the homogeneity of space, or the conservation of energy, and so on ... Homogeneity in general can never be proven by experiment, simply because it is a general proposition ... Experiment can, if it wants to, even prove the validity of spiritualism, or any other stupidity; our only escape from it lies in reason." [32]

They also disagreed on specific questions about organic development. Strakhov had been interested in the question of continuous organic development since his university days; his thesis had been concerned with embryonic transfers as the foundation for comparative anatomy, using the specific case of mammalian wristbones. But Strakhov's conception of the process of organic development, as well as his understanding of evolutionary recapitulation, differed in detail from Danilevsky's, as their correspondence makes clear.

Nevertheless, despite the arguments, Strakhov made himself responsible for Danilevsky's book, as he later did for *Russia and Europe*. He saw Darwinism through the press in the fall of 1885, even though it delayed publication of his own book on Turgenev and Tolstoy.[33] Then, soon after publication, Danilevsky died. Strakhov found himself shortly engaged in a campaign to honor Danilevsky's memory and establish his reputation, in speeches,[34] articles, and eventually a second volume to *Darwinism* in 1889.[35]

Strakhov's articles reviewing *Darwinism* were intended mainly to draw attention to Danilevsky's work. "A Full Refutation of Darwinism" outlined Danilevsky's major points: that natural selection does not necessarily function like artificial selection in breeding; that there are no transitional types in evidence in

32. Strakhov to Danilevsky, November 29, 1883, in *Russkii vestnik* (March 1901), p. 126. The most damaging insult that Danilevsky could think of for Darwin was to call him "philosophical and *a priori.*"
33. Strakhov to Danilevsky, July 29, 1885, in *Russkii vestnik* (March 1901), p. 141.
34. To the Slavic Benevolent Committee, reprinted as "O knige N. Ia. Danilevskogo 'Rossiia i Evropa" in its *Izvestiia* (December 1886), pp. 556–570.
35. Volume II contained a final chapter and an index prepared on the basis of Danilevsky's manuscript notes.

the natural world, as Darwin's theory would lead us to expect; that heredity acts in a conservative manner, tending to destroy weak (Mendel would call them "recessive") traits, and hence chance variations would not be perpetuated; that crossbreeding within species would tend to disallow the operation of Darwinian selection.[36]

Strakhov's article had the desired effect. In April 1887 he was answered by Professor Timiriazev in a public lecture at the St. Petersburg Polytechnical Museum.[37] Strakhov replied.[38] The polemic rested for a year, in the course of which Strakhov took up the defense of *Russia and Europe* and Danilevsky's name became a general subject for discussion.

When another scientist, Andrei Famintsyn, took up the argument again, it was in a different spirit.[39] Danilevsky had called Darwin "irreligious"; Famintsyn, a religious man, found no such contradictions to the religious world view in Darwin. Strakhov's reply emphasized that such arguments were completely irrelevant to the issue, although he insisted that Darwin's rejection of teleological evolution had an antireligious implication.[40] Professor Timiriazev was provoked to re-enter the debate with attacks on both Famintsyn[41] and Strakhov.[42]

The final incident in the polemic was an article by Strakhov in which he attempted to answer both Timiriazev and Solovev's

36. N. N. Strakhov, "Polnoe oproverzhenie darvinizma" (A full refutation of Darwinism), *Russkii vestnik* (January 1887), pp. 9–62.

37. K. Λ. Timiriazev, "Oprovergnut-li darvinizm?" (Is Darwinism Really Refuted?), *Russkaia mysl* (May and June 1887), pp. 145–180.

38. N. N. Strakhov, "Vsegdashniaia oshibka darvinistov" (The Habitual Mistake of the Darwinists), *Russkii vestnik* (November and December, 1887), pp. 98–129.

39. Andrei Famintsyn, "N. Ia. Danilevskii i darvinizm" (N. Ia. Danilevsky and Darwinism), *Vestnik evropy* (February 1889), pp. 616–643.

40. N. N. Strakhov, "A. S. Famintsyn o 'Darvinizme' N. Ia. Danilevskogo" (Famintsyn's judgment on Danilevsky's *Darwinism*), *Russkii vestnik* (April 1889), pp. 225–243.

41. K. A. Timiriazev, "Strannyi obrazchik nauchnoi kritiki" (A peculiar form of scientific criticism), *Russkaia mysl* (March 1889), pp. 90–102.

42. K. A. Timiriazev, "Bezsilnaia zloba antidarvinista" (The feeble malice of the anti-Darwinist), *Russkaia mysl* (1889), May, pp. 17–52; June, pp. 65–82; July, pp. 58–78.

attack on *Russia and Europe*.[43] He accused them both of deferring to European authorities without meeting the intellectual issues. But he ended his article on a note of relief: he could now close the polemic in the knowledge that he had done his duty toward popularizing Danilevsky's books. "It is hoped that they will be met by more perceptive critics in the future."[44]

This final remark represented more than mere petulance. Strakhov had, indeed, become bored by the debate; he felt an obligation to continue it long after he had any desire for it. "It has been a year now since I have been working for Danilevsky's memory, and sometimes I get very bored . . . It is an important question, but hardly spiritual nourishment and not even terribly interesting for me as a naturalist."[45] And finally, in triumph, "With Timiriazev's attack on Famintsyn, I can consider the matter closed . . . and won: i.e., everyone is now talking about Danilevsky's *Darwinism!*"[46]

Strakhov became impatient with the debate about Darwinism once he had made his initial point, but his conviction that science was a significant area of human experience which must be kept within its limits to remain uncorrupted involved him in another polemic in which he felt very much at home. In the 1870's the University of St. Petersburg was seized by an enthusiasm for spiritualism and seances led by the chemist A. M. Butlerov and the zoologist N. P. Vagner. Spiritualism was a popular fad all over Europe at the time; Strakhov found it neither surprising nor worthy of attention under ordinary circumstances that Russians should be imitating their Western neighbors once again. But when he found that respectable scientists were becoming mediums

43. Strakhov combined the issue of *Darwinism* and *Russia and Europe;* Vladimir Solovev had attacked them both as mere imitations of western European arguments, in connection with Danilevsky's supposed indebtedness to Heinrich Rückert.
44. Strakhov, *Borba s zapadom*, 3rd ed., II, 567.
45. Strakhov to Tolstoy, November 5, 1887, in *Perepiska*.
46. Strakhov to Tolstoy, May 18, 1889, in *Perepiska*.

and trying to experiment with transsensory phenomena, he felt impelled to intervene.

As a philosophical idealist, Strakhov well understood that dissatisfaction with the empirical world that led people to hope for something better in another realm. One of his first essays, "Life on Other Planets," had been devoted to this search. "Man's idealism . . . his search for moral perfection, leads him to postulate a superior life on other planets . . . a Golden Age . . . an Eldorado . . . a new Atlantis." Even political radicals try to escape from the facts of this world. "Political fanatics dream of transcending man and changing the course of history . . . They kindle in themselves dissatisfaction with the present order, and then they dream of some new humanity that will be free from the innate characteristics of human nature; this, in essence, is the same fantasy about the future that the spiritualists indulge in when they converse with dwellers on others planets in the present." [47]

Such an attempt was bound to be futile, he thought. *The World as a Whole* was an attempt to deal with these spiritual demands by guiding them away from science and into metaphysics. [48] The physical world as we know it is a harmonious whole in which each part obeys the same laws. Strakhov preached a message of rationalist faith in the operation of the laws of nature; man may protest against the rational structure of the world, but he cannot escape it within the realm of this world. Man's idealism must operate in a world that is separate from the world of matter. "There can be no escape from rationalism within the world of rationalism itself . . . The solution is not to reject science but to leave it alone and to pass into a higher sphere of thought." [49]

"I suppose that spiritualism is part of our desire for the irrational, but it seeks irrationalism in the wrong place." [50] Strakhov's major objections to Vagner and Butlerov was that they

47. Introduction to *Mir kak tseloe.*
48. The book was a collection of articles from the 1860's.
49. N. N. Strakhov, *O vechnykh istinakh* (St. Petersburg, 1887), pp. xxxiv and xxxv. This book was a collection of his articles against the "spiritualists."
50. Strakhov to Tolstoy, December, 1875, in *Perepiska.*

used their authority and training as scientists to propagate their spiritualism.[51] They shout as slogans "the Progress of Knowledge, the Empirical Method, and Freedom of Research," and maintain that only initiates who have listened to mediums can understand. Hence, they suggest "experiments." As Strakhov had many times maintained, empiricism is misleading because naked facts explain nothing. The results of an experiment depend on the conditions of an experiment. Despite the apparent conclusions of certain experiments, it is nevertheless true that there are certain physical truths as indubitable as mathematical axioms, and one of these truths is the conservation of matter. "I well understand the thirst with which these rationalists pounce upon impossible facts, after so many years of working in their science with them . . . These facts answer an inner need . . . But their conclusions simply will not do." [52]

Strakhov rested his case against spiritualism on the eternal validity of "those physical truths which are as indubitable as mathematical axioms." When his article produced no immediate response, his disappointment led him to continue the discussion in a more general form, in—as it were—an appendix to *The World as a Whole*. In 1878 he wrote "The Basic Concepts of Psychology."[53] It was followed in time by "The Basic Concepts of Physiology"[54] and "The Chief Problem of Physiology." [55] These articles were eventually collected and published in *The Basic Concepts of Psychology and Physiology* in 1886. The least known of all his work, these articles are obviously intimately connected with his polemic against spiritualism. The two problems, the validity of

51. Expounded in Strakhov's articles in *Grazhdanin* (1876), nos. 41–42, pp. 981–983; no. 43, pp. 1015–18; no. 44, pp. 1056–59.
52. Strakhov, *O vechnykh istinakh*, p. 36.
53. N. N. Strakhov, "Ob osnovykh poniatiiakh psikhologii" (The basic concepts of psychology), *Zhurnal Ministerstva Narodnogo Prosveshcheniia* (1878), May, pp. 29–51; June, pp. 133–164.
54. N. N. Strakhov, "Ob osnovykh poniatiiakh fiziologii" (The basic concepts of physiology), *Russkaia mysl* (May and June 1883), pp. 1–32.
55. N. N. Strakhov, "Glavnaia zadacha fiziologii" (The chief problem of physiology), *Zhurnal Ministerstva Narodnogo Prosveshcheniia* (1886), August, pp. 311–338; September, pp. 149–241.

scientific laws and the pretense to scientific scholarship of the spiritualists, were connected in Strakhov's mind.

One must suppose that it was the publication of Strakhov's "The Basic Concepts of Physiology" in 1883 that was the impetus for the eventual resumption of the discussion. Strakhov took as his theme: "There is nothing vacillating or accidental in Nature; at the base of all things are firm laws and principles." He took as his example the law of the conservation of matter. After a seven-year silence, Vagner suddenly decided to answer Strakhov's "Letters on Spiritualism" of 1876.[56] Vagner denied that there were irrefutable physical laws. There is no boundary between apprehensible and superapprehensible, or between natural and supernatural; there is only infinite gradation. The logic of facts is inexorable, and it can disprove the truth of axioms. For instance, Vagner said, in effect, that God can, if he wishes, create a triangle in which the sum of two sides is smaller than the third. If Strakhov denies this, if he relies on the truths of science, he is a materialist.

Strakhov replied to the challenge in a fourth "Letter on Spiritualism."[57] He warned that the spiritualists were perverting the idea of science by going beyond its legitimate borders in their "mediumistic experiments." He sneered at Vagner's attempt to reject the eternal laws of space and time: "let him fly beyond them if he wishes, but he can't call this 'science.'" The accusation of materialism he found absurd. "That which we call our fate is beyond science; it lies in what we call God, conscience, happiness, worthiness . . . All this is inside us and not in the region of the stars . . . It permeates our daily life . . . None of us is a cog in a machine; each of us is the hero of that comedy and tragedy which we call our life . . . The miracles we need, the forces we must submit to, are not where the spiritualists seek

56. N. P. Vagner, "Peregorodochnaia filosofiia i nauka" (Compartmentalized philosophy and science [an open letter to Mr. Strakhov]), *Novoe vremia*, July 13 and 20, 1883.

57. N. N. Strakhov, "Eshche pismo o spiritizme" (Another letter on spiritualism), *Novoe vremia*, February 1, 1884, pp. 37–58.

them . . . One seeks for God in the depths of one's heart, and not in the Fourth Dimension."[58]

Strakhov's article provoked a reply from Butlerov.[59] Strakhov had denied the existence of "spirits" by citing the law of the conservation of matter. Butlerov objected that the law tells us only that "something" is conserved, but it need not be in the form of matter; it may be in the form of immaterial energy. Vagner also replied, once again claiming that aspirations of the human heart can overturn the truths of science.[60] Strakhov answered them both; Butlerov replied; Strakhov replied again:[61] one cannot invent a fourth dimension in which all things are equally possible and impossible; this soon leads to a fifth and to a sixth dimension. Man of course has a soul, but it is not a physical phenomenon. It has no weight and no force; man falls with exactly the same acceleration as a stone. Here Strakhov found himself once again repeating the arguments that Bernard had used against the vitalists.

Butlerov never replied to Strakhov; their positions were really too far apart for fruitful discussion. On the matter of the conservation of matter, both Strakhov and Butlerov were correct in their own ways. The modern conception of the interchangeability of mass and energy in some sense vindicates Butlerov, but that the spirits of the dead fall into the category of "energy" still remains to be proved! Butlerov died in 1887, and Strakhov published their polemic in book form as *On Eternal Truths;* he took the opportunity to express his respect for his opponent if not his opponent's position; the debate was conducted on a tedious, but decorous, level.

---

58. Strakhov, *O vechnykh istinakh*, pp. 54–56.
59. A. M. Butlerov, "Umstvovanie i opyt" (Speculation and experiment), *Novoe vremia*, February 7, 1884.
60. N. P. Vagner, "Razdvoennaia filosofiia" (A bifurcated philosophy), *Novoe vremia*, April 3, 1884.
61. N. N. Strakhov, "Fizicheskaia teoriia spiritizma" (A physical theory of spiritualism), *Novoe vremia*, February 26, 1885; A. M. Butlerov, "Mediumizm i umozrenie bez opyta" (Mediumism and speculation without experiment), *Novoe vremia*, August 27, 1885; N. N. Strakhov, "Zakonomernost stikhi i poniati" (The lawfulness of elements and concepts), *Novoe vremia*, November 11 and 26, 1885.

There was a personal ramification to the fight against spiritualism which led to far more acrimony. Vladimir Solovev was passionately involved in spiritualistic adventures. He had originally met his philosophical mentor Pamphilus Danilovich Iurkevich[62] at a seance in 1874, and he remained "in communication" with him by the same method after his death. Solovev's *The Philosophical Principles of Integral Knowledge* was a partial statement of his spiritualistic views. In 1878 he began a series of lectures on his mystical philosophy which alarmed Strakhov: "Solovev's teachings about Sophia and Godmanhood sound like Gnosticism to me . . . He deduces a priori what he knows a posteriori."[63] It was at this point that the friendship began to deteriorate, and Strakhov, in Tolstoy's company, attended Solovev's lectures in a very skeptical mood.

Soon after the debate began with Butlerov, Solovev wrote to Strakhov: "Let me ask you only one question, which you are fully competent to answer, being (1) a zoologist, (2) a literary critic, and (3) latterly interested in spiritualism: Why did Horace call the medium an invulnerable Ibis? (Medio tutissimus ibis.)"[64] The jocularity soon evolved into bitterness. "Your arguments against Butlerov and Vagner are applicable also to *all* miracles and against the existence of any spiritual beings and hence against all religion; for, although there can be a religion without God (Buddhism), there can never be one without devils and angels . . . Don't be annoyed that I am reluctant to concede to you my heavenly hierarchy . . . Remember our old friendship!"[65] "You know that you are dearer to me than all the spiritual quasi-devils and mediums of Vagner . . . [but] verity can be conceded to mechanics only insofar as it does not contradict the higher religious-metaphysical truths . . . You know how the freethinkers in the fourth and fifth century were wont to deny the Trinity on the basis of arithmetic, because $3 \neq 1$ and $1 \neq 3$; in the same way you deny miracles on the basis of physics . . . I must say I find

62. The same Iurkevich who appears in the 1861 polemic.
63. Strakhov to Tolstoy, March 15, 1878, in *Perepiska*.
64. Solovev to Strakhov, March 2, 1884, in Radlov, *Pisma*, vol. I.
65. Solovev to Strakhov, March 9, 1887, in Radlov, *Pisma*.

your arguments illusory."[66] "Your haughty phrases about faith in miracles has led me to add to my daily prayers the request that you be granted such faith; one mystic experience is all you need for the objective demonstration of the reality of miracles."[67] Solovev, in his own way, also took Strakhov's defense of science for materialism, but it was merely a philosophical dualism which Solovev, ever the harmonizer and unifier, found impossible to understand.

Strakhov's polemics with the Darwinists and the spiritualists on behalf of the purity of science were dispassionate excursions; even Solovev's personal intervention was no more than an annoyance. But Strakhov was to find that his commitment to the discipline as an intellectual satisfaction would cause great personal pain in his relations with his most valued confidant and friend, Leo Tolstoy.

Strakhov had very early found in Leo Tolstoy a symbol for his Russian answer to Europe's cultural pretensions. Tolstoy appreciated the incisive analysis of *War and Peace* and the rigorous attack on John Stuart Mill; when they finally met in person, Tolstoy found empathy and intellectual excitement in Strakhov. Tolstoy also made use of him, as Dostoevsky and Danilevsky had done; Strakhov was his literary agent and his continual defender. Strakhov played the role with love and pleasure: Tolstoy was the repository of his hopes for Russia.

It must have been very disturbing to Strakhov, therefore, when he finally met Tolstoy in 1871, to find him in the midst of a crisis of self-doubt about his artistic vocation. Strakhov had called *War and Peace* the masterpiece of Slavophile literature, but Tolstoy was no longer so sure that literature was the proper medium for his Slavophilism. He began to turn to more and more direct action, in particular to the campaign for popular education for the Russian peasant. In his enthusiasm for his projects he eventually evolved a position that could only be called anti-

66. Solovev to Strakhov, April 12, 1887, in Radlov, *Pisma*.
67. Solovev to Strakhov, May 20, 1887, in Radlov, *Pisma*.

intellectual; his rejection of both literature and science as unworthy disciplines could not but lead to conflict with Strakhov.

Tolstoy had always been interested in the problem of education. He had set up a peasant school on his estate in the early 1860's and had even published a pedagogic journal for a time. In the 1870's education was the issue of the day. Whereas the radicals on *Sovremennik* had parodied the pochvennik slogan of literacy in the 1860's,[68] the populists of the 1870's turned to education as the major item in their "movement to the people." *Narodnost* was the slogan for both Left and Right, radical populist and conservative Pan-Slav. Even the reactionary Prince Meshchersky was interested in popular education. Concerned with the decline of the prestige of the nobility since the reforms, he saw a possible resurgence for them as molders of the consciousness of the liberated peasantry. In 1874 he published a series of articles in *Grazhdanin,* calling on the nobility to take over responsibility for the popular schools.[69]

Tolstoy's attitude toward education also reflected the mentality of the patriarchal aristocrat. His hostility to the government's bureaucracy is evident from his novels. Who could be better equipped to help the peasant than the agrarian nobleman who had refused government service and remained close to the land? But Tolstoy's views were even more directly Slavophile, however unconventional, and it was on these grounds that he made his appeal to Strakhov. "Have you noticed, in our time in the world of Russian poetry, the link that exists between two related phenomena: the decline in every type of poetic creativity (music, painting, poetry) and the rise in the desire to study every kind of Russian popular poetics? It seems to me that this is not at all a decline, but rather a death with a redeeming resurrection in *narodnost.*"[70] Hence he rejects conscious intellectual activity

68. *Sovremennik* published a parody about a "General Postepennikov," who wanted to educate Russia district by district one a year; it would take only 600 years.
69. Eikhenbaum, *Lev Tolstoi,* p. 37.
70. Tolstoy to Strakhov, March, 1872, in P. Sergeenko, ed., *Pisma L. N. Tolstogo* (Moscow, 1910), vol. I.

for spontaneity, moving into an area which Strakhov, for all his narodnost, would never accept.

In 1871 Tolstoy began work on the *Azbuka*. He intended it as a basic children's reader, based not on current pedagogic theories but instead on the child's instinct toward morality and religion. It taught not history, but historical anecdotes with a moral lesson and liberal doses of biblical illustrations. It taught not science, but practical answers to practical questions: "What is the wind for?" Tolstoy's *Azbuka* was intended as a blow not only to German pedagogy but also to radical populism, which had made an idol of science and history.

Tolstoy finished the manuscript in May of 1872 and he got Strakhov's help in the editing and publishing. *Azbuka* was, predictably, not a great success. It was attacked by both radicals and pedagogues as reactionary. Tolstoy made the book a pretext for a major polemic on the subjection of education.

Strakhov advised caution. "I sympathize with you completely, I will follow what you say with interest, and I am sure that you will say marvelous things. But just think, Lev Nikolaevich, there are millions of them; they are stupid and fierce; and the entire progressive press is behind them. It would sadden me to see you waste your strength and time on the analysis and refutation of each little piece of dirt . . . You could fight all your life and still make only a very small dent in your opponents." [71] Strakhov was, as we have seen, not afraid of polemics, but he felt that this argument would detract from the real genius of Tolstoy.

Tolstoy did not take the advice. He even approached *Otechestvennye zapiski* with his articles. Mikhailovsky was hesitant; he recognized the populist elements in Tolstoy's message but he also saw the authoritarian side of it. But Tolstoy bribed the journal by offering them his new novel (*Anna Karenina*). Thus, "On Popular Education" appeared in the September 1874 issue as the culmination of Tolstoy's views. It described his dream of an ideal peasant school which was very close to the old Slavophile idea of the simple domestic schoolroom on the estate of a noble-

71. Strakhov to Tolstoy, May–June, 1874, in *Perepiska*.

man, run by a rural personage who resembled the village priest, ignorant of "German" science, history, and pedagogy.

As it turned out, *Otechestvennye zapiski* had only embarrassment from the article. Tolstoy's novel appeared four months later in *Russkii vestnik*.[72] Mikhailovsky was left with the job of justifying Tolstoy to his readers, which he did very cleverly. He accepted the radical Tolstoy and rejected the conservative Tolstoy.[73]

Grazhdanin showed its approval by reprinting parts of Tolstoy's article (it had only been a year since those by Meshchersky on the same subject). Finally, discounting his own advice, Strakhov entered the polemic with two essays in *Grazhdanin*.[74] Strakhov sidestepped the methodological issue: the important question was what was taught and by whom. His special target was the schoolteacher who thought he was superior to his pupils and had the right to teach everything about everything simply because he had a "higher" education: in other words, the populist schoolteacher who "went to the people," on the assumption that by molding the environment he could mold the man.[75]

Pedagogues assume that they have more influence on a
man's soul than on his body, that they can develop his soul
in the way that food and exercise develops his body . . . But
the character of man's moral and intellectual forces are

72. This was only after complicated negotiations and against Strakhov's advice to favor the larger circulation of *Otechestvennye zapiski* and the greater business acumen of Nekrasov over Katkov (Strakhov to Tolstoy, November 8, 1874, in *Perepiska*). Strakhov was proved right later on when Katkov refused to print the radical epilogue of the novel.
73. N. K. Mikhailovsky, "Desnitsa i shuitsa Lva Tolstogo" (The Right Hand and the Left Hand of L. Tolstoy), *Otechestvennye zapiski* (May–July 1875), and in N. K. Mikhailovsky, *Literaturno-kriticheskie stati,* ed. G. A. Bialyi (Moscow, 1952), pp. 59–113.
74. N. N. Strakhov, "Ob uchenie naroda" (About the education of the people), *Grazhdanin* (1874), no. 48, pp. 1213–16; no 50, pp. 1272–75.
75. Leskov had made the same point in his novel, *The Cathedral Folk,* which contrasted the good and wise village priest to the stupid and materialistic rascal who taught his pupils about "bones and frogs." Leskov did not meet Tolstoy until 1887 when he became one of the most faithful Tolstoians; he knew Strakhov, however, through *Zaria* and the Academic Committee.

defined by Nature, not by education . . . The pedagogue is
mistaken if he thinks the child is completely unformed . . .
Hence, the teacher's role is simple and natural: he must
have the tact to understand what is going on in the soul
of a child . . . He is the servant rather than the master
of the child.[76]

In making these points, Strakhov was only elaborating on Tolstoy's article. But there is a dissenting note in Strakhov's essay,
although it is very subtle; this dissonance was to grow in the
course of their friendship. It betrays a difference of opinion that
dates as far back as 1863 when Strakhov reviewed Tolstoy's pedagogical journal *Iasnaia Poliana* for *Vremia*.[77] He very much approved of Tolstoy's basic method which rejected dry manipulative
psychology and emphasized the vital spiritual essence of the "living soul" of the child. But Strakhov also suggested that Tolstoy
did not go far enough in his respect for the true potential of the
child. Tolstoy imagines that, in our desire to respond to a child's
natural inclinations, we must throw out all the learning which
has been accumulated over the centuries in our universities.
This, Strakhov warned, would be hasty; he cautioned against
condescension to the child. One must awaken the highest pos-
sibilities, rather than limit him to the lowest common denominator. One must not underestimate the child's soul, "which includes
within itself both Pushkin and the legacy of our universities."[78]
Strakhov had worked too hard for his own education to be cava-
lier about its importance.

Now, a decade later, Strakhov differed with Tolstoy's interpretation of a proper curriculum. "The student should be taught an
educated way of thinking as a model; this is epitomized in the
study of science . . . which is the record of human achievement

76. Strakhov, *Turgenev i Tolstoi*, 3rd ed. pp. 404–413.
77. N. N. Strakhov, "Novaia shkola" (A new school), *Vremia* (January 1863),
pp. 150–168.
78. Strakhov, *Kriticheskie stati*, p. 399.

throughout the ages . . . [Education] should encompass the entire cultural, religious, intellectual and artistic milieu."[79] Although agreeing on the importance of reading, writing, and arithmetic, Strakhov stressed the significance of the artistic and scientific heritage.[80]

Tolstoy's rejection of the poetry of Pushkin as a subject to be taught in the schools had a nihilist ring to it and serious personal implications. He was never superficial in his enthusiasms, and this rejection of literature included his own work, also. At this most Slavophile period of his life he decided to abandon literature and devote himself entirely to the Russian peasant. The *Azbuka* was the clearest example of his dedication, but it had a curious preview in Tolstoy's version of Pushkin's "A Prisoner of the Caucasus." Published in *Zaria* in 1872, the story was a rewriting of Pushkin's romantic tale into peasant language: it was, in short, a "demonstration" against Pushkin. "I have betrayed the devices of my own style because even Pushkin seems ridiculous to me . . . The language which our people speak, which has all the sounds for the expression of everything a poet might wish to say, is very dear to me."[81]

The "demonstration" against Pushkin was also, of course, a demonstration against Strakhov's interpretation of Tolstoy himself. Strakhov, as we have seen, considered Tolstoy not only Pushkin's greatest follower but also the perfect reconciliation of literary culture and the popular spirit. "I am sad at your saying that your pedagogic activities are more important than your art, even though you know how highly I value them."[82]

Each time that Tolstoy decided to abandon art (and this was a

79. Strakhov, *Turgenev i Tolstoi*, 3rd ed., pp. 400–402.
80. It is ironic that, of all commentators on the polemic, only Mikhailovsky was perceptive enough to see the contradiction between Tolstoy's article and Strakhov's. He noted the excessively pragmatic aspect of Tolstoy's question, "Why study geography?" "Even Mr. Strakhov, whom it would be difficult to describe in relation to Tolstoy except as a worshipper, even he, although he strokes Tolstoy's head, does it to a great degree against the grain" (Mikhailovsky, "The Right Hand," p. 61).
81. Tolstoy to Strakhov, March 25, 1872, in Sergeenko, *Pisma*.
82. Strakhov to Tolstoy, June 20, 1874, in *Perepiska*.

periodically recurring crisis in his life), Strakhov tried to dissuade him. The very appearance of *Anna Karenina* was in a way a victory for Strakhov; the novel was the most Pushkinian of Tolstoy's works, almost a continuation of the theme of *Eugene Onegin*. But after the novel was finished, Tolstoy once again decided to abandon literature. "God help you, Lev Nikolaevich, don't bury your talent!"[83] In the 1880's, Tolstoy began to occupy himself with composing pseudo-peasant stories. "I was terribly unhappy with your 'Tale about Ivan-the-fool' . . . I never question an author's intention if I get a sense of clear expressiveness, creativity, liveliness . . . but if the work is just a *sochinenie,* verses without poetry, etc., then it seems unnatural and a waste of energy, and therefore the utilization of sublime means for petty ends . . . You, a great artist, have no right to write in such a way."[84]

Tolstoy finally carried his literary nihilism to the extreme of *What Is Art?* (1897–1898), which Strakhov fortunately did not live to witness. But they continued to quarrel about the significance of literature to the end. A friend of both described a moving scene which took place at Iasnaia Poliana during the summer of 1894. Tolstoy suddenly announced that he did not like poetry. Strakhov reminded him that he had once praised Fet. Tolstoy replied that that had been a long time ago. "Nikolai Nikolaevich, the specialist on matters of poetry, did not defend it and did not argue. He was too sensitive to start a bitter quarrel in Tolstoy's home."[85] The conversation turned to de Maupassant. Tolstoy had just finished an essay on the French writer in which he said, among other things, "Content is everything; form is inessential. Pushkin's 'Egyptian Nights' and Lermontov's *Demon* are nothings." "Strakhov was silent; he kept his quite different aesthetic views to himself."[86]

The utilitarianism of Tolstoy's views on art carried over to other disciplines, especially to science, as the *Azbuka* makes clear. Thus,

83. Strakhov to Tolstoy, October 16, 1879, in *Perepiska.*
84. Strakhov to Tolstoy, October 26, 1885, in *Perepiska.*
85. Lazursky, "Diary," p. 445.
86. Lazursky, "Diary," p. 455.

very early in the friendship, Strakhov found himself locked in an intellectual quarrel with Tolstoy over science. Unlike the Darwinists and Renan, Tolstoy made no obeisance to the scientistic heresy; he was ready to accept Strakhov's assurances that the worlds of nature and morality were forever separate. But for precisely that reason he considered the world of nature detestable. Strakhov found truth and beauty in the fact that $2 \times 2 = 4$ simply *because* it does not testify to anything; Tolstoy found it a triviality and said so in the introduction to *Azbuka*.

For a student who does not know anything about the apparent movement of the heavenly bodies, the sun, the moon, the planets, the eclipses, and about observations of these events from various points on the earth,—for such a student, the explanation that the earth revolves on its axis is not an answer to a question, but without doubt is merely an obtrusive bit of senselessness. The student who supposes that the earth stands in the water on fishes is judging more truly than he who believes that the earth rotates without knowing how to understand and explain this.[87]

The publication of *The World as a Whole* in 1872 was to be the focus of the confrontation. Strakhov's book, the second such venture, was a compilation of his articles on the philosophy of nature from the 1860's. It was the most open statement that he ever made of his faith in the beauty of the world of nature as an integral phenomenon; the articles on spiritualism are in a sense only an appendage to this book.[88]

Tolstoy saw that it was an important book, but he did not like it. "Your idea that the goal of life is perfection is simply wrong;

87. Quoted in Eikhenbaum, *Lev Tolstoi*, p. 40.
88. The book included "Letters on Life" and "The Significance of Heglian Philosophy in our Time," which had originally attracted the attention of Grigorev and Dostoevsky in 1860; "Life on Other Planets," his inaugural article in *Vremia;* and several shorter pieces published at various times, including a critique of the atomic theory and also of the chemical theory of elements.

it lowers the significance of human life . . . It is a fact that poets, and millions of Christians and Buddhists, both find dissatisfaction in life . . . You err in not recognizing that the essence of life is a reflection of this dissatisfaction."[89] Tolstoy, under the influence of Schopenhauer and in the midst of a period of Christian pessimism, found Strakhov's devotion to nature distasteful.

There was, however, something perverse about Tolstoy's rejection of *The World as a Whole,* because he, perhaps unwittingly, used part of it for his *Azbuka.* In a review of Alfred Brehm's *Life of the Birds* in 1866, Strakhov had had sharp words for "those educated people who take such pride in the fact that they know the system of Copernicus," despite the fact that they do not really understand it. He remarked in particular about

one scholar (if the reader does not know of him, so much the better) who continually laughs at the simple folk prejudice that the earth *stands on three whales.* This is great ignorance to someone who knows that the earth goes around the sun! This scholar always mentions those whales whenever he talks about the people; you can tell his articles, even when he does not sign them.[90]

For human beings, the whale theory and the sun theory are of equal value, being of only theoretical interest . . . The scholar, who does not know either the reasoning of Copernicus or contemporary astronomy, is obviously not interested in the underlying scientific explanation . . . And in fact, the reason for the origin of the whale theory is still in operation: it has to do with human physiology—just as we see the shore moving when we are on a boat, even though we "know" that the opposite is true . . . If today someone were to "scientize" the whale theory, no doubt our scholar would accept it as completely as he does Copernicus . . . This kind of "knowing" has little value.[91]

89. Tolstoy to Strakhov, November 12, 1872, in Sergeenko, *Pisma.*
90. The scholar he had in mind was A. N. Pypin, Chernyshevsky's cousin and Strakhov's polemical enemy on *Vestnik evropy;* see Rozanov, *Literaturnye izgnanniki,* p. 225.
91. Strakhov, *Mir kak tseloe,* 2nd ed., pp. 285–288.

It is easy to see the relationship between this passage (which was reprinted in *The World as a Whole* in 1872) and Tolstoy's preface to the *Azbuka*.[92] But there is a subtle difference in Strakhov's paragraph, just as there was in his defense of Tolstoy's views on popular education. Strakhov does not deny either the significance of the Copernican theory or its place in a school curriculum. He is merely ciriticizing the condescension of the would-be intellectual who, like the village schoolteacher, thinks he knows everything because he has read a few books. In fact, Strakhov makes a rather stringent demand of the intellectual: in order to really understand the undoubtedly significant Copernican theory, one must, and should, read Copernicus.

Nevertheless, Strakhov at first seemed to capitulate to Tolstoy's attack. "You are distressed at the pantheism which you see in *The World as a Whole* . . . and the absence of a moral sense in the book . . . This was written a long time ago . . . You note that I spoke too easily of life's dissatisfactions and too little about religion . . . I did not understand at the time; only later it came to me, with Schopenhauer . . . At that time I put great faith in human progress and literature and similar stupidities and that is why the poets were far more important to me than the current state of Christianity . . . As I publish the book now I have severe doubts: is it not immoral?"[93]

This letter to Tolstoy might appear to be a complete repudiation of Strakhov's life-long position on the relationship between science and metaphysics. But it represents only a temporary aberration under the influence of his love and respect for the great Tolstoy and his own diffidence and self-doubts. He never abandoned his former views, and even in this very letter he made a retraction: "I still ascribe to pantheism a great importance as the movement which enlightened the entire intellectual development of the West . . . We know no other 'science' besides pantheism; I see no way out of this dilemma." Strakhov's continued loyalty to *The World as a Whole* belied his first disavowal to Tol-

92. See above, p. 175.
93. Strakhov to Tolstoy, January 8, 1873, in *Perepiska*.

stoy. In the 1892 preface to the second edition he wrote: "I have never written anything better than this book."

Tolstoy was irritated by Strakhov's rebellion, by his dualistic refusal to be totally occupied with a religious search and to abandon a science which gives no answers. "Strakhov is like a piece of rotten wood," he wrote to a friend; "you poke and poke with your finger at him, you think there will be something there, but no—your finger passes right through, where there is no texture—there is, precisely, no center in him, it is all eaten away by science and philosophy."[94] And Solovev, the spiritualist, reported to Strakhov with some satisfaction: "Yesterday I saw Tolstoy, and he maintained that the earth does not rotate around the sun but is immobile. I have nothing against that in principle, of course, but I referred him to an astronomer and also to you. But he said that you are too much in love with science and hence would contradict him. I suppose he is right, although you love him no less than science."[95]

It is the clarity and consistency of Strakhov's approach which is most impressive. He was completely cognizant of the achievements of science and even of the details of the course which it was taking in his own day. This made him a perceptive, but not necessarily a unique, personage in his time; science, after all, was its chief preoccupation. But he was also aware of the limitations of this development, aware in a way that our century has learned to appreciate but which his century tended to overlook. He was able to avoid the simplistic materialism of a monist such as Chernyshevsky, who could not accept the intricacies of non-Euclidian geometry or forgive Dubois-Reymond for his "ignorabimus."[96] That he never gave in to the temptation to immerse himself completely in science because of its power or to betray science because of its limitations makes Strakhov a true modern.

94. Letter to V. I. Alekseev in 1879, quoted in Eikhenbaum, *Lev Tolstoi*, p. 172.
95. Solovev to Strakhov, October 19, 1884, in Radlov, *Pisma*.
96. Charles Moser, *Antinihilism in the Russian Novel of the 1860's* (The Hague, 1964), p. 28.

[VI]

The Hermit

Strakhov's defense of science from Tolstoy's disdain involved more than the issue of Strakhov's alleged "pantheism"; the differences between them illustrate a very fundamental aspect of Strakhov's life. Tolstoy was moved by an impatient desire to carry his inclinations to the extreme conclusion; Strakhov was always restrained by a cool moderation. It is this contrast between the two that gives the Tolstoy-Strakhov correspondence its special significance to anyone interested in Strakhov.

There is no doubt that Tolstoy's friendship played a large role in Strakhov's later life. But Tolstoian scholars such as V. P. Kranikhfeld and P. I. Biriukov tend to exaggerate its importance. Their image of Strakhov, from the vantage point of Iasnaia Poliana, is of a solitary man behind a desk in St. Petersburg, concerned mainly with writing letters to Tolstoy or arranging to publish his books or making plans to visit Tolstoy in the summer. But Strakhov, of course, had a life of his own, too, and his intellectual disagreements with the Sage of Iasnaia Poliana were extensive.

The essence of the gulf between Tolstoy and Strakhov was religious. They were both men who were obsessed with questions which other men would call "religious"; but the quality of their interest was very different. Tolstoy had little patience with rationalism; Strakhov was unable to move outside its bounds. Although Tolstoy tried hard to convert Strakhov to his own passion, he understood the detached nature of his friend very well from the beginning:

Once, when you did not know I was in the room, I
observed an expression on your face which was both severe
and intense . . . I understood at that moment that you are
destined for *pure* philosophical activity . . . I mean pure in
the sense of not poetic and not religious . . . this approach
to philosophy is an indigenous Western characteristic:
neither Plato, nor Schopenhauer, nor any of the Russians

have it . . . *You* have, thus, a trait I have never encountered
in a Russian before: it is clarity and conciseness, and yet
a softness which is merged with strength.[1]

A tiny incident early in their relationship illustrates the elusive-
ness of the issue of religiosity in Strakhov's personality. In 1877
Strakhov and Tolstoy decided to make a pilgrimage to the Optina
Cloister. Not far from Iasnaia Poliana, the cloister was famous as
a monastic retreat. It was fashionable for writers to come; Kireevsky and Gogol had visited in the 1850's, and Leontev spent the
last years of his life there in permanent residence. (In 1878 Dostoevsky and Solovev made a similar pilgrimage; the literary result was the monastic scenes in *The Brothers Karamazov*.)

Strakhov became interested in a pilgrimage in 1875 when he
was touring Italian convents,[2] and in 1876 a young friend, Pavel
Aleksandrovich Matveev, urged a visit.[3] Tolstoy became excited
by the idea, but by summer Strakhov had become disenchanted.
"It has ceased to attract me for some time, ever since I tried to
read all those books which are in favor there."[4] Tolstoy lured him
on, though, and in June they made the journey.

The most direct account of the visit comes from Dmitry Ivanovich Stakheev, a writer with a minor but amiable talent who lived
in the midst of the St. Petersburg literary world.[5] Strakhov had an
apartment in the Stakheev house during the last twenty years of
his life. Their friendship was close, although one more of personal loyalty than intellectual affinity. Stakheev wrote several
reminiscent pieces about Strakhov, one of which is about the
visit to the cloister. Stakheev tells the following story:

When Strakhov and Tolstoy approached the famous *starets*

1. Tolstoy to Strakhov, 1872, in Sergeenko, *Pisma* I, p. 94.
2. Strakhov to Tolstoy, May 4 (April 22), 1875, in *Perepiska*.
3. Strakhov to Tolstoy, November 4, 1876, in *Perepiska*.
4. Strakhov to Tolstoy, May 18, 1877, in *Perepiska*.
5. He had worked on *Russkoe sloso* in the 1860's; he was an editor of *Niva* and
Cherniaev's *Russkii Mir* in the 1870's; he was part of the circles surrounding the
publishing firms of A. F. Marks and M. O. Volf.

(elder) of Optina Cloister, Father Ambrosy inquired who they were. Tolstoy was silent. Strakhov, after some embarrassment, finally said, "I am a scholar, I am interested in the sciences." "What kind?" asked the elder. "Philosophy," Strakhov answered. "And who is he?" asked the elder, pointing to Tolstoy. Tolstoy, very insulted, was still silent. Strakhov answered for him, saying that he was a great and famous writer, Count Tolstoy. "Ah," said the elder, "a C-oun-t!" And then, "I had a brother who was a general. My own brother, a general."

Stakheev's story about the visit has a polemical history. It was published in *Istoricheskii vestnik* in January 1907 and immediately challenged by Pavel Matveev in the April issue.[6] Among other things, Matveev questioned the reliability of Stakheev as a source about Strakhov's life. What he did not mention is that Stakheev obviously disliked Tolstoy. He strongly disapproved of his religious heterodoxy, and he always avoided him when he came to visit Strakhov.

Matveev reported that he had visited Optina Cloister several days after the Strakhov-Tolstoy visit and heard a very different account of it. According to Matveev, Tolstoy and Father Ambrosy talked long and seriously about humility, Strakhov remaining perfectly silent. Finally, Ambrosy turned to Strakhov and dismissed him, saying "Our philosophy is not that which you are interested in; I will introduce you to our Father Kliment." (Father Kliment had a master's degree in philosophy from Moscow University.) Father Kliment later reported to Matveev: "Strakhov is just a bibliophile; books interest him more than anything else. He questioned me about Mt. Athos and was most of all intrigued with our collection of old manuscripts and rare books." When Father Ambrosy later complained to Matveev about Tolstoy's lack of humility, Matveev suggested that Strakhov might have a good influence on him. "Oh no," replied Father Ambrosy, "that

6. Pavel Matveev, "L. N. Tolstoi i N. N. Strakhov v Optinoi pustyni" (L. N. Tolstoy and N. N. Strakhov at Optina Cloister), *Istoricheskii vestnik* (April 1907), pp. 151–157.

Strakhov is a hardened man. *His* unbelief is even more firm and more profound." Father Kliment agreed: "Strakhov is a lost soul, for whom faith is only a matter of poesy."

The evidence would indicate that Matveev's version was the more accurate. Strakhov wrote to Tolstoy in August: "Matveev came to see me . . . He visited Optina after we did, and he told me about it . . . The Fathers praised you and compare you to Gogol . . . Father Ambrosy accused me of lack of faith."[7]

How much of a "believer" *was* Strakhov? There is a great deal of information, but much of it is contradictory. That he was raised in a strictly clerical manner and was very religious as a child makes him no different from the positivist Renan or, for that matter, the atheist Chernyshevsky. He was a philosophical idealist, and his writings usually associate idealism with the search for God. His admiration for Renan was based on what he sensed were Renan's latent religious sensibilities. His admiration for Tolstoy had the same basis. It would be absurd to deny that Strakhov was a "religious" man in the most ordinary sense of the word. But there is a real question as to the quality of his religious commitment.

Strakhov's later followers in the 1890's were very insistent on the orthodoxy of Strakhov's views.[8] Both V. V. Rozanov and Boris Nikolsky emphasize this quality. Rozanov gives us a touching description of Strakhov's apartment as a monk's cell, filled only with hard chairs and books, and of his life as a solitary ascetic. He insists that Strakhov believed in the literal truth of the Gospel and in the real meaning of Holy Communion.[9] At one point in his edition of his own correspondence with Strakhov, Rozanov commented: "Although a famous critic and philosopher, Strakhov retained the primitive faith of the Belgorod seminary all his life."[10]

Nonetheless, it is clear that Rozanov spoke of Strakhov's faith only in a relative sense. "Strakhov lived as an eternal slave to the

7. Strakhov to Tolstoy, August 16, 1877, in *Perepiska*.
8. I shall discuss this circle in the following chapter.
9. V. V. Rozanov, *Literaturnye ocherki* (St. Petersburg, 1899), p. 245.
10. Rozanov, *Literaturnye izgnanniki*, p. 347.

Holy Father, Turgenev as a slave to [Pauline] Viardot"[11] Obviously, compared to Turgenev, Strakhov was a religious man! As insistent as Rozanov is on Strakhov's religiousness, he admitted that he died with a faith "unclear," without hearing those "voices" (the miracle – of faith?) which he was always expecting.[12] Matveev related that in 1895, when Strakhov was about to enter the hospital for what was to be his final operation for cancer, it was suggested that a priest be called. "Strakhov, ordinarily so gentle, grew enraged at the suggestion, and he died without the intervention of a priest."[13]

Boris Nikolsky made the same point as Rozanov but in a more decisive manner.[14] He spoke of the religious discipline of his childhood, of his "monastic tone when talking of secular matters," of his Church-like vocabulary. He claimed that Strakhov studied science at the university only in order to defend his faith by refuting the unbelieving materialists. Nikolsky spoke with some authority, since he was using as a basis for his analysis an unpublished autobiographical essay that Strakhov had written for him.

Strakhov indeed had a few periods of intensified mysticism over the years. One was in 1886 after Danilevsky's death when he was convinced that his own end was near. "I'd like to write just one more book," he wrote to Tolstoy, "about how to seek God, and about how everything works for God's glory, and how all knowledge leads to a knowledge of God."[15]

During the 1880's both Tolstoy and Strakhov became seriously involved with mysticism. They read Buddhist tracts together; Strakhov kept Tolstoy well supplied with such items as the writings of Lao-Tse and Griesebach (Schopenhauer's editor), and Emile Burnouf's *Le Lotus de la bonne foi*. When Strakhov went to Germany in the summer of 1884 ("for a rest and to hear Wagner"), he came back with armfuls of books, including those of the Quietists.

11. Rozanov, *Literaturnye izgnanniki*, p. 349.
12. Rozanov, *Literaturnye ocherki*, p. 245.
13. Matveev, "Tolstoy and Strakhov at Optina Cloister," p. 156.
14. Nikolsky, "Strakhov," *passim*.
15. Strakhov to Tolstoy, August 22, 1886; also, April 25, 1887, in *Perepiska*.

The product of all this ferment for Strakhov was a curious essay about "Righteousness, Charity, and Saintliness."[16] He described almost in an Augustinian way the three stages toward moral perfection. The first stage, that of justice and righteousness, is dependent on law and is a product of reason and history: we call a righteous man "honorable." The second stage encompasses love for others and it operates within the rule of law to mediate between our own desires and those of others: we call a charitable man "good." But the purest stage is that of saintliness, in which we rise above our own natures and enter into the realm of disinterested chastity: this is the world of eternal passionless indifference. This final stage is well understood by the common people; Mitrich teaches it to Nikita in Tolstoy's play *The Power of Darkness*.

The essay is curiously unrelated to anything Strakhov wrote before or later. Vladimir Solovev was very puzzled by it, and he reacted sharply against the attempt to elucidate a moral system unconnected with Christian dogma.[17] He accused Strakhov of being either a Stoic or a Schopenhauerian, but not a follower of Christ. Solovev denied that Strakhov's notion of saintliness, with its passionless indifference, had anything to do with the Gospel. He amassed biblical quotations to prove that Christ had seen the height of saintliness in a remedy for the world of sorrows, not a rejection of it; the resurrection, he felt, was a real victory over the finality of life and death.

It must be admitted that Solovev was correct within the context of Christian dogma. What Strakhov described in his essay, and what Tolstoy was also preaching at this time, was indeed a kind of Buddhist Nirvana. Strakhov was more like Tolstoy in this mood than at any other point. Nevertheless, one gets the impression that Strakhov never reached his goal or even came near it. It is

16. N. N. Strakhov, "Spravedlivost, miloserdie i sviatost" (Righteousness, charity, and saintliness), *Novoe vremia*, no. 5784 (April 1892).

17. Vladimir Solovev, "Otritsatelnyi ideal nravstvennosti" (A negative ideal of morality), *Russkoe obozrenie* (April 1892), pp. 804–811.

his questionings that strike us, not his certainties, and even his questions are more often in response to Tolstoy's proddings than to spontaneous anguish.

One thing is certain: Strakhov had no love for the organized church despite his sentimental memories of his seminary days. He even had occasion to seduce Tolstoy away from the church. In 1879, when Tolstoy was engaged in a frantic search for certainty, Strakhov wrote to him: "Your letter worries me . . . The bishops cannot help you . . . They are believers, but their faith turns all their judgments into sophistries and rhetoric . . . They do not give themselves the right to make rational judgments . . . They never speak to the point . . . They only know how to confuse things . . . I hate all these devices, even though I know that such men are often humble and full of love . . . Only in India can one find a comparable intellectual stagnation."[18] Thus Strakhov's ambiguous behavior at Optina Cloister.

Tolstoy soon followed Strakhov's lead and later became famous (and infamous) for his battle against the Orthodox Church; in this he found Strakhov a great supporter. Strakhov once sarcastically said of Tolstoy's powerful antagonist, John of Kronstadt: "It doesn't surprise me that such a man appeared at the point of our greatest contact with Europe—not just in St. Petersburg, but on the very island of Kronstadt!"[19]

The response to Tolstoy from the orthodox side sometimes took the form of official persecution, and Strakhov tried to write an apologia of Tolstoy's religious views that would soften the blows. But Tolstoy was under such a cloud that Strakhov found difficulties in publishing his own essay in any journal. The article finally appeared, after censorship delays, in September 1891.[20] He described Tolstoy's position as that of an independent Christian

18. Strakhov to Tolstoy, October 16, 1879, in *Perepiska.*
19. Rozanov, *Literaturnye ocherki,* p. 246.
20. N. N. Strakhov, "Tolki o Tolstom" (Sense about Tolstoy), *Voprosy filosofii i psikhologii* (September 1891). The censorship difficulties are described in Strakhov's letters to the editor, N. Ia. Grot, between May and July, 1891. See *N. Ia. Grot v ocherkakh, vospominaniiakh i pismakh,* pp. 236–260.

evangelist. "Tolstoy at the time of his disillusion turned to examine the faith of Katkov and Aksakov and Metropolitan Makary and found it wanting . . . Only the faith of the simple people would do."[21]

Nevertheless, Strakhov found it necessary in a later article to insist that he himself did not necessarily recommend either Tolstoy's path or that of the church toward truth. "I make no positive suggestion about religion, except to follow Christ."[22] But the search must be continued, he said. The religious man who recognizes his own sinfulness and then turns to authority for leadership is renouncing his own responsibilities. "One should try to heighten the sensitivity of one's own reason and conscience . . . In fact, we are all wretched and pitiful not so much because we fall so easily into sin, but because we do not often use our own minds; almost all of us can distinguish between good and evil . . . One must be careful when rejecting rationality not to deny one's own intelligence."[23] Hence, what Strakhov conceded about religion with one hand he retracted with the other, and his mystical moments give no definitive clue to his real position.

The intellectual ambiguities aside, there was a psycholgical inclination toward the religious life in Strakhov, a personal identification with monasticism, which in a way makes all his religious skepticism appear to be a self-delusion. Ernest Renan once spoke of himself as "un prêtre manqué";[24] this would do as well for a description of Strakhov.

The monastery runs as a motif in his letters. Not only his friends described him as a monk; he himself used the image often. "There is scarcely a monk who lives such a solitary life as I do now."[25] He often described his bachelor existence as a celibacy. When he visited the Italian monasteries in 1875, he wrote: "The real life

21. "Sense about Tolstoy," in Strakhov, *Vospominaniia i otryvki*, p. 142.
22. "An Answer to an Anonymous Letter," in Strakhov, *Vospominaniia i otryvki* p. 188.
23. Strakhov, *Vospominaniia i otryvki*, pp. 190–193.
24. *Souvenirs de l'enfance et de jeunesse, Oeuvres Complètes*, II, 800.
25. Strakhov to Tolstoy, July 21, 1886, in *Perepiska*.

of man is in religion, art, some kind of Ideal . . . Catholicism is a great religion . . . Asceticism, for me, is the ultimate expression of religiosity; I know, having spent my first seventeen years among clerics and monks."[26] He later wrote of the Italian trip, "I left St. Martin's monastery satiated . . . The life of a monk is a complete thing . . . They build their lives as they wish, in harmony with absolute spiritual devotion . . . Whatever the person, whatever his life in reality, as an Ideal he would wish it to be as in this monastery."[27]

The culmination of Strakhov's attraction to the monastic life was his pilgrimage to Mt. Athos in 1881. It was in the summer after the assassination of the tsar, and Strakhov, in severe depression, wished to get away from everything "European"; he blamed the disaster of the First of March on the Westernization of Russian intellectuals. The Athos visit made an indelible impression, so much so that he was unable to commit it to paper when he returned; he tried twice, but failed. In 1889 Father Makary at Athos died, and Strakhov finally expressed himself in a memorial to the dead monk.[28] "I only wish to relate the joy that one can find in monasticism and which shone so strongly in Makary."[29] "My Athos article is, in essence, a small defense of the monastic life."[30]

It is ironic that the historian can see Strakhov's essay not only from the point of view of Strakhov's biography, but also as a delayed reaction to one of the "scandalous incidents" of the 1860's. Nikolai Blagoveshchensky, an editor of *Russkoe slovo*, had written a series of travel impressions about Athos in 1863 that had caused a minor sensation at the time. His tone was the opposite of Strakhov's: cool, critical, sacrilegious. He described the financial and political maneuvers by which the despotic monastic authority maintained its independence from the secular Turkish authorities. He detailed the endless feuds among the various

26. Strakhov to Tolstoy, May 4 (April 22), 1875, in *Perepiska*.
27. Strakhov, *Vospominaniia i otryvki*, p. 74.
28. Strakhov to Tolstoy, July 24, 1889, in *Perepiska*.
29. Strakhov to Tolstoy, August 13, 1889, in *Perepiska*.
30. Strakhov to Tolstoy, August 31, 1889, in *Perepiska*.

monasteries for land and revenue and the rivalries between Slavs and Greeks, Ukrainians and Russians. He outlined the financial system by which the monks raked in money on pilgrimages through Russia as holy wanderers; he claimed that Athos had enormous coffers, despite the fact that pilgrim monks often absconded with the funds. He evoked the gloominess of the monastic life in which each small slip is a sin, and the apathy and temerity of the individual monk who is a victim of such a life. The entire article was a Voltairian performance in mockery of those who went to Athos in search of peace and answers. It is not surprising that such a piece was printed in *Russkoe slovo* in 1863 or that it raised such a furor. One wonders, however, whether Strakhov remembered this scandal when he visited Athos twenty years later and whether the contrasting irony was a conscious one.

However, even the Athos piece, which is the most direct and unambiguous appreciation of the religious life that Strakhov ever wrote, cannot be taken as evidence that Strakhov was a "believer." His nostalgia for the contemplative life was not necessarily predicated upon a belief in the Christian God. In April 1890 Strakhov wrote to Tolstoy: "I finally met Aleksandra Alekseevna,[31] and she praised my Athos piece and said, 'I read it and I see that you are a believer . . . ' I tried to deny it and to show her that there was nothing of the sort in my story." [32] A month later he wrote: "I said to Aleksandra Andreevna, 'No, Countess, I never said that I was a believer,' when she tried to number me among her like-minded group. I never thought that *you* would like my Athos piece, but how is it that none of those Church-believers noticed that the Athos essay was written by a nonbeliever?" [33]

One could perhaps summarize Strakhov's religious position with a quotation from a letter which he wrote to V. V. Rozanov in response to an article in which the young Rozanov made the same mistake Countess Tolstaya had made. "Thank you for your article

31. Strakhov means Aleksandra Andreevna Tolstaia, Tolstoy's cousin.
32. Strakhov to Tolstoy, April 24, 1890, in *Perepiska*.
33. Strakhov to Tolstoy, May 21, 1890, in *Perepiska*.

about me . . . But I don't know how you can write about my 'religiousness'; I suppose, of course, that you are right in the final
analysis because all serious matters eventually lead to the realm
of the religious." [34] It is the tension between his philosophical rationalism, his emotional mysticism, and his psychological asceticism which creates the religious drama in Strakhov's life.

The asceticism has particular psychological poignancy because
his religious posture was so anchored in his personal image of
himself. Throughout his correspondence we find him speaking
of himself as a man without vitality, detached and alone and
somehow inhuman. As counterpoint, there was his admiration
for people who were full of life, such as Grigorev, Dostoevsky,
Tolstoy, and the fictional Bazarov. To Tolstoy he wrote: "You
asked, how have I lived up till now? – The answer is that I have
not lived as I should have . . . In the period of my greatest development (1856-1867) I did not, as it were, live life; I only gave
myself to life, I submitted myself to temptation; but I so exhausted
myself, I became so jaded, that from that point on I rejected
life . . . I acted as old men act, lived-out men . . . I protected
myself . . . And in particular I protected myself morally, for I
have a weak and restless conscience . . . I worked and wrote
only so much as not to depend on others . . . In times of great
activity, I stopped as soon as I had enough money . . . I never
worried about acquiring a position or property . . . Hence, I
didn't *live,* but only accepted life as it came . . . I have no family,
no possessions, no position, no circle, no ties which would connect
me with life." [35] "You ask how I live, I *told* you: I don't live . . . I
get up, get dressed, etc., like other people, and that is all." [36] "I am
not so much a man who has 'sinned,' as – much worse – a man who
has not lived . . . a man with no will and no desires." [37]

This image of the detached, theoretical personality, oblivious to
the details of everyday life around him, was naturally accepted by

34. Strakhov to Rozanov, June 30, 1890, in Rozanov, *Literaturnye izgnanniki.*
35. Strakhov to Tolstoy, April 25, 1878, in *Perepiska.*
36. Strakhov to Tolstoy, May 1878, in *Perepiska.*
37. Strakhov to Tolstoy, November 17, 1879, in *Perepiska.*

others also. Grigorev once told Strakhov to be grateful for it. "You are insane to regret that you have never lived – do you know what life gives to her lovers? God preserve you from life – the torments of a doubting mind are nothing compared to the torments of a doubting heart!" [38] It is not surprising that V. Kranikhfeld, in an essay on the relationship between Strakhov and Tolstoy based on their letters, should make the point that Strakhov's was an "inactive will in an active intelligence" and that he had "a dread of drawing any conclusion from his thought which would have practical implications for living." [39] More surprising is the insight of Strakhov's populist contemporary Mikhail Protopopov, who called Strakhov's relationship to life "a Cemetery Philosophy." "There are people who talk in vaccums, optimistically and ideally . . . Nevertheless, one must come to terms with life . . . In certain times, good Christians took up the sword when necessary . . . [Strakhov] is a pure metaphysician, he gives no attention to the elementary interests of reality and life." [40]

Strakhov himself made literary material out of his sense of alienation. One of his earliest poems speaks with poignancy of alienation, and it would seem to be more than mere literary posturing.

> Confusing dream – days follow after days,
> And each one paler than the day before.
> My mind breathes not some lofty aspiration;
> My heart is mute, asleep among the living.
> I am, in light of better days, oppressed
> By listlessness as if by heavy chains.
> I languish from the cheerlessness of life
> As from a painful, stinking wound.
>
> Why did you then, oh cruel fate,
> Create in me a sacred spark?
> Why then for struggle destine me,

38. Grigorev to Strakhov, September 23, 1861, in "Memoirs of Grigorev."
39. V. Kranikhfeld, "L. N. Tolstoi i N. N. Strakhov v ikh perepiske" (L. N. Tolstoy and N. N. Strakhov in their correspondence), *Sovremennyi mir* (December 1912), p. 330.
40. "A Cemetery Philosophy," *Delo* (June 1882), pp. 1–3.

But give me not the strength to fight?
Why make my heart and hand so weak
Yet place inside a burning fire—
Live fire, unquenchable, of longing,
Fire of shame and harsh regret.[41]

When Tolstoy once asked for information about Strakhov's life, Strakhov sent him instead a fragment from a short story which he had written, called "The Last of the Idealists."[42] The story, told in first person, is about a certain Pavel Nikolaevich T---khov, a "superfluous man" of the Turgenev type who was an enigma to his friends because of his Hamlet-like qualities. The feeling of alienation first descended on him "the night my father died, when I was six." "My alienation from life was expressed positively in the creation of my own ideals . . . and negatively in not caring a nickel for anything." "Living in the ideal life, I postponed the business of living to another time . . . I lived, but I did not recognize it." Tolstoy, when he read the story, claimed to recognize the autobiographical portrait as that of a spiritual twin: he said that he himself had always felt as Strakhov's hero and as Hamlet of the Shchigryi District (Turgenev's hero), and that he was *proud* of it![43] Tolstoy did not seem to realize that the final phrase, "I am *proud* of it!" completely negated any sense of kinship he may have felt; it nicely illustrates the difference between the vital Tolstoy and the emotionally anesthetized Strakhov.

In concrete terms, Strakhov's alienation from life was symbolized by the fact that he never married. There were, no doubt, profound psychological reasons for his solitary personality, reasons which we can now scarcely have the information to resurrect. But one can see in his bachelor existence another aspect of the abstraction and dispassionate quality of his thought in general.

The biographer is fortunate in having an informative psycho-

41. "Lamentation," 1853, in Strakhov, *Vospominaniia i otryvki*, p. 310.
42. It was published as "Poslednyi iz idealistov" in *Otechestvennye zapiski* (July 1866). Quoted from Strakhov, *Vospominaniia i otryvki*, pp. 281, 284.
43. Tolstoy to Strakhov, 25 August 1875, in *Literaturnoe Nasledstvo* XXXVII-XXXVIII (1939), pp. 155-156.

logical portrait of this side of Strakhov's life in a short story by his friend Stakheev, called "The Hermit." Strakhov is never mentioned by name, but it is so obviously Strakhov that one may use it as corroborative evidence almost without scruple—always keeping in mind that this is a story rather than a memoir and that imaginary details are inserted for poetic effect. The details are easy to isolate if one knows enough about Strakhov.

"The Hermit" ("Pustynnozhitel")[44] concerns a certain Nikolai Aleksandrovich Klimentov, who lives a life obsessed with books; he spends whole days among the bookdealers, bargaining and fondling the rare texts. Nikolai Aleksandrovich lived comfortably, because he had a salary from two jobs, one in the "Academic Archive" and the other in the "Committee." He was an old bachelor. Once, long ago, when he was just completing his university course, "something dangerous" (as he put it) happened. This "something dangerous" lived in the same rooming house and had generous proportions, a contralto voice, dark eyes, and a bold manner. Nikolai Aleksandrovich at the time was a clean-shaven young man, very well dressed; the girl took his modesty as a sign that he was a lamb ready for the slaughter. Once, during a walk in the park, he quite unexpectedly found himself in her arms. He protested, confusedly. "I love you," she said. "But we must be calm about this," he answered. "I cannot," she said, "you have captivated me!" The next morning he fled from the rooming house to the apartment of a friend. "I am terrified, on the verge of an abyss," he shouted to him. The friend was incredulous, pointing out that the girl was from a wealthy family; he berated Nikolai Aleksandrovich for not taking the opportunity to better himself. The narrator comments at the end of the incident: "Whether this was the reason for his noted alienation from the fairer sex or not, I do not know; but his consequent mistrust of women was quite apparent. Moreover, this was hardly the only such occasion for a flight from the rooming house; there were, it seems, several such flights; moreover, some of them were not entirely successful in terms of

44. In Stakheev, *Sobranie sochinenii*, II, 163–255.

avoiding a prudent yielding to opportunity. 'Of course, who has not sinned before God,' he always would say when talking about his distant youth, 'and I had my enthusiasms, heh heh . . . there was a certain young lady, very special and quite attractive, hm hm . . . ' And on such occasions he would usually look around the room carefully, glancing to the right and to the left, and, sharply lowering the tone of his voice, say, 'She died a very long time ago.'"

The narrator also tells the story of Nikolai Aleksandrovich's unsuccessful academic career; others with better connections got the desired job instead. "Nikolai Aleksandrovich was just not right for the job, with his silent bookishness . . . and instead of a professorship he drank the bitter cup of want for many years." The "Academic Archive" was unexpected good fortune for him; he now could devote himself to "book monasticism." His habits were regular, and his neighbors set their clocks by his comings and goings. His love of books was inherited, he said, from his father; his parents had quarreled about the money spent on books. "It's a good thing I'm not married," he used to say. When asked if he had actually read all the books he owned, he admitted that he had not: "I'm afraid of books a little; a book which I do not have in my hand I can imagine to be full of all sorts of wisdom; only when I can examine it am I quieted."

The tragedy of Nikolai Aleksandrovich's life, to which only his books and his housekeeper were witness, was his brother. The brother was also gifted in science, a doctor. His rare visits to Nikolai Aleksandrovich were always painful. He would burst into the room, upsetting all the books, and behave outrageously. Nikolai Aleksandrovich was patient; this would evoke screams in protest to his condescension, an all-night stay, and finally a departure in the morning with a demand for some money. Then he would scream at the paltriness of the amount he received. Nikolai Aleksandrovich soothed him: "I do what I can. I give your landlord fifteen rubles a week for your board . . . I cannot give you more . . . How many times have I tried to change you, and what comes of it?" The brother sneered at the lectures, demanded (and received) more money, and left.

Nikolai Aleksandrovich kept his brother's existence a secret.
But he was profoundly affected when he died. He castigated himself for having condescended to the man and walked about
pinched and sunken for a long time after the funeral. The death
of his brother "brought him face to face with certain unpleasant,
and hitherto unfaced, facts of life—namely, that the dust heap
awaits us all." He found it harder to work, and wished to retire
from the Archive. The narrator comments: "He went on in this
way without suspecting how comical and annoying such thoughts
of his might appear to a man who had to live among *real* fears
and disturbances."

Nikolai Aleksandrovich tried to retire, but found instead that
his superior wanted to promote him to a Moscow position, with
6,000 rubles a year. He became so agitated at the offer that he
returned home that night with the wrong overcoat. "Who needs
a seven-room apartment? Who needs 6,000 rubles?" The daughter
of the man whose overcoat he had taken by mistake came in the
evening for the coat. She complained to Nikolai Aleksandrovich
that her father, now 64 years old, does nothing but run after
women. Nikolai Aleksandrovich was astounded; that night he
mused, "Why shouldn't *I* get married? Perhaps to that young
woman . . . Am I so old, in fact?" and other such thoughts. But
the idea of the new responsibilities inherent in the 6,000 rubles
deterred him; he finally refused the new job, explaining to his
superior that "such a conspicuous job does not correspond to my
nature, if you'll excuse me . . ."

Many years later, when an old friend came to call, he found
Nikolai Aleksandrovich quite ill. He was sure that he was dying;
"Nonsense," said the friend, quoting the Bible for words of encouragement. Nikolai Aleksandrovich immediately perked up,
corrected the quotation, and took down the Bible from his shelf
to verify it. He expounded for a moment on the meaning of the
text, and then suddenly felt faint again. "I'm dying," he insisted.
The housekeeper wanted to call a priest. Nikolai Aleksandrovich
protested. "But don't you believe in an afterlife?" asked the
friend. "I don't know—I am disposed to believe—" The friend

insisted: "Then you must do your Christian duty." But Nikolai Aleksandrovich said weakly, "I must assume that to God, my Creator, — I can go — without any intermediaries!" But they sent for a doctor and a priest anyway. Nikolai Aleksandrovich suddenly sat up, pointed toward his books, and said insistently, "I have Dmitry Vasilev's book here; return it to him." When the priest arrived, he was only permitted to recite the Lord's Prayer; Nikolai Aleksandrovich died while repeating it after him. Nikolai Aleksandrovich left his money (three hundred rubles) to his housekeeper and his books to the Humane Society to be sold for charity. And so his library was once again returned to the Apraksin book markets which he had haunted all his life.

The details of the story are almost all matched by the facts of Strakhov's life. Stakheev used poetic license, but the insertion of incidents tends to emphasize the solitariness of Strakhov's existence. The two major dramatic incidents in the story, concerning his relations with women and with his brother, illustrate this point.

We have corroboration in Strakhov's letters for the authenticity, if not the precise accuracy, of Stakheev's account of Strakhov's ineptitude with women. He was not completely innocent, despite his determination to avoid a marriage. He wrote to a young friend that he had had a licentious youth, but that it "began to oppress me and I grew silent" around 1863.[45] At about this time, Dostoevsky had written to Strakhov from Europe, planning their trip: "We shall see Naples and Rome and with luck caress Venetian girls in a gondola (eh, Nikolai Nikolaevich) . . . But 'never mind, never mind, silence!' as Poprishchin said."[46]

In reaction to the interested questionings of Countess Tolstaia, Strakhov wrote to Tolstoy: "Tell the Countess the following story: There once was a young girl whom everyone urged me to marry

45. Strakhov to Rozanov, June 6, 1890, in Rozanov, *Literaturnye izgnanniki*, vol. I.
46. Dostoevsky to Strakhov, June, 1862, in Dostoevsky, *Pisma*, I, 310. Dostoevsky's mock conspiratorial tone referred to the main character of Gogol's *Diary of a Madman*, who uses the words he quotes to silence his own lascivious thoughts.

... But because she was rich and wry-mouthed, and for various other reasons, I did not give in to the urgings ... Still, I found her very pleasing ... This very spring her forthcoming marriage was announced; I know her fiancé ... He had to go away for business for several months and returned just in time for the wedding, only to find her bathed in tears and begging to be released ... The very next day she married someone else ... So there's marriage for you!"[47]

Another time he wrote: "An old friend, whose wife has deceived him, came to me for advice ... He says he has proof, and wants a divorce to marry again and perhaps beget a son and heir (his wife had given him only a daughter)—what insanity! What a thirst for life! ... It is all madness ... All these anguishes seem to me foolish. Is it not because my heart is all dried up, because I am a bachelor and have never married?"[48] And later, in a mood of self-castigation: "I never knew how to live ... My relations with women reflect this best ... I never really felt any passion or planned on marriage ... My two relationships came from the fact that these women wanted it, not me ... This is a shameful thing for a man to say ... As in other spheres, I never acted on my own initiative, but only acceded to what happened to me, and I avoided the dangers as I could."[49]

Despite this ambivalence about women and families for himself, Strakhov was strongly attracted to the warmth of the households of his friends, especially Danilevsky and Tolstoy. The swarm of children, the liveliness, was a haven for him, an Eden to which he fled once or twice a year from St. Petersburg. He played a very special role in the Tolstoy house; the Countess loved and trusted him and he was often the mediator between her and Tolstoy; Tolstoy named him executor of his papers in his will (although, as it turned out, Strakhov died first). Tolstoy's reaction to Strakhov's solitariness was characteristically egotistical, al-

47. Strakhov to Tolstoy, September 12, 1871, in *Perepiska*.
48. Strakhov to Tolstoy, March 5, 1876, in *Perepiska*.
49. Strakhov to Tolstoy, November 17, 1879, in *Perepiska*.

though shrewd. He insisted that Strakhov's position was desirable; he became more vocal about it as he grew older and entered his "Kreutzer Sonata" phase. "I know that you are often sad about your aloneness, probably now [Strakhov was ill] more than before. But do not be sad; appreciate your freedom, which you are unaware of as a healthy man is unaware of his health." [50]

In the light of the situation, it is all the more surprising that Strakhov should have been so interested in "the female question" and to have approached it with such insight. His companion in the polemic, Tolstoy, was on the contrary very personally involved in the issue. The first half of Tolstoy's personal and literary life was a vigorous defense of the institution of the family; the second half was an attempt at escape and ascetic withdrawal from it. But Strakhov had no real relationship to the problem at all. "None of you, who strive so hard for action, can understand the difference between action and the complete absence of any desire for it whatsoever, between action and pure contemplation. There, for me, is the center of gravity." [51]

50. Tolstoy to Strakhov, June 13, 1895, in Chertkov and Gusev, *Tolstoi i o Tolstom*, vol. II.
51. Strakhov to Tolstoy, February 6, 1882, in *Perepisku*. Strakhov's peculiar family history also complicated his solitariness. His father had died; the role was taken over by an uncle whom he detested, and his mother died not long afterward. Although his uncle took him to Kostroma, he always considered the Ukraine and sunny Belgorod his home; what relatives he had remained there, in Kiev and Poltava and Belgorod. There was an older brother, who appears in Stakheev's "The Hermit." We know little about Petr Nikolaevich. He lived in St. Petersburg and was part of the *Vremia* circle; Dostoevsky sends him greetings in a letter (Dostoevsky to Strakhov, September 18 [30], 1863, in *Shestidesiatye gody*). He was still in St. Petersburg in the 1870's, and a great financial drain on Strakhov. When he died, the funeral expenses and the debts he left were a great worry. These facts are all incorporated into Stakheev's story although he telescoped them. (It was Danilevsky's death, a decade after the brother's death, which prompted Strakhov's retirement from the Library. He had, in fact, just accepted the job when the brother died.) Petr Nikolaevich appears to have been another "demonic" type, like Dostoevsky, and Strakhov's reaction to him was similarly ambivalent. There was a sister, also, who died rather young; her daughter, Olia, was Strakhov's closest family contact as he grew older. This niece married I. P. Matchenko, who was later to publish Strakhov's writings posthumously and (if anyone) could be truly said to have been Strakhov's heir. He "worked for his memory," as Strakhov would have

Nikolai Strakhov

Strakhov's personal sense of detachment is almost emblematic of his intellectual positions (although the psychologists would probably make a reverse formulation). On almost every issue he expressed sweet reasonableness. He refused to let his opinions involve him in the actual business of living, and thus he was able to avoid political conflict, personal confrontation, and emotional turbulence. For someone who is following his writings, the tone of moderation is at times almost unbearable. On the other hand, it is just this sense of flexibility and multidimensionality that makes him seem, in retrospect, so often right. Tolstoy appreciated this more than anyone else, but Tolstoy was rare among his contemporaries.

---

said. But, after all, they were not spiritual or emotional nourishment for him: "When I arrived at Fet's, I realized how my dear relatives bore me . . . I feel more at home with Fet and you" (Strakhov to Tolstoy, July 28, 1879, in *Perepiska*). With the exception of another young cousin, a nurse who cared for him during his last illness, this was the only family that Strakhov ever had.

[VII]

The Final Triumph

Strakhov's public reputation in his later years was a final vindication of his consistent integrity. In contrast to the solitariness of his personal existence, he found respect and even a following for his intellectual work. This new success was not due to any change on Strakhov's part, for he was a remarkably consistent thinker throughout life. It was the society around him which had changed.

It is usual to speak of the 1880's as "the conservative decade" in Russian history; the shock of the First of March, the assassination of the tsar, quieted the liberals and created a stalemate among the radicals. Mikhail N. Katkov is the dominant figure and the symbol of these years. Under these circumstances it would be easy to explain Strakhov's popularity as that of a conservative in a monochromatic conservative society; his popularity would have been reinforced by the fact that Strakhov had become integrated into the bureaucratic establishment by his position on the Academic Committee. His success would then appear to be due to a social aberration caused by an excessive reaction to the terrorist crime of 1881.

However, the degree of abnormality of the 1880's has been distorted by liberal historians. The period was in fact a very normal one if one takes as a standard of normalcy the condition of most European societies at the time; it was a period of pluralism and intellectual diversity everywhere. The 1860's, that supposed high-water mark of Westernism, was in fact the most "abnormal" period in Russia in the nineteenth century. The domination of radical public opinion and of the notion that to be Westernized meant to be radical was a distortion of European reality. Chernyshevsky may have taken Büchner, Buckle, and Feuerbach for his idols, but his was a Westernism which reflected only one aspect of European life. Even in Chernyshevsky's time, Thomas Carlyle had an important impact on European thought. I have tried to show that the 1860's were not exclusively radical even in Russia; there were other visible and significant intellectual forces at the time, such as pochvennichestvo. Nevertheless, it is undeniable that the radicals exerted a public influence that was out of proportion to either their intellectual worth or their numbers. This influence tended to silence other views, and Strakhov was a victim of it.

By contrast, the period after the Paris Commune and the assassination of Alexander II was more normally diversified. Part of the explanation, certainly, lies in a social reaction to revolutionary extremism which made radicalism less appealing. But it would be a mistake to think that the radical journals, for instance, disappeared. *Otechestvennye zapiski* and *Delo* were important populist forums; *Vestnik Evropy* and *Golos* were significant liberal publications. In the late 1880's *Russkaia mysl* (Russian Thought) appeared to champion the populist cause. Moreover, the next decade witnessed the birth of the Russian labor movement and the foundation of radical political parties; radicalism was still a vital phenomenon.

The difference between this radicalism and that of the 1860's was that it was no longer the only intellectual trend. Whereas one had to be radical to be "respectable" in the former period (all other viewpoints were considered "ultrareactionary," both by contemporaries and by future historians of *obshchestvennoe dvizhenie*), this was no longer true in the following generation. A large spectrum of political and philosophical opinion existed in the later period.

Strakhov, who had a fondness for the morphological approach, found the explanation for the new phenomenon in "intellectual maturity." He attributed the fanaticism of earlier Russian social thought to its youth: Bazarov was an intellectual adolescent. His enthusiasm and his honesty appealed to Strakhov, but adolescence is undesirable as a permanent state. Post-1848 Europe presented a more diversified intellectual spectrum, especially as the myth of radicalism grew less strong. It took Russia twenty-five years to catch up with Europe's state of consciousness, but after the traditional time lag, Russia found more varied sources of inspiration when it looked to Europe. On the other hand, Russians also began to grow sophisticated themselves, and this native development produced a natural diversification.[1]

The most important sign of this new Russian maturity was the growth of philosophical studies. Isaiah Berlin has often remarked that there has never been "philosophy" in Russia. This may be fair enough in reference to his "remarkable decade" (1838–1848), but it is not applicable to the later period – unless one were willing to apply the statement to most of Western Europe at the end of the century. Russia certainly did not develop *famous* philosophers as she did musicians and novelists; some scholars think that she did not even develop *interesting* philosophers until Nikolai Berdiaev in the twentieth century, but she certainly had *professional* philosophers – men who studied philosophy as a discipline, often at a European source, and returned to Russia to teach and to write philosophical tracts. Russia's philosophical awakening corresponded to a similar development in Europe and America; the proliferation of philosophical journals provided a new stimulus for widespread intellectual confrontation and mutual influence in the 1880's.

It is a fact of the history of philosophy that thinkers in the latter part of the nineteenth century were all in some way antipositivists. Philosophy at the time was defined as a critique of materialism, a "reazione idealistica contro la scienze."[2] In Germany Dubois-Reymond made an important modification of positivism. The neo-Kantians, beginning as early as the 1860's with Friedrich Lange and Kuno Fischer, revived an interest in ethical idealism. Schopenhauer and Eduard von Hartmann popularized the philosophy of voluntarism. British neo-Hegelians, led by T. H. Green, returned to the speculative method. At the end of the century, pragmatism and empiriocriticism finally routed positivism as a dogma. Even in the area of pure science the old certainties

1. N. N. Strakhov, "Zametki o tekushchei literature" (Remarks about current literature), *Grazhdanin*, no. 15–16, 18–22 (1873); reprinted in Strakhov, *Kriticheskie stati*, pp. 46–98.
2. Antonio Aliotta, *La Reazione idealistica contro la scienza* (1912); *The Idealistic Reaction against Science,* trans. Agnes McCaskill (London, 1914).

were effectively questioned. Lübeck Ostwald attempted to show that the idea of the conservation of energy was in no way a confirmation of the exclusive operation of mechanism in nature. New chemical discoveries about the divisibility of the atom undermined both the atomic theory and the notion of chemical elements as primary particles.[3]

In such an atmosphere, it is not surprising that Strakhov's books seemed more relevant to his readers; the maverick of the 1860's was now fully within the group. The Hegelianism of his youth was again fashionable; Strakhov found in Schopenhauer and Lange kindred voices. On the purely scientific issues Strakhov turned out to be particularly on the mark. His essays of the early 1860's were republished in 1892 and praised as examples of the latest in scientific thought.[4] One notes especially the timeliness of the section of *The World as a Whole* entitled "A Critique of Mechanism", which included "On the Atomic Theory" (1858–1860), "On the Theory of Elements" (1865), and "The Law of the Conservation of Energy" (1890).

Another aspect of Russian intellectual development at this time was a revival of interest in aesthetic questions. The 1860's had rejected aesthetics for social utility, but, as the intellectual spectrum broadened, the impact of "useful" civic poetry weakened. The revival can be dated from the Pushkin celebration in 1880 at which Dostoevsky's famous speech routed Bazarov's ideas about Pushkin's worthlessness. This native impulse was strengthened by emerging European Symbolism; the Russian response was the aesthetic manifesto written by the poets Minsky and Ieronim Iasinsky and Dmitry Merezhkovsky's "On the Reasons for the Decline of Russian Literature." It is natural that Strakhov, who had fought his whole life against utilitarian aesthetics and the denigration of Pushkin, should find a new circle of readers in the wake of this new aestheticism.

The shape of Strakhov's career in the last quarter-century of his life shows a steady growth of his reputation and his stature.

3. Aliotta, passim; see also, Cassirer, *The Problem of Knowledge.*
4. *Mir kak tseloe,* 2nd ed.

In December 1889 he was elected to the Academy of Sciences. In 1894 he (and Solovev and Tolstoy) were elected to the Moscow Psychological Society. To its president Strakhov wrote at the time: "I cannot thank you enough for this honor . . . I fully realize that this means more than a Doctorate in Philosophy."[5]

Strakhov supplemented his income in later years by publishing his own journal articles in book form, and his books now sold well. He did one more translation, out of love rather than financial need: Lange's *History of Materialism*. There were also two editions of *Borba s zapadom* in the 1880's and one in the 1890's, with a supplementary volume. There were two editions of *Kriticheskie stati ob I. Turgeneve i L. Tolstom* in the 1880's and one in the 1890's (and two posthumous ones). *Mir kak tseloe* had a second edition in 1892; *Ob osnovnykh poniatiiakh psikhologii i fiziologii* had a second edition in 1894 (and a posthumous one). *Zametki o Pushkine i drugikh poetakh* (1882) had two posthumous editions. *O vechnykh istinakh* (1887) sold out. *Iz istorii literaturnogo nigilizma* appeared in 1890 and was immediately recognized by literary historians as an important source for the 1860's. In 1895, Strakhov published his *Filosofskie ocherki* as a fulfillment of his commitment to the philosophical renaissance.[6] Strakhov's memoirs (*Vospominaniia i otryvki*) and some of his poems and stories appeared in 1892. Add to this list the biography of Dostoevsky (1883), the Grigorev *Sochineniia* (1876), and the editions of works by Danilevsky and Fet, and one sees that Strakhov's publishing activities were quite extensive.

Friendships substituted for the family that was missing in his life, although none meant as much to him as Tolstoy, whom he saw rarely, and Danilevsky, who had died in 1886. His oldest friend was the poet Platon Kuskov, whom he had known since his arrival in St. Petersburg as a young student; Kuskov was with him when he died. Another old acquaintance was I. A. Vyshnegrad-

---

5. Strakhov to Grot, 31 January 1894, in *N. Ia. Grot v ocherkakh, vospominaniiakh i pismakh*.

6. His heir, Matchenko, edited and published a supplementary volume of philosophical articles called *Kriticheskie stati*, containing all the previously unpublished essays in 1901; a second edition appeared in the following year.

sky from the Pedagogical Institute; from his later position as Minister of Finance, he allowed Strakhov to help some of his more radical friends by intercession with government officials. In the Slavic Benevolent Committee he met a group of historians attached to the University of St. Petersburg: V. V. Grigorev, N. P. Semenov, and K. N. Bestuzhev-Riumin, who was a co-editor with Strakhov of the fifth edition of *Russia and Europe*. The closest of his purely literary friends was Apollon Maikov. Mark Osipovich Volf's bookstore acted as a sort of literary club for these gentlemen, especially in that six-by-six corner where the Russian and French sections were to be found.

Konstantin Leontev played a rather confused role as a friend. Leontev's character was in some ways an elaboration, in other ways, a morbid exaggeration, of the characteristics of Strakhov's personality. Leontev had been trained as a biologist in the late 1840's, and he always retained a naturalist framework in his writings. Although he was regarded as a Slavophile after his "conversion," his love of European medievalism and his Byzantinist predilections made him much less Russia-centered than most Slavophiles. He appreciated Strakhov's praise of cultural diversity in the latter's polemic with Solovev over *Russia and Europe*. He was a convinced antinihilist and attributed his "conversion" to hostility to the bourgeois ethics of the 1860's.

Nevertheless, Leontev's perceptions were of a different order than Strakhov's. Nothing illustrates this more than their respective literary tastes; they admired the same writers, but for different reasons. Leontev appreciated Apollon Grigorev's poetry more than his criticism, and he wrote a study of the poems which emphasized the erotic elements in the verse. When Leontev suggested to Strakhov that this essay be published in *Zaria* in 1869, Strakhov refused.[7] Leontev wrote a superb formalistic analysis of Tolstoy (*Analysis, Style, Tendencies*); its technique was the opposite of Strakhov's ideological approach. Leontev liked *Anna*

7. It appeared posthumously in Konstantin Leontev, "Neskolko vospominanii i myslei o pokoinom A. Grigoreve" (Some reminiscences and reflections about the late A. Grigorev), *Russkaia mysl* (September 1915), pp. 109–124.

Karenina better than *War and Peace* and appreciated most of all the aristocratism in Tolstoy's novels.

The monastic suggestions in Strakhov's personality were exaggerated in Leontev. His conversion to orthodoxy and its ritualism had begun with a pilgrimage to Mt. Athos; it ended with a final apotheosis in the Optina Cloister and ordination as a monk.

Leontev's conversion brought him into personal contact with the Slavophile circle in the 1870's, and especially with Dostoevsky and Solovev; he spent many evenings in Strakhov's sitting room, and it is from this period that the anecdote which began this study of Strakhov was taken. Leontev was shocked by Solovev's subsequent polemic with Strakhov and the Slavophiles, but he loved Solovev more than either, and in the 1880's Strakhov and Leontev rarely met. At the very end of his life, however, he began to correspond with V. V. Rozanov, who was at the time Strakhov's disciple; after Leontev's death, Rozanov published their correspondence. Leontev became a topic of conversation between Strakhov and Rozanov, and thus we learn something about Strakhov's reaction to this perverse alter ego.

When Rozanov wrote Strakhov that he had discovered that Leontev had been a homosexual, Strakhov replied: "I knew all that about Leontev, but I never mentioned it to you . . . You know, 'de mortibus' and all that . . . It is one of the more disgusting symptoms . . . in religion, 'holy sorcery' and that sweet struggle between sin and fear; in scholarship, merely dilettantism; in art, the cultivation of dirtiness, artificiality, sumptuousness, and superficial beauties (Leontev did not really understand poetry); and in politics, dreams of aristocratism, power, and pride . . . I know quite a few people of this inclination: Prince Meshchersky, the poet Apukhin, etc. – others incline that way but control themselves by conscience and intellect; one had better not name them – this moral depravity upsets me; I cannot reconcile myself to it . . . And such people dare to call Leo Tolstoy harmful!"[8] When

8. Strakhov to Rozanov, April 22, 1892, in Rozanov, *Literaturnye izgnanniki*, vol. I.

Rozanov protested the harshness of the judgment, Strakhov replied: "Leontev's sins are his own affair; who are we to throw stones? And they are not important . . . But intellectual lewdness *is* important, it is a sin against the Holy Ghost."[9] Strakhov's distaste for Leontev as a man reveals, one would suppose, his own uneasiness about their spiritual affinities; Leontev had developed to their farthest extent some of the eremitic inclinations buried deep in Strakhov.

If the last decade of Strakhov's life can be characterized by popular acceptance, the symbol of this acceptance is the discipleship of Vasily V. Rozanov. In the 1880's Rozanov was a minor teacher in the provinces with great intellectual ambitions. He had published one book (*O ponimanii,* 1886) and had already prepared manuscripts for several others. He very clearly identified himself with the Dostoevsky cult (which would soon be institutionalized by Merezhkovsky) by marrying Polina Suslova, the "infernal woman" of Dostoevsky's early novels. At the end of 1887 Rozanov wrote an ardent letter to Strakhov asking for permission to visit him. The letter overflowed with philosophical and religious musings. Strakhov postponed a meeting, suggesting instead that they correspond; he praised the philosophical enthusiasm which revealed itself in Rozanov's letter but suggested more discipline in thought. Rozanov answered with a bombardment of letters and a translation of Aristotle's *Metaphysics.* Strakhov promised to get the translation published, but he made many technical corrections of the text. Thus, a cautionary note, which was to be a hallmark of the relationship, entered from the very beginning.

Rozanov had all the impulsiveness and perversity that had marked Grigorev and Dostoevsky. The difference in Strakhov's reaction to it is explained by the fact that Strakhov was twice Rozanov's age; in the calm of his later years he was able to dominate, rather than submit to, the passion of the younger man. "Your personal troubles seem to stem from a lack of control and idle-

9. Strakhov to Rozanov, May 11, 1892, in Rozanov, *Literaturnye izgnanniki.*

ness; get yourself in hand." [10] "Why are you so depressed? . . . You are the type of person who always irritates me. You do not control yourself; something always controls you instead. With complete shamelessness you can say 'I *can* not.' To me this means 'I do not want to be a man and I refuse self-awareness.' How can you speak of suicide? To kill oneself out of melancholy is like killing yourself because of a pimple on the nose . . . Disenchantment leads to great discoveries . . . I can't help you by mail; you will simply have to learn to help yourself." [11]

Rozanov was wildly unhappy in the small town of Elets and he begged Strakhov to find him a job in the city. "What will you do here? I think your Elets resembles my Belgorod: a good place, with sunshine and forests and sweet air, and you wish to come instead to St. Petersburg, whose muck I still have not yet gotten accustomed to! Teachers are a dime a dozen here." But in 1893 Strakhov finally got Rozanov a job in the Department of State Control, and their relationship continued to flourish on personal contact.

Strakhov acted as Rozanov's literary protector, and through his help Rozanov became well-known in the journals. But he continued to send his manuscripts first to Strakhov for criticism and help. "Why do you always act through me when dealing with Maikov [12] or the Academic Committee? You can act for yourself without me now . . . You are like a child and one must watch you carefully . . . You must take yourself in hand and answer for your own actions . . . After all, you are a respectable personage now, you appear in *Russkii vestnik,* etc. . . . You can turn to the editors yourself." [13] "I've grieved long enough about your literary troubles . . . You need a literary nursemaid to follow you about . . . I performed this function for a while, but I think it is time you were on your own." [14]

10. Strakhov to Rozanov, November 9, 1888, in Rozanov, *Literaturnye izgnanniki.*
11. Strakhov to Rozanov, January 5, 1890, in Rozanov, *Literaturnye izgnanniki.*
12. L. N. Maikov, editor of *Zhurnal Ministerstva Narodnogo Prosveshcheniia.*
13. Strakhov to Rozanov, April 17, 1890, in Rozanov, *Literaturnye izgnanniki.*
14. Strakhov to Rozanov, April 22, 1892, in Rozanov, *Literaturnye izgnanniki.*

Strakhov tried to reject Rozanov's emotional dependence, but he was delighted by his *intellectual* dependence. Rozanov shared Strakhov's evaluation of Danilevsky and wrote several articles in defense of him during Strakhov's polemic with Solovev; he also later attacked Darwinism in *Priroda i istoriia* (1900). *O ponimanii* (1886) was an idealist philosophical tract directed against empiricism. Rozanov's appreciation of Dostoevsky in "The Legend of the Grand Inquisitor" (1890) started from the premises of Strakhov's biography of Dostoevsky and was one of the first and most perceptive studies in the cult of Dostoevsky which dominated the renascence of aethetics in the 1890's. But Strakhov was uneasy at the quality of Rozanov's enthusiasm for the great writer; he wrote, prematurely, in 1888: "I am glad that you are beginning to see the essential sickness in Dostoevsky . . . I think he is harmful for many people, and for you in particular." [15] Strakhov tried to awaken Rozanov to Tolstoy instead, but in vain; nevertheless, Rozanov later used his friendship with Strakhov to get an introduction to Iasnaia Poliana.[16]

In 1890 Rozanov wrote the first of his essays on Strakhov himself: "On the Struggle with the West, in Connection with the Work of One of Our Leading Slavophiles." [17] In surveying Strakhov's work he underlined the importance of *The World as a Whole* and *On Eternal Truths:* that is, of the purely scientific aspect of his thought, which he characterized as "organicism" and a belief in a "rational science." He discussed the body of literary criticism and the significance which Pushkin and Tolstoy had for Strakhov. But the strongest element in Rozanov's essay is his insistence on Strakhov's religiosity: "Just as those very religious people, the Jews, never spelled out the name of God, so Strakhov never actually spelled out his central idea, but instead, always wrote around it." [18]

15. Strakhov to Rozanov, December 14, 1888, in Rozanov, *Literaturnye izgnanniki.*
16. *Letopisi gosudarstvennogo literaturnogo muzeia: L. N. Tolstoi* (Moscow, 1938), p. 224. (Rozanov's letters to Tolstoy)
17. V. V. Rozanov, "O borbe s Zapadom v sviazi s deiatelnostiu odnogo iz slavianofilov," *Voprosy filosofii i psikhologii* (March 1890), pp. 27–63.
18. Rozanov, *Literaturnye ocherki*, p. 66.

It was to this interpretation of himself that Strakhov objected.[19] Nevertheless, Strakhov was moved by the adulation. "I kiss you for it . . . I never thought I'd live to read such an appreciation."[20]

Through Rozanov, Strakhov became associated with a small neo-Slavophile circle in St. Petersburg. The chief figure in the group was Iury Govorukha-Otrok, who used the pen name Iu. Nikolaev. He wrote several articles about Strakhov in the 1890's for *Moskovskie vedomosti.* Govorukha-Otrok was a renegade populist who had become converted to patriotism in exile and returned to Russia as a conservative journalist.[21] His attacks on the "liberal" literary critics pleased Strakhov, although he regretted their sharply polemical tone. Rozanov wrote a joint obituary of the two men, who died in the same month in 1896; Rozanov later published the essay, together with Strakhov's letters and his own articles about Strakhov, in a volume entitled *Literary Exiles.* He meant the title as a symbol for the social ostracism encountered by conservative thinkers in Russia (himself most of all).

Terty Ivanovich Filippov was the head of the department in which Strakhov had acquired a job for Rozanov. Filippov provided a living link between Strakhov's last disciple and his earliest mentor, Grigorev, for Filippov had once been a member of the "Young Editorial Board" on Pogodin's *Moskvitianin.* He was later on the executive committee of the Slavic Benevolent Committee. Filippov was the center of Rozanov's neo-Slavophile group; Strakhov found them a little extreme and stood aloof. "They are intelligent and honest men . . . Rozanov is the best of the lot . . . But it is my duty, it seems, to inspire a little free-thinking in them; they throw themselves into conservatism with the same passion as the nihilists once threw themselves into nihilism!"[22]

19. See chapter VI, p. 188.
20. Strakhov to Rozanov, September 13, 1890, in Rozanov, *Literaturnye iz-gnanniki.*
21. His former colleagues accused him of being an informer. Mikhailovsky even started to write a novel about a revolutionary-turned-traitor based on Govorukha-Otrok's life. See Billington, *Mikhailovsky and Russian Populism,* p. 103.
22. Strakhov to Tolstoy, June 29, 1893, in *Perepiska.*

On the fringes of the group was Boris Nikolsky, who was a lecturer in law at the University of St. Petersburg and also an editor of *Novoe vremia*. In later years Nikolsky became well-known for his reactionary political views.[23] But in the 1890's he was mainly a literary man; like Strakhov, for instance, he edited a volume of Fet's verses. Nikolsky's essay on Strakhov, published just after the latter's death, is the most complete study of the man's thought. But, as in the case of Rozanov, Nikolsky overemphasized the religious aspects of Strakhov's life. His justification for this interpretation was Strakhov's several autobiographical pieces which were written at Nikolsky's urging but never published.[24] They seem to represent more the musings of Strakhov's final year than a true culmination of his life's thought.

The admiration of Rozanov and Nikolsky was naturally a great pleasure for the aging philosopher. "You cannot imagine what a joy it is after all these years to hold a conversation with one of *my readers*!" he once said to a young man respectfully disputing a point with him.[25] But far greater in significance was the creation of a journal which epitomized Strakhov's convictions during his thirty-year career and which was a symbol of the new intellectual mood of the 1890's: *Voprosy filosofii i psikhologii* (Questions of philosophy and psychology).

The journal owed its conception to N. Ia. Grot, a lecturer in philosophy at the University of Moscow and founder of the Moscow Psychological Society; Grot was an example of the new professional interest in philosophy as a discipline. Strakhov had known his father, Ia. K. Grot, and his uncle, N. P. Semenov, from the Slavic Committee. Grot was also a close personal friend of Vladimir Solovev, with whom he sympathized in the controversy over spiritualism without losing respect for the older Strakhov. Grot wanted to publish a journal which would deal with philo-

23. Hans Rogger, "The Formation of the Russian Right," in *California Slavic Studies,* vol. III (Berkeley, 1964).

24. See chapter I and chapter VI.

25. K. N. Bestuzhev-Riumin, obituary in *Zhurnal Ministerstva Narodnogo Prosveshcheniia* (February 1896), p. 117.

sophical issues in a more erudite manner than was current in, for instance, *Russkii vestnik* or *Vestnik Evropy,* the "fat journals" which had in the past almost singlehandedly substituted for academic sophistication in the minds of Russian intellectuals.

The first issue of Grot's journal appeared in 1889. His introductory remarks are significant for an understanding of the kind of appeal it made to Strakhov.

There is no doubt that the periodical press which now exists does not cover all tendencies of social thought, nor does it give a place to certain forms of thought and aspirations which are newly arisen in our society . . . The positive sciences in the last fifty years have had such huge successes that they have almost superseded all the previous centuries of achievement. And with all this, the happiness of humanity has not only not grown, but it has suffered a decline, as is shown by the new pessimism which has developed and spread so quickly in our time . . . [A new all-encompassing metaphysics] is especially important for us Russians, who have still not learned to live in abstractions with our *own* minds and hence have up to now, with greater or lesser subservience to the various directions of Western philosophical speculation, continued to change our idols and become disenchanted with them with the same speed as we were beguiled by them. For the sake of these needs we are now undertaking to publish a special *Russian* journal devoted to the basic questions of philosophy and psychology. We wish to offer a new organ, with a special content, and special problems, to that part of Russian society which aspires to the deepest analysis of the questions of life.

Grot gave a thumbnail sketch of the history of European philosophy, as it had been reflected on the Russian scene: French skepticism, then German idealism, then German materialism, then the German reaction in Hartmann and Schopenhauer, coincident with British empiricism and Comte. "But fortunately, still in the 1870's, there began among us the first attempts at an independent criticism and our own philosophical constructions. It is enough to mention the works of V. S. Solovev, B. N. Chicherin, N. N. Strakhov, and A. A. Kozlov." Grot noted that the Greeks had been concerned most with aesthetic truths, the Romans with mathematical truths, the British with empirical truths, and the Germans with logical truths. "We Russians, if we can be judged by the previous history of our self-consciousness, are apparently inclined to give most weight to the religious-ethical element, that is—the guidance of the will in relation to the final goal: the Good . . . Does not the historical problem of Russian thinkers lie in a certain profound synthesis of various ideals, from the point of view of the Good? Perhaps, indeed, the dominance of the ideal of the Good over other ideals is a rightful dominance."

One need not elaborate on the elements in Grot's introduction which echo Strakhov's thought. The plea for philosophical professionalism and for independence from Western ideas, the historical approach to the history of philosophy with a special role for Russian thought, all these are familiar. There is even a pochvennik element in the Russian messianic synthesis. Moreover, Grot appreciated the role that Tolstoy was playing in exactly Strakhov's terms. "Perhaps none of the specialists have been as influential for the reawakening of the philosophical spirit in Russian society as L. N. Tolstoy . . . Profound human questions, newly understood and newly presented by our Artist-Thinker, can be seriously and basically elucidated and answered only on the basis of a new, many-sided critique of general philosophical questions."

The title of the new journal was meant to emphasize the multiplicity of serious world views to which it would cater. Grot and his colleagues, Strakhov included, thought of psychology as one approach to the study of man's spirit, without the positivist connotation that we find today in "psychology" as a discipline within the natural sciences.

Psychology is a special science, which studies human phenomena internally, illuminating the process of self-consciousness. If it uses for its study the devices of external

experiment, then this is only as an aid, elucidating through
the study of external laws the means, expression, condition, and instruments by which one can better penetrate
the inner meaning of life . . . But Psychology as a special
science of internal experiment cannot itself decide the
problems of the meaning and the laws of life . . . Together
with Psychology, one needs the results of all the other
special sciences for a rounded solution; one must try in
this way to build a whole teaching about life and the world,
without logical contradiction, and be able to satisfy not only
the demands of our minds but those of our hearts, also.

Grot combined respect for science with an acknowledgement of
its potential limitations; this is precisely what Strakhov had tried
to expound in his investigations of the problem.

Strakhov's reaction to the announcement of the new journal
was jubilant. He immediately offered them an article by Rozanov,
"written with a love for philosophy." [26] But the syncretic tone of
Grot's introduction made him uneasy. "I do not think that Solovev
and Trubetskoy will make their points well; nevertheless, that's
beside the point . . . To argue is no crime . . . Still, I think my
Rozanov is a far better writer." Grot published Rozanov for many
years, including Rozanov's panegyric to Strakhov. In 1891 the
journal compiled a bibliography of Strakhov's philosophical
writings.

Voprosy filosofii i psikhologii took as one of its missions the
popularization of Nietzsche. Grot asked Strakhov to contribute an
article. "My slowness in responding to your letter is due to thought-
fulness . . . I have known Nietzsche since his first book appeared,
and I understand him . . . At first I read him with great interest,
but when I saw that he misunderstood Schopenhauer and such, I
put him aside . . . I could write something for you, but I can't say
exactly when." [27] In fact, he never did.

Although the journal was intended as a forum for a variety of

26. Strakhov to Grot, December 18, 1889, in *N. Ia. Grot*.
27. Strakhov to Grot, December 30, 1892, in *N. Ia. Grot*.

philosophical views, it became more and more identified with neo-Kantianism. The contributions of Aleksandr I. Vvedensky played an important role here. Vvedensky had studied in Germany with Eduard Zeller, Kuno Fischer, and Wilhelm Windelband and then had become a professor at the University of St. Petersburg. Strakhov greeted neo-Kantianism with enthusiasm as a sign of serious philosophical commitment, but he was inclined to underestimate its impact.[28] He thought of it as a temporary stage on the road to the rediscovery of Hegel. He admired Vvedensky's work, however, and the admiration was reciprocated. Reviewing the second edition of *The World as a Whole* in 1892, Vvedensky said: "I always recommend *The World as a Whole* and *The Basic Concepts of Physiology and Psychology* to my new students; many of them have abandoned materialism as a result of reading Strakhov."[29]

Vvedensky wrote a short pamphlet about Strakhov after the latter's death ("The General Sense of Strakhov's Philosophy") in which he stressed the antirational elements of his thought; he interpreted Strakhov's development much as Rozanov had, as a progressive disassociation from scientific rationalism to an acceptance of philosophical and religious idealism. It is thus difficult to understand why he so admired the two books which he recommended to his students; they were the epitome of Strakhov's rationalistic approach to the world of nature. Vvedensky deliberately misunderstood the limited positivist approach to science which Strakhov tried so carefully to outline.

The philosophical revival in Russia had its parallel in an aesthetic revival with which Strakhov was also personally associated and not only because of his friendship with Dostoevsky. The movement centered around the journal *Severnyi vestnik* (Northern messenger), which was edited by the poets Merezhkovsky and Minsky (whose aesthetic manifestoes in the late 1880's had been the spark for the revival itself) and the critic A. L. Volynsky (this

---

28. In a review of a book by Heinrich Struve in 1890, and in "Problems in the History of Philosophy" in 1893, both in Strakhov, *Filosofskie ocherki*.
29. A. I. Vvedensky, review in *Obrazovanie* (November 1892), p. 370.

was the pen name used by A. L. Flekser). Volynsky eventually became famous in Russian literary history for several perceptive studies of Dostoevsky, but his earliest success was a history of Russian literary criticism which first appeared as a series of articles in *Severnyi vestnik*.[30] Volynsky devoted many pages to Grigorev and to *Vremia*'s polemic with the nihilists. He did not particularly single out Strakhov as a critic; he confined his discussion of him to the journalistic rout of Chernyshevsky in the 1860's. Nevertheless, his book was posited on Strakhov's premises that "the criticism of artistic works ought not to be journalistic, but philosophical—and ought to base itself on a firm system of idealistic philosophical concepts."[31] Thus Volynsky was no more than Strakhov or Solovev an "art for art's sake" critic.

Volynsky's philosophical work *The Struggle for Idealism* illustrated both the neo-Kantian and the aesthetic inclinations of Merezhkovsky's journal (although the book itself appeared after the journal was closed). One of its chapters, "Christianity and Buddhism," took as its starting point Strakhov's "Righteousness, Charity, and Saintliness."[32] Volynsky's approach to Strakhov's article was similar to Solovev's, although he exhibited none of the antagonism of the latter. Volynsky had only praise for Strakhov, "this literary monk . . . [his] whole life is only contemplation, only peaceful and balanced meditation, only silent and tranquil prayer with a faith turned toward the heavens."[33] Other articles in his book dealt with the limitations of science (in Kantian terms: time and space are merely categories of thought and not realities), with the delusions of materialism, and with the identification of religion with philosophical idealism.

The similarity between Strakhov's ideas and those of the found-

30. Volynsky, *Russkie kritiki*.

31. Volynsky, *Russkie kritiki*, p. ii. Although he admitted that "Strakhov's short remarks more profoundly penetrate the essence of *Fathers and Sons*, more truly elucidated the poetic value of the novel, than all the judgments of Pisarev," Volynsky nevertheless devoted ten pages to Pisarev's critique and less than a page to Strakhov. Thus, he also bowed to historical criteria.

32. See chapter VI, pp. 184–185. The article first appeared in *Severnyi vestnik* in February 1893.

33. A. L. Volynsky, *Borba za idealizm* (St. Petersburg, 1900), p. 73.

ers of *Voprosy filosofii i psikhologii* and *Severnyi vestnik* illustrates how much Strakhov was associated with the modernist movement of the 1890's. But his identification with it was retrospective rather than active; his creative intellectual life was over by the time the modernist movement began. The intellectual heritage of a lifetime became respectable and even favored, but he never had the chance to develop and revise his thoughts under the beneficent influence of receptive appreciation. Strakhov's books all had second editions in the decade of the 1890's, but to the new generation (sympathetic as it was) they could not but appear slightly archaic.

Strakhov's life proceeded quietly in the last years. There were regular Wednesdays in his apartment and yearly visits to Iasnaia Poliana. His personal library grew and grew; "books were the only sport of this secular monk."[34] Friends tell us that it was difficult to find a sitting place because the books were scattered everywhere: on chairs, on the divan, on the floor. One was always afraid of stepping on some rare edition of Newton or Linnaeus or Bruno. In the sitting room he had a statue of Buddha, a portrait of Grigorev, and a portrait of himself painted by Ilya Repin. Over his bed was a photograph of Tolstoy and prints of Michelangelo's *Day and Night* and Raphael's *Madonna della Seddia.*[35]

In the spring of 1895 at the age of sixty-seven Strakhov became seriously ill. He constantly had a cigarette in his mouth, and the years of smoking finally caught up with him. He fell ill in February and cancer of the tongue was diagnosed. He underwent a painful operation which deprived him of speech for a while. After years of hypochondria (his letters to his friends are filled with complaints about his eyes, his leg, his colds), this final illness seemed to throw him back on himself; he did not tell a soul. When Tolstoy heard about the operation, he wrote Strakhov an agitated letter: "I am very angry that you did not let us know . . . We are

34. Nikolsky, "Strakhov," p. 219.
35. Rozanov, *Literaturnye izgnanniki,* p. 344.

with you in heart and spirit, you are not alone . . . I order you to recover quickly and come to us soon to recuperate."[36] Strakhov did visit Iasnaia Poliana that summer; he also visited Danilevsky's family and his own relatives in Belgorod and Kiev. It was to be a last visit with all his loved ones.

He seemed to make a good recovery; he attended the opening session of the Academic Committee immediately upon his return, and his friends thought he looked well. But in fact he was getting much worse; the cancer soon spread to throat and lungs. He had trouble with articles he was supposed to write for Grot: "I can't seem to overcome a certain heaviness of head and pen."[37] Nevertheless, this last year saw the publication of two large compendia: his *Philosophical Works* and the third volume of *The Struggle with the West*. He was quite sure that he would finish the article for Grot by January.

But he did not live to finish it. Death came quite suddenly. He began to feel ill on the morning of the 23rd of January and called in a distant cousin, a nurse who had tended him after his operation the previous year. Kuskov was with him. At the last moment, suddenly feeling better, he sat up in bed and said, "Well, I've had a good rest, and now I can write again." Georgievsky, arriving on business from the Academic Committee, found him already dead.

The funeral at Novodevichy Cemetery was small and relatively quiet. There were speeches by Kuskov, Nikolsky, and one of the young neo-Slavophiles from Rozanov's group; Kuskov's theme was "Philosophari nihil aliud est, quam Deum amare." But at the very end a strange incident occurred, which was very consistent with the ambiguities of Strakhov's life. Just as people were beginning to disperse, a young man, unknown to everyone, jumped up to speak. He was obviously unsure of himself, and he stuttered and stammered for a while. Finally, he dragged it out: "Dear one . . . you are gone, and after you only Lev Nikolaevich Tolstoy and

36. Tolstoy to Strakhov, June 13, 1895, in Chertkov and Gusev, *Tolstoi i o Tolstom*, vol. II.
37. Strakhov to Grot, December 8, 1895, in *N. Ia. Grot*.

Vladimir Sergeevich Solovev are left!" Then he hurriedly fled.
Rozanov's comment was typically wrong-headed: "Those were
two very strange names to mention at this Orthodox grave."[38]

Strakhov died, then, as he had lived: in solitude. He was misunderstood even by the men who loved him. His complexities were
alien to his generation, which tended to more monolithic commitments. He had once been ridiculed by radicals who did not realize
the extent to which he sympathized with them; the inappropri-
ate later appreciation of orthodox conservatives did more to hurt
his reputation than to strengthen it.

The mildness of Strakhov's personality forbids the term "tragic"
to describe his career; it would be more fitting to say simply that
his was a sad life. He was as erudite and as able as the best of his
generation, but he lacked the forcefulness to make his voice
heeded; most of all, he refused to worship current fashion. Thus
he was denied even the acclaim that comes to mediocre but timely
talents.

Strakhov's career is a case study of a particular kind of historio-
graphic problem: oversight. On the most obvious level, he has
been ignored by liberal historians who tried to forget the existence
of other than liberal viewpoints. But Strakhov presents a problem
even for those historians who hold no particular brief for liberalism; he had too much of the "modern" in him for full compre-
hension within the nineteenth-century conservative framework.
Hence Strakhov was pigeonholed; he was placed into categories
("Slavophile" or "Slavophile literary critic") which were easy for
admiring historians to utilize, but unelucidating. They hardly do
justice to the subtlety of his thought.

It is obvious, for instance, both that Strakhov was a Slavophile
and that his Slavophilism was not a distinguishing characteristic. If Strakhov were limited to his Slavophilism, he would appear
a mediocre thinker indeed. He had neither the passion of Khomiakov as a Slavophile "explorer" nor the political hard-headedness

38. The source is "Pamiati usopshikh" (In memory of departed ones), in Rozanov, *Literaturnye ocherki*, p. 273. It was written in 1896.

of Danilevsky as a Pan-Slav ideologue. Those interested in literary history have often categorized Strakhov as a literary critic. Yet that definition, while more apt than "Slavophile," still leaves him unappreciated. He is an interesting literary critic, but hardly a distinguished one.

His real métier was what he himself called "philosophy," and it was here that his gifts were most brilliantly displayed. Tolstoy recognized Strakhov's mastery, and the popularity of his writings in the 1890's indicates that the new philosophical generation concurred. Strakhov had neither a "system" nor a talent for synthesis; rather, he had an extraordinary ability to understand the ramifications of other systems, no matter how divergent from his own instincts. Thus, he understood Feuerbach better than Chernyshevsky did, and Comte better than Taine. He had a precise appreciation of the possible implications of the positivist movement, and especially of the kind of philosophical dualism that could emerge from it. In fact, Strakhov's understanding of positivism belongs less with Comte and the 1860's than with Ernst Mach and the early twentieth century. Hence, the triumph of his last decade reflects the excellence of a man who not only refused to submit to the intellectual despots of his time, but also had an intimation of the future.

Bibliography

Major Works by N. N. Strakhov (The first edition has been cited.)

Bednost nashei literatury: Kriticheskii i istoricheskii ocherk. St. Petersburg, 1868.

Borba s zapadom v nashei literature. 3 vols. St. Petersburg, 1882–1887–1896. The second edition of vols. I and II, 1887–1890 is expanded. The third edition follows the second edition, 1897–1898.

Filosofskie ocherki. St. Petersburg, 1895.

"Iz bumag N. N. Strakhova." *Russkii vestnik* (January 1898), pp. 143–154.

Iz istorii literaturnogo nigilizma (1861–1865). St. Petersburg, 1890.

Kriticheskie stati (1861–1894). Kiev, 1902.

Kriticheskie stati ob I. Turgeneve i L. Tolstom (1862–1885). St. Petersburg, 1885.

Mir kak tseloe. St. Petersburg, 1872. The second edition (St. Petersburg, 1892), is expanded.

"Nasha iziashchnaia slovesnost. Prestuplenie i nakazanie." *Otechestvennye zapiski,* no. 3 (March 1867), pp. 325–334, and no. 4 (April 1867), pp. 514–527.

"Novosti po chasti nauk estestvennykh." *Zhurnal Ministerstva Narodnogo Prosveshcheniia* (May 1857–May 1860).

"O kostiakh zapiastia mlekopitaiushchikh." *Zhurnal Ministerstva Narodnogo Prosveshcheniia* (September 1857), pp. 274–332.

O metode estestvennykh nauk i znachenii ikh v obshchem obrazovanii. St. Petersburg, 1865.

O vechnykh istinakh (Moi spor o spiritizme). St. Petersburg, 1887.

Ob osnovnykh poniatiiakh psikhologii i fiziologii. St Petersburg, 1886.

"Pisma o filosofii." *Voprosy filosofii i psikhologii* (January 1901), pp. 783–793.

Vospominaniia i otryvki. St. Petersburg, 1892.

"Vospominaniia o Fedore Mikhailoviche Dostoevskom," in *Biografiia, pisma i zametki iz zapisnoi knizhki F. M. Dostoevskogo.* Ed. O. F. Miller and N. N. Strakhov. St Petersburg, 1883.

"Vospominaniia ob A. A. Grigoreve," in A. *Grigorev: Vospominaniia i stati.* Ed. R. V. Ivanov-Razumnik. Moscow, 1930.

Zametki o Pushkine i drugikh poetakh. St. Petersburg, 1882. The second edition (Kiev, 1892) is expanded.

Strakhov's Correspondence

N. Ia. Danilevsky (1873–1885). "Pisma N. N. Strakhova k N. Ia. Danilevskomu." *Russkii vestnik,* January 1901, pp. 127–142; February 1901, pp. 453–469; March 1901, pp. 125–141.

F. M. Dostoevsky (1862–1875). Strakhov published most of Dostoevsky's letters to him (1868–1871) in an appendix to his reminiscences in *Biografiia, pisma i zametki iz zapisnoi knizhki F. M. Dostoevskogo.* The more complete selection is in F. M. Dostoevsky, *Pisma,* ed. A. S. Dolinin, 4 vols. Moscow, 1928–1930–1932–1959. Strakhov's letters to Dostoevsky, edited by A. S. Dolinin, are in "Pisma N. N. Strakhova k F. M. Dostoevskomu," in N. K. Piksanov and O. V. Tsekhnovitser, eds., *Shestidesiatye gody.* Moscow, 1940.

A. A. Grigorev (1861–1862). Strakhov published Grigorev's letters to him in "Vospominaniia ob A. A. Grigoreve."

N. Ia. Grot (1887–1895). Strakhov's letters to Grot are in *N. Ia. Grot v ocherkakh, vospominaniiakh i pismakh.* Ed. K. Ia. Grot. St. Petersburg, 1911.

V. V. Rozanov (1888–1896). Strakhov's letters to Rozanov were published in V. V. Rozanov, *Literaturnye izgnanniki.* St. Petersburg, 1913.

V. S. Solovev (1877–1890). Solovev's letters to Strakhov are in *Pisma V. S. Soloveva,* ed. E. L. Radlov, St. Petersburg, 1908. Vol. I.

L. N. Tolstoy (1870–1896). The major volume of correspondence with Tolstoy is *Perepiska L. N. Tolstogo s N. N. Strakhovym.* Ed. B. L. Modzalevsky. St. Petersburg, 1913. Other important letters from Tolstoy to Strakhov are in the following volumes:
Chertkov, V. G., and N. N. Gusev, eds. *Tolstoi i o Tolstom.* Vol. II. Moscow, 1926.

Gusev, N. N., ed. *Letopisi gosudarstvennogo literaturnogo muzeia: L. N. Tolstoi.* Moscow, 1938.

"Pisma Tolstogo N. N. Strakhovu." *Literaturnoe nasledstvo,* XXXVII–XXXVIII (1939), 151–182.

Sergeenko, P. A., ed. *Pisma L. N. Tolstogo.* 2 vols. Moscow, 1910–1911.

Memoirs About Strakhov and His Circle

Avseenko, V. G. "Kruzhok." *Istoricheskii vestnik* (May 1909), pp. 438–451. These memoirs relate specifically to *Zaria* and its circle.

Boborykin, P. D. "Za polveka." *Minuvshie gody* (November 1908), pp. 111–149.

Fet (Shenshin), A. A. *Moi vospominaniia (1848–1889).* Moscow, 1890. Although Strakhov and Fet were good friends, they were scarcely ideological allies. Fet speaks very reservedly of Strakhov in his memoirs and reproduces almost none of their correspondence. The memoirs were published while Strakhov was still alive.

Gradovsky, G. K. "Iz minuvshego." *Russkaia starina* (October 1908), pp. 57–74. This section of Gradovsky's memoirs relates specifically to his participation in the Pan-Slav movement and, hence, to *Zaria* and *Grazhdanin.*

Lazursky, V. F. (Diary). *Literaturnoe nasledstvo*, XXXVII–XXXVIII (1939), 444–491. Lazursky was a Tolstoian. He often met Strakhov at Iasnaia Poliana in the 1890's and even contemplated writing a biography of Strakhov. This article and the two following bibliographical items comprise his memoirs of Tolstoy, which were later published in a heavily edited form as V. F. Lazursky, *Vospominaniia*, (Moscow, 1914).

Lasursky, V. F. "Iasnopolianskie posetiteli v 1894 g." *Golos minuvshego* (March 1914), pp. 119–134.

Lazursky, V. F. "L. N. Tolstoi i N. N. Strakhov (iz lichnykh vospominanii)." In *L. N. Tolstoi: Biografiia, kharakteristiki, vospominaniia.* Russkaia byl, ser. III. Moscow, 1910.

Librovich, S. F. *Na knizhnom postu.* Moscow, 1916. Librovich was a bibliophile, an intimate of the publishing circles in St. Petersburg and particularly of M. O. Volf; it was in this connection that he knew Strakhov.

Matveev, Pavel. "L. N. Tolstoi i N. N. Strakhov v Optinoi pustyni." *Istoricheskii vestnik* (April 1907), pp. 151–157.

Meshchersky, V. P. *Moi vospominaniia.* 3 vols. St. Petersburg, 1897–1917. Meshchersky's memoirs elucidate the ambiguous role which Strakhov played on *Grazhdanin:* Meshchersky actually knew Strakhov only very slightly.

Miliukov, A. P. *Literaturnye vstrechi i znakomstva.* St. Petersburg, 1890. Miliukov, as a friend of Dostoevsky and Grigorev in the 1860's, provides insights into the editorial problems of *Vremia* and *Epokha*.

Panteleev, L. F. *Iz vospominanii proshlogo.* Moscow, 1934.

Shemanovsky, I. M. I. "Vospominaniia o zhizni v glavnom pedagogiches-kom institute, 1853–1857 gg." *Literaturnoe nasledstvo,* XXXV–XXXVI (1936), 271–299. This is a description of a university experience which presumably resembled Strakhov's very much; Shemanovsky entered just a year after Strakhov left the institute.

Shtakenshneider, E. A. *Dnevnik i zapiski (1854–1886).* Moscow, 1934.

Stakheev, D. I. "Gruppy i portrety." *Istoricheskii vestnik* (1907), January, pp. 81–94; February, pp. 464–478, March, pp. 846–854; July, pp. 130–142; August, pp. 424–437. As a close friend and neighbor for twenty-five years, Stakheev is able to provide numerous insights into Strakhov's life; his observations, in this and the two following bibliographical items, are of a personal rather than an intellectual nature.

Stakheev, D. I. *Sobranie sochinenii.* St. Petersburg, 1902. Vol. II. "Pustynnozhitel," pp. 163–255.

Stakheev, D. I. "Stanislav pervoi stepeni i enotovaia shuba." *Istoricheskii vestnik* (February 1904), pp. 464–478.

Veinberg, Petr. "Bezobraznyi postupok *Veka.*" *Istoricheskii vestnik* (May 1900), pp. 472–489. Memoirs of the famous "Egyptian Nights" episode in 1861.

Other Primary Sources Cited in the Text

Antonovich, M. A. *Literaturno-kriticheskie stati.* Moscow, 1961.

Antonovich, M. A. "Liubovnoe obiasnenie s *Epokhoi.*" *Sovremennik* (October 1864).

Antonovich, M. A. "O dukhe *Vremeni* i o g. Kosits., kak nailuchshchem ego vyrazhenii." *Sovremennik* (April 1862).

Bernard, Claude. *An Introduction to the Study of Experimental Medicine.* New York, 1927.

Carlyle, Thomas. *Carlyle's Collected Works. 30 vols.* London: "Library Edition", 1869–71. Vol. V. "The Life of Friedrich Schiller."

Chernyshevsky, N. G. "The Anthropological Principle in Philosophy." In *Selected Philosophical Essays.* Moscow, 1953.

Danilevsky, N. Ia. *Darvinizm: Kriticheskoe issledovanie.* 2 vols. St. Petersburg, 1885–1889.

Danilevsky, N. Ia. *Rossiia i Evropa: Vzgliad na kulturnye i politicheskie otnosheniia slavianskogo mira k germano-romanskomu.* 5th ed. St. Petersburg, 1895.
Danilevsky, N. Ia. *Sbornik politicheskikh i ekonomicheskikh statei.* St. Petersburg, 1890.
Mikhailovsky, N. K. "Analogicheskii metod v obshchestvennoi nauke." *Otechestvennye zapiski* (July 1869).
Mikhailovsky, N. K. "Desnitsa i shuitsa Lva Tolstogo." In *Literaturno-kriticheskie stati.* Ed. G. A. Bialyi. Moscow, 1952.
Mikhailovsky, N. K. "Iz literaturnykh i zhurnalnykh zametok 1872 g." *Sochineniia N. K. Mikhailovskogo.* St. Petersburg, 1896. Vol. I, pp. 1–53.
Pisarev, D. I. "Nineteenth Century Scholasticism." In *Selected Philosophical, Social and Political Essays.* Moscow, 1958.
Renan, Ernest. *Essais de morale et de critique* and *Souvenirs d'enfance et de jeunesse.* In *Oeuvres complètes.* Ed. Henriette Psichari. Paris, 1947–61. Vol. II.
Solovev, V. S. *Sobranie sochinenii V. S. Soloveva.* Ed. E. L. Radlov. St. Petersburg, 1901–1907. Vol. V. *Natsionalnyi vopros v Rossii.*

Secondary Works

Aliotta, Antonio. *The Idealistic Reaction Against Science.* London, 1914.
Belchikov, N. F. "Chernyshevskii i Dostoevskii." *Pechat i revoliutsiia* (July–August 1928), pp. 35–53.
Bentley, E. R. *A Century of Hero-Worship.* Philadelphia. 1944.
Berliner, G. O. "Literaturnye protivniki N. A. Dobroliubova." *Literaturnoe nasledstvo,* XXV–XXVI (1936), 32–69.
Berliner, G. O. *N. G. Chernyshevskii i ego literaturnye vragi.* Moscow, 1930.
Bestuzhev-Riumin, K. N. "N. N. Strakhov (nekrolog)." *Zhurnal Ministerstva Narodnogo Prosveshcheniia* (February 1896), pp. 114–117.
Billington, J. H. *Mikhailovsky and Russian Populism.* Oxford, 1958.
Borshchevsky, S. S. "Raskol v nigilistakh." *Literaturnyi kritik* (November–December 1940), pp. 65–92.
Borshchevsky, S. S. *Shchedrin i Dostoevskii.* Moscow, 1956.

Byrnes, R. F. "Dostoevsky and Pobedonostsev." In *Essays in Russian and Soviet History.* Ed. J. S. Curtiss. New York, 1963. Pp. 85–102.

Cassirer, Ernst. *The Problem of Knowledge: Philosophy, Science, and History Since Hegel.* New Haven, 1950.

Charlton, D. G. *Positivist Thought in France During the Second Empire.* Oxford, 1959.

Chizhevsky (Cizevski), D. I. "Dostoevskij und Strachov." *Zeitschrift fur Slawischen Philologie,* X (1933), 388ff., and XIII (1936), 70.

Chizhevsky, D. I. *Gegel v Rossii.* Paris, 1939.

Dolinin, A. S. (Iskoz, A. S.). *Dostoevskii, stati i materialy.* 2 vols. Moscow, 1922–1925.

Dolinin, A. S. "F. M. Dostoevskii i N. N. Strakhov." In N. K. Piksanov and O. V. Tsekhnovitser, eds. *Shestidesiatye gody.* Moscow, 1940. Pp. 238–254.

Dolinin, A. S. *Poslednie romany Dostoevskogo.* Moscow, 1963.

Dorovatovskaia-Liubimova, V. S. "Dostoevskii i shestidesiatniki." In *Dostoevskii.* Gosudarstvennaia Akademiia Khudozhestvennykh Nauk, Literaturnaia sektsiia, no. 3. Moscow, 1928. Pp. 5–60.

Eikhenbaum, Boris. *Lev Tolstoi: Semidesiatye gody.* Leningrad, 1960.

Galaktionov, A. A., and P. F. Nikandrov. *Istoriia russkoi filosofii.* Moscow, 1961.

Galand, René M. *L'âme celtique de Renan.* Paris, 1959.

Georgievsky, A. I. "K istorii uchenogo komiteta ministerstva narodnogo prosveshcheniia." *Zhurnal Ministerstva Narodnogo Prosveshcheniia,* October 1900, pp. 25–61; November 1900, pp. 17–61; December 1900, pp. 74–121; April 1902, pp. 33–72; May 1902, pp. 21–56.

Gillispie, C. *The Edge of Objectivity.* Princeton, 1960.

Gippius, V. V. "Saltykov i zhurnalnaia polemika 1864 g." *Literaturnoe nasledstvo,* XI–XII (1933), 87–112.

Goltsev, V. A. "N. N. Strakhov, kak khudozhestvennyi kritik." In his *O khudozhnikakh i kritikakh.* Moscow, 1899. Pp. 114–126.

Grossman, L. P. *Tri sovremennika (Dostoevskii, Tiutchev, Grigorev).* Moscow, 1922.

Grot, N. Ia. "Pamiati N. N. Strakhova." *Voprosy filosofii i psikhologii* (February 1896), pp. 299–336.

Guralnik, U. A. "*Sovremennik* v borbe s zhurnalimi Dostoevskogo." *Izvestiia Akademii Nauk SSSR* (Otdel Literatury i Iazyka), vol. IX, no. 4 (1950), pp. 265–285.

Istoriia russkoi kritiki. Vol. II. Moscow, 1958.

Ivanov, I. I. *Istoriia russkoi kritiki s XVIII v.* 2 vols. St. Petersburg, 1898–1900.

Karpovich, Michael. "Vladimir Solovev on Nationalism." *Review of Politics*, VII (April 1946), 183–191.

Kirpotin, V. Ia. *Dostoevskii i Belinskii.* Moscow, 1960.

Kirpotin, V. Ia. *Dostoevskii i shestidesiatye gody.* Moscow, 1966.

Kirpotin, V. Ia. *Publitsisty i kritiki.* Moscow, 1932.

Kohn, Hans. *Pan-Slavism: Its History and Ideology.* 2nd ed. New York, 1960.

Kolubovsky, Ia. N. "Materialy dlia istorii filosofii v Rossii 1855–1888 gg: N. N. Strakhov." *Voprosy filosofii i psikhologii* (March 1891), pp. 99–121.

Komarovich, V. L. "Dostoevskii i shestidesiatniki." *Sovremennyi mir* (January 1917), pp. 129–138.

Komarovich, V. L. "Dostoevskii i 'Egipetskie nochi' Pushkina." *Pushkin i ego sovremenniki,* XXIX–XXX (Petrograd, 1918), pp. 36–48.

Kozmin, B. P. "Raskol v nigilistakh." *Literatura i marksizm* (February 1928), pp. 51–107.

Kranikhfeld, V. "L. N. Tolstoi i N. N. Strakhov v ikh perepiske." *Sovremennyi mir* (December 1912), pp. 327–342.

Lemke, M. K. *Epokha tsenzurnykh reform, 1859–1865 gg.* St. Petersburg, 1904.

Literaturnoe nasledstvo, XXXV–XXXVI and XXXVII–XXXVIII (1939). The two volumes are devoted to Tolstoy.

MacMaster, R. E. *Danilevsky, a Russian Totalitarian Philosopher.* Cambridge, Mass.: Harvard University Press, 1967.

MacMaster, R. E. "Danilevsky: Scientist and Panslavist." Ph.D. Diss., Harvard, 1952.

MacMaster, R. E. "The Question of Heinrich Rückert's Influence on Danilevsky." *American Slavic and East European Review* (February 1955), pp. 59–66.

Moser, Charles. *Antinihilism in the Russian Novel of the 1860's.* The Hague, 1964.

Nazarevsky, Λ. "Pomety Nekrasova na rukopisi N. N. Strakhova." *Literaturnoe nasledstvo,* LIII–LIV (1949), 85–87.

Nikitin, S. A. *Slavianskie komitety v Rossii v 1858–1876 gg.* Moscow, 1960.

Nikolsky, B. V. "N. N. Strakhov: Kritiko-biograficheskii ocherk." *Istoricheskii vestnik* (April 1896), pp. 215–268.

Nikolsky, B. V. "Pamiati N. N. Strakhova." *Russkii vestnik* (March 1896), pp. 231–255.
Radlov, E. L. "Neskolko zamechanii o filosofii N. N. Strakhova." *Zhurnal Ministerstva Narodnogo Prosveshcheniia* (May 1896), pp. 339–361.
Rogers, J. A. "Darwinism, Scientism, and Nihilism." *Russian Review*, XIX (January 1960), 10–23.
Rozanov, V. V. *Literaturnye izgnanniki.* St. Petersburg, 1913.
Rozanov, V. V. *Literaturnye ocherki.* St. Petersburg, 1899.
Rozanov, V. V. *Priroda i istoriia.* St. Petersburg, 1900.
Sanine, Kyra. *Les Annales de la patrie*, Paris, 1955.
Skabichevsky, A. M. *Istoriia noveishei russkoi literatury.* St. Petersburg, 1891.
Stammler, Heinrich. "Vladimir Soloviev as a Literary Critic." *Russian Review* (January 1963), pp. 68–81.
Thaden, E. C. *Conservative Nationalism in Nineteenth-Century Russia.* Seattle, 1964.
Titlinov, A. V. *Dukhovnaia shkola v Rossii v XIX st.* 2 vols. Vilna, 1909.
Volynsky (Flekser), A. L. *Borba za idealizm.* St. Petersburg, 1900.
Volynsky, A. L. *Russkie kritiki.* St. Petersburg, 1896.
Vvedensky, A. I. *Obshchii smysl filosofii N. N. Strakhova.* Moscow, 1897. (25 pp.)
Vvedensky, A. I. Review of *Mir kak tseloe. Obrazovanie* (November 1892), pp. 369–371.
Vvedensky, A. I. "Znachenie filosofskoi deiatelnosti N. N. Strakhova." *Obrazovanie* (March 1896), pp. 1–8.
Wardman, H. W. *Ernest Renan: A Critical Biography.* London, 1964.
Wellek, René. *A History of Modern Criticism.* 4 vols. New Haven, 1955–1965.
Zapadov, A. V., ed. *Istoriia russkoi zhurnalistiki XVIII–XIX vv.* Moscow, 1963.
Zenkovsky, V. V. *A History of Russian Philosophy.* Trans. G. L. Kline. 2 vols. New York, 1953.
Zenkovsky, V. V. *Russian Thinkers and Europe*, Trans. G. Bodde. Ann Arbor, 1953.

Index

1. *Public Opinion in Soviet Russia: A Study in Mass Persuasion*, by Alex Inkeles
2. *Soviet Politics — The Dilemma of Power: The Role of Ideas in Social Change*, by Barrington Moore, Jr.*
3. *Justice in the U.S.S.R.: An Interpretation of Soviet Law*, by Harold J. Berman. Revised edition, enlarged
4. *Chinese Communism and the Rise of Mao*, by Benjamin I. Schwartz
5. *Titoism and the Cominform*, by Adam B. Ulam*
6. *A Documentary History of Chinese Communism*, by Conrad Brandt, Benjamin Schwartz, and John K. Fairbank*
7. *The New Man in Soviet Psychology*, by Raymond A. Bauer
8. *Soviet Opposition to Stalin: A Case Study in World War II*, by George Fischer*
9. *Minerals: A Key to Soviet Power*, by Demitri B. Shimkin*
10. *Soviet Law in Action: The Recollected Cases of a Soviet Lawyer*, by Boris A. Konstantinovsky; edited by Harold J. Berman*
11. *How Russia Is Ruled*, by Merle Fainsod. Revised edition
12. *Terror and Progress USSR: Some Sources of Change and Stability in the Soviet Dictatorship*, by Barrington Moore, Jr.
13. *The Formation of the Soviet Union: Communism and Nationalism, 1917–1923*, by Richard Pipes. Revised edition
14. *Marxism: The Unity of Theory and Practice — A Critical Essay*, by Alfred G. Meyer
15. *Soviet Industrial Production, 1928–1951*, by Donald R. Hodgman
16. *Soviet Taxation: The Fiscal and Monetary Problems of a Planned Economy*, by Franklin D. Holzman
17. *Soviet Military Law and Administration*, by Harold J. Berman and Miroslav Kerner*
18. *Documents on Soviet Military Law and Administration*, edited and translated by Harold J. Berman and Miroslav Kerner
19. *The Russian Marxists and the Origins of Bolshevism*, by Leopold H. Haimson
20. *The Permanent Purge: Politics in Soviet Totalitarianism*, by Zbigniew K. Brzezinski*

21. *Belorussia: The Making of a Nation* — A Case Study, by Nicholas P. Vakar
22. *A Bibliographical Guide to Belorussia*, by Nicholas P. Vakar*
23. *The Balkans in Our Time*, by Robert Lee Wolff (also American Foreign Policy Library)
24. *How the Soviet System Works: Cultural, Psychological, and Social Themes*, by Raymond A. Bauer, Alex Inkeles, and Clyde Kluckhohn†
25. *The Economics of Soviet Steel*, by M. Gardner Clark*
26. *Leninism*, by Alfred G. Meyer*
27. *Factory and Manager in the USSR*, by Joseph S. Berliner†
28. *Soviet Transportation Policy*, by Holland Hunter
29. *Doctor and Patient in Soviet Russia*, by Mark G. Field†
30. *Russian Liberalism: From Gentry to Intelligentsia*, by George Fischer
31. *Stalin's Failure in China, 1924–1927*, by Conrad Brandt
32. *The Communist Party of Poland: An Outline of History*, by M. K. Dziewanowski
33. *Karamzin's Memoir on Ancient and Modern Russia: A Translation and Analysis*, by Richard Pipes
34. *A Memoir on Ancient and Modern Russia*, by N. M. Karamzin, the Russian text edited by Richard Pipes*
35. *The Soviet Citizen: Daily Life in a Totalitarian Society*, by Alex Inkeles and Raymond A. Bauer†
36. *Pan-Turkism and Islam in Russia*, by Serge A. Zenkovsky
37. *The Soviet Bloc: Unity and Conflict*, by Zbigniew K. Brzezinski. Revised and enlarged edition‡
38. *National Consciousness in Eighteenth-Century Russia*, by Hans Rogger
39. *Alexander Herzen and the Birth of Russian Socialism, 1812–1855*, by Martin Malia
40. *The Conscience of the Revolution: Communist Opposition in Soviet Russia*, by Robert Vincent Daniels
41. *The Soviet Industrialization Debate, 1924–1928*, by Alexander Erlich
42. *The Third Section: Police and Society in Russia under Nicholas I*, by Sidney Monas
43. *Dilemmas of Progress in Tsarist Russia: Legal Marxism and Legal Populism*, by Arthur P. Mendel

44. *Political Control of Literature in the USSR, 1946–1959,* by Harold Swayze
45. *Accounting in Soviet Planning and Management,* by Robert W. Campbell
46. *Social Democracy and the St. Petersburg Labor Movement, 1885–1897,* by Richard Pipes
47. *The New Face of Soviet Totalitarianism,* by Adam B. Ulam
48. *Stalin's Foreign Policy Reappraised,* by Marshall D. Shulman
49. *The Soviet Youth Program: Regimentation and Rebellion,* by Allen Kassof
50. *Soviet Criminal Law and Procedure: The RSFSR Codes,* translated by Harold J. Berman and James W. Spindler; introduction and analysis by Harold J. Berman
51. *Poland's Politics: Idealism vs. Realism,* by Adam Bromke
52. *Managerial Power and Soviet Politics,* by Jeremy R. Azrael
53. *Danilevsky: A Russian Totalitarian Philosopher,* by Robert E. MacMaster
54. *Russia's Protectorates in Central Asia: Bukhara and Khiva, 1865–1924,* by Seymour Becker
55. *Revolutionary Russia,* edited by Richard Pipes
56. *The Family in Soviet Russia,* by H. Kent Geiger
57. *Social Change in Soviet Russia,* by Alex Inkeles
58. *The Soviet Prefects: The Local Party Organs in Industrial Decision-making,* by Jerry F. Hough
59. *Soviet-Polish Relations, 1917–1921,* by Piotr S. Wandycz
60. *One Hundred Thousand Tractors: The MTS and the Development of Controls in Soviet Agriculture,* by Robert F. Miller
61. *The Lysenko Affair,* by David Joravsky
62. *Icon and Swastika: The Russian Orthodox Church under Nazi and Soviet Control,* by Harvey Fireside
63. *A Century of Russian Agriculture: From Alexander II to Khrushchev,* by Lazar Volin
64. *Struve: Liberal on the Left, 1870–1905,* by Richard Pipes
65. *Nikolai Strakhov,* by Linda Gerstein

*Out of print.
†Publications of the Harvard Project on the Soviet Social System.
‡Published jointly with the Center for International Affairs, Harvard University.